I SING OF A MAIDEN

THE MACMILLAN COMPANY
NEW YORK · BOSTON · CHICAGO
DALLAS · ATLANTA · SAN FRANCISCO

MACMILLAN AND CO., LIMITED
LONDON · BOMBAY · CALCUTTA
MADRAS · MELBOURNE

THE MACMILLAN COMPANY
OF CANADA, LIMITED
TORONTO

I SING

OF A MAIDEN

The Mary Book of Verse

EDITED BY SISTER M. THÉRÈSE

of the Congregation of the Sisters of the Divine Savior

New York ·1947

THE MACMILLAN COMPANY

Nihil obstat:

JOHN A. SCHULIEN, S. T. D.
Censor Librorum

Milwaukee, Wis.
April 21, 1947

Imprimatur:

✠ MOYSES E. KILEY
Archiepiscopus Milwaukiensis

Milwaukiae, Die 22 Aprilis, 1947

TO MARY

MOTHER OF THE SAVIOR

I SING OF A MAIDEN

I sing of a maiden that
  Matchless is,
King of all Kings is her son
  I wis.

He came all so still
  Where his mother was
As dew in April
  That falleth on grass.

He came all so still
  To his mother's bower
As dew in April
  That falleth on shower.

He came all so still
  Where his mother lay
As dew in April
  That falleth on spray.

Mother and maiden
  Was ne'er none but she
Well may such a lady
  God's mother be.

Anonymous—Fifteenth Century

CONTENTS

ix

CONTENTS

xi

CONTENTS

PART III

"MY THOUGHT WAS ON A MAID SO BRIGHT"
Medieval Mary-Songs

PART IV

"MARY IS A FLOWER FIELD"
From Chaucer to Donne

CONTENTS

xiii

CONTENTS

PART V

"MOST BLESSÈD LANTERN"

The Age of Transition: Seventeenth and Eighteenth Centuries

PART VI

"LADY, THOU ART A FLAME!"

The Romanticists

CONTENTS

PART VII

"THE LADY OF MY DELIGHT"

Nineteenth Century and Modern (European)

XV

CONTENTS

CONTENTS

xvii

PART VIII

"LADY OF LETTERS"
Early and Contemporary American

CONTENTS

CONTENTS

CONTENTS

CONTENTS

xxii

CONTENTS

INTRODUCTION

From the most ancient years *woman* has been the perennial theme of song. This is as it should be, for, as Archbishop Richard J. Cushing of Boston remarked in an address to some two thousand Jewish women, "Outside the realm of religion, the most reverent thing on the face of the earth is a woman!" Apart from being, with man, a *person, the noblest thing in nature,* according to St. Thomas, and the very masterpiece of God's creativeness, she possesses in her own uniqueness a deep cosmic quality which binds her in a singular way to the destinies of all mankind. She is to man, or should be, the most nearly perfect finite manifestation of God's infinite Beauty—of God, who is "eternal youth." Hence, through all the centuries man, uplifted by the charm, joy, and "otherworldliness" of her presence, or the sublime renunciation of that presence, has loosed his spirit in ecstatic song. He has been lyric alike in the delight of her immediacy and closeness, as the Lover of the Bride of the *Canticle,* and Homer of Helen, as in the pain beyond healing of her absence, as Petrarch of Laura, and Dante of Beatrice. Thus divinely has woman been hymned.

Yet, who will question the statement that, of all women who have lived, there is *one* incomparable among them, whose beauty has summoned the singers of all ages to unremitting praise—the young Jewish maid of Nazareth, Mary the Mother of Jesus Christ, and hence the Mother of God. The poems of this book are gathered praise of her.

From *Genesis* wherein she is first pre-figured, to its earliest luminous commentary in the *Apocalypse,* this "woman clothed

xxv

with the sun" breaks through the mists of the Old Dispensation
in the texts of the *Psalms, Proverbs, The Canticle of Canticles,
Wisdom, Ecclesiasticus and Isaias,* until in the *Gospels* she appears startlingly in the flesh as "His mother Mary." Her coming
had been a living progressive revelation in both spoken and written word, the utterance of Isaias, its most signal instance:

> Behold a virgin shall conceive,
> and bear a son,
> and his name shall be called Emmanuel.
>
> *Isaias VII, 14*

From the earliest years of Christianity the Church in her liturgy
has taken passages of sublime poetry from the *Psalms, Canticle,*
and the *Sapiential Books*—notably the description of Divine Wisdom—and applied them to Mary by appropriation.

> The Lord possessed me in the beginning of his way,
> before he made anything from the beginning.
>
> . . . .
>
> I was with him forming all things:
> and was delighted every day,
> Playing before him at all times;
> Playing in the world.
>
> *Proverbs VIII, 22, 23*

In the ancient liturgies Mary is expressly referred to as the
Theotokos, "God-bearer," a title which was first conceived in
the writings of Origen in the third century and has since held an
integral place in the edifice of Catholic theology known as Mariology. It is from this her highest prerogative, the Divine Maternity, that all her other privileges flow. Light was successively
focused on some one of her privileges. In the first five centuries
the emphasis was placed on her maternity and virginity (*ante et
in partu*). The Martyr Justin stressed the Eve-Mary contrast.
Origen insisted on the perpetual virginity of Mary. And the
Council of Ephesus (431 A.D.) condemning Nestorianism which
attacked the Divinity of Christ directly, thereby assailing Mary's
divine motherhood, firmly insisted on the *Theotokos* as a sign of
orthodox thought on the Virgin Mary. In the fourth century the
voice of Ephrem the Syrian, first poet of the Virgin, stressed her
immunity from original sin, and St. John Damascene in the

eighth century emphasized her holiness and dignity as Mother of God. The concept of Mary, Mediatrix of Grace, makes its appearance early, centralized by the doctrine of her Assumption into heaven, celebrated by an appointed feast in the Churches of the East and West. The history of Mariology, then, has its roots in antiquity.

It is fitting that the first complete Marian poem should have been written by one of her own countrymen, Ephrem of Syria. The first references to Mary in Christian Latin poetry—barring Virgil's rendition of the Sybilline prophecy in his *Fourth Eclogue* —occur incidentally in the course of the poems. The first appears in the *Carmen adversus Marcionem,* of the second half of the third century, wherein its unknown author refers to man after the fall as renewed by Christ—

> . . . . the flower of flesh and host
> Of peace—a flesh from espoused Virgin born.

References to Mary continue to emerge in Latin poetry: in the *Laudes Domini* of the fourth century, the verse Gospel-histories of Juvencus, in a poem of the Roman Proba, in the *Carmen de Salvatore* ascribed to Pope Damasus of the fourth century, and the *Carmen de Christo* of the fifth century soldier-poet, the Spaniard Merobaudes. In the incomparable hymns of St. Ambrose there is casual allusion to Mary, and in Hymn XI of the *Cathemerinon* by Prudentius, we find the first direct apostrophe to Our Lady in Latin poetry—the spontaneous, lyrically beautiful *"Sentisne virgo nobilis"*:

> Know thou, O Virgin, noble-blest,
> That through the timeless tunneled glooms
> The blinding beauty of thy soul
> With childbirth splendor flames and blooms?
>
> What joys are fountained for the world
> Within thy womb's well, deep and white,
> Whence streams a new-created age
> And golden light, and Golden Light!
> *From the Latin by Raymond F. Roseliep*

In Paulinus of Nola, Fortunatus, and Hilary of Arles lyrical praise of Mary abounds. From the *Carmen Paschale* of Sedulius issue some of the most exquisite lines of Marian poetry ever penned, the *"Salve, sancta Parens"*—lines which have been taken into the liturgy of the Votive Mass for Mary's feasts and sparkle gemlike in the variegated tapestry of her Little Office. Father Roseliep gracefully renders them:

Hail, Maiden Root! whence lithely mounts a Kingly Flowering,
That since our time unwound has petaled world and heaven with spring;
Whose word, whose whispered name sends life rebounding through earth's
  wheel,
While thy most envied vestal womb makes centuries rock and reel;
Though virgin still, thou hast the rapture every mother knows,
Thou more-than-root, thou stem and sap for one Eternal Rose—
Christ-gladness with no equal, and His everlasting snows.

In Ennodius' *"Ut Virginem Fetam Loquar"* at the beginning of the sixth century, direct invocation to Mary becomes apparent; and with it begins a cycle of Latin poetry addressed entirely to the Virgin.

That from out these early beginnings Marian lyricism gathered momentum, amplification, and startling beauty is abundantly clear from the utter profusion of rare parchments treasured in libraries throughout the world.

In Bodleian and Harleian
  Lurk ambushes of grace—
A secret siege Our Lady lays
  To many an ancient place . . .

The Primer's gilded hieroglyphs
  Her lyric names conceal,
From manuscripts like winding-sheets
  Her risen praises steal!
                    Sister Mary Ignatius

Early in England, Cynewulf sang of her in *The Christ* as the "maiden ring-adorned":

                    Young was the woman
a stainless maiden,   whom He chose for Mother,
and without man   was that wonder wrought,
that the young bride   brought forth her Bairn.
Never was it so   before or since
in the wide world,   such a Child-bearing.
        From the Old English by Margaret Williams
                    xxviii

In the isles of Greece, Cosmas the Melodist made songs for her;
on the shores of the northern sea, Eysteinn of Thykkvabaer in
a long and moving poem acclaimed her his "Lily." On the continent the meistersingers and minnesingers were her loyal-hearted
troubadours; and as varied a group as Walther von der Vogelweide, Adam of St. Victor, Saint Bonaventure, Jacaponi da Todi
and Francesco Petrarch sang of her, until the chorus mounted to
its grand apotheosis in Dante's ecstatic prayer of St. Bernard, "O
Virgin Mother, Daughter of thy Son," in the twenty-third canto
of the *Paradiso*.

But it was in the Middle Ages that the tide of Marian poetry
was at its flood. If England, "Mary's dower," was at that time "a
nest of singing birds," the most thrilling and frequent note was
that of "a maiden who matchless is," "Godes Moder Milde," as
Chaucer sang of her. England was a land of Mary-shrines; and
even on the quarter-decks of her ships that sailed the seas were
shrines to the Virgin. In those days

> . . . . Albion's seamen knew
> Why they salute the quarter deck
> (It held a shrine to Mary),
> They named the hungry fowl that flew
> About the galley at their beck
> 'Chickens Matris Carae.'
> *Fray Angelico Chavez*

Among the Marian lyrics were various types and genres illus-
trating many facets of the singers' devotion. There were the short,
spontaneous lyrical lullabies, the extended dialogues between
the small Christ and His Mother, and the *plaintes* of the Virgin
in which she laments the death of her Son. The joys of Mary were
also a favorite theme, and they are to be found preserved in sixteen distinct lyrics. Even up to the very eve of the Reformation,
England's poets were singing carols as exquisite as,

> There is no rose of swich vertu
> As is the rose that bare Ihesu,
> Alleluia!

Thought of her would influence the conduct of men toward
all women—

In worship of that mayde swete
Mild Mary, Mother May,
All good women will I greet.

That the pages of Chaucer are verily permeated by "Christes mooder deere" is immediately apparent to even the most casual reader. *The A B C of Our Lady,* which he wrote for Blanche of Lancaster, is a glorious prayer and hymn of honor to Mary. So too, the glowing "Prioress's Tale," a medieval miracle story of Our Lady, which is one of his *Canterbury Tales.* The famous Hoccleve portrait, preserved in the Harley MS. at the British Museum and considered to be the most authentic in existence, depicts Chaucer holding a black rosary in his hand. In the last months of his life when he lived on the monastery property at Westminster, his home was significantly situated in the garden of Our Lady's chapel; and one can readily picture him, rosary in hand, pacing the grey cloisters saying his *Aves.* When Chaucer had been laid to rest in the south transept of Westminster Abbey, his friend and poetic disciple, Thomas Hoccleve, asks Mary to be his advocate in paradise:

> As thou wel knowest, O Blissid Virgyne,
> With lovying hert and hye devocioun
> In thyne honour he wroot ful many a lyne;
> O now thine helpe and thi promocioun,
> To God thi sone make a mocioun,
> How he thi servaunt was, Mayden Marie,
> And that his love floure and fructifie.
>
> *From The Regiment of Princes*

All the age echoed this Marian devotion. John Lydgate named Mary "Celestial Cypress set upon Syon"; Luigi Pulci begged her to illuminate the verses of *Morgante Maggiore,* and François Villon wrote charmingly of "His Mother's Service to Our Lady." During the great plague in Florence, Savonarola sent up a sincere poetic plea to her:

> O Star of Galilee,
> Shining over earth's dark sea,
> Shed thy glorious light on me.

William Dunbar wrote stirring ballades to Our Lady, and in 1511 the staunch humanist, Erasmus, visited the chapel at Walsingham, her most famous English shrine, and there left hanging among the ex-votos a touchingly penitent ode in Greek:

> . . . . I, poor bard,
> Rich in good will, but poor in all beside
> Bring thee my verse—nought have I else to bring—
> And beg, in quital of this worthless gift,
> That greatest meed—a heart that feareth God,
> And free for aye from sin's foul tyranny.
> Erasmus, his vow.

But not long after Erasmus' visit, Our Lady's shrine was stripped, and, at Cromwell's orders, her image was brought to Chelsea in a cart and there publicly burned. From their deepest hearts came the people's lament:

> Weep, weep, O Walsingham,
> Whose days are nights;
> Blessings turned to blasphemies,
> Holy deeds to despites.
> Sin is where Our Lady sate,
> Heaven is turned to hell;
> Satan sits where Our Lord held sway—
> Walsingham, oh, farewell.

They had been comforted had they known that though for centuries her shrine lay desecrate, in 1897 Our Lady returned, and the Slipper Chapel was fittingly restored. It is significant that in 1934, the First Mass since the English Reformation was offered in this chapel by the late Cardinal Bourne, who had personally led a pilgrimage to "England's Mary-land."

The tragic road that led to Tyburn was a lyrically piercing one. Months and years in the stern Tower of London were paradoxically redolent of song. Those so-called *Recusants,* who had made the great refusal joyfully—St. Thomas More, and the *Beati,* Edmund Campion, Robert Southwell, Philip Howard, and Henry Walpole were poetically eloquent. Robert Southwell hymned Mary in stanzas of laud and lament, and Walpole's poignant understanding of her sorrow at the foot of the cross has echoed down the succeeding centuries. The clustered sweetness of these Mary-songs is among the most tender lyrics of our tongue. Of the same period was Richard Verstegan (Rowlands), the charm of whose Marian lullaby, first published anonymously in Martin Peerson's *Private Musicke* in 1660, is unequalled perhaps by any other with its wistful refrain—

> Sing lullaby, my little Boy,
> Sing lullaby, my life's Joy!

When the medieval unity based on Christianity was broken, and its dispersed threads caught up into the dual strand of the Renaissance dichotomy, John Donne, though abandoning the Faith of his youth, nevertheless retained much of the inspiration which that Faith had given him. First of the moderns in the world of letters, he wrote felicitous poems to Mary. It is further significant that in his will he bequeathed to his intimate friend, Lord Hay, a picture of the Blessed Virgin which had hung in his private dining room during all the years of his Deanship of St. Paul's. In his quaint "Ghyrlond of the Blessed Virgin Marie," Ben Jonson, too, gives evidence of understanding her place in orthodox theology and titles her "Daughter, and Mother, and the Spouse of God."

Despite an ingrained Puritan prejudice, Milton strikingly states the role of Mary in the "Nativity Hymn" and in both the Paradises, speaking of her with tenderness as the "Virgin blest" and the "Second Eve." In his rapturous singing, Crashaw was her devoted laureate. And in the very conventional eighteenth century there was a group of minor poets including Thomas Ken, Nahum Tate, John Norris, and John Byrom, who in the stereotyped idiom of their day wrote extended poems on some aspect of the Virgin Mary's life.

In the most unlikely periods and places there has not lacked praise of her. In that great unrest that was the Romantic Movement, Mary also had her poets, and some of the most widely celebrated of her lyrics were written in that day. Among the nostalgic souls who longed for that of which they knew not the name, yet called it by a thousand titles, and loosed all their being in flight for it, were those who glimpsed, if by blurred vision, that woman because of whom all womankind is sacred. Goethe and Schiller have named her with reverence. Wordsworth's "Sonnet to the Virgin" is known wherever the English tongue is spoken. Coleridge, Scott, and Byron have reverently sung of her, and Shelley, in the passage of *Epipsychidion,* "Seraph of heaven, too gentle to be human," may have expressed the beauty of the "greatest among women."

But in that spiritual and literary emergence following close upon the Oxford Movement and coming into the present century with an ever increasing resonance, was a chorus of authentic voices among which were those of Coventry Patmore, Alice Meynell, Francis Thompson, Gerard Manley Hopkins, Hilaire Belloc, and G. K. Chesterton. Each of this lyric galaxy has left Mary-poems of rare beauty. Theirs was an intimacy with God's Mother not witnessed since the days of her medieval troubadours. Chesterton may stand as their spokesman when he speaks with heavenly daring and possessiveness of Our Lady—

> . . . . for she was ours
> And had run on the little hills behind the houses
> And pulled small flowers;
> But she rose up and went into a strange country
> With strange thrones and powers.

Yet distance would present no barrier to her love, and he rises in her defense. Though she now "wears a crown in a strange country"—

> . . . . she has not forgotten to call to her old companions,
> To call and crave;
> And to hear her calling a man might arise and thunder
> On the doors of the grave.

On the continent, Rainer Maria Rilke wrote a long and arrestingly beautiful *Life of Mary;* the young and tragic Rupert Brooke told touchingly of "Mary and Gabriel." France had its Charles Péguy, and has still its Paul Claudel, both of whom are Marian poets of superb strength and power. And the chorus of her praise has been joined in recent years by two contemporary major poets—W. H. Auden and T. S. Eliot, the latter of whom in "The Dry Salvages" calls to her:

> Lady, whose shrine stands on the promontory,
> Pray for all those who are in ships . . .
>
> . . . .
>
> Also pray for those who were in ships, and
> Ended their voyage on the sand, in the sea's lips
> Or in the dark throat which will not reject them
> Or wherever cannot reach them the sound of the sea bell's
> Perpetual angelus.

In America, Marian lyricism has been a thing to gladden the heart. From Transcendentalist New England, Longfellow in his *Golden Legend* places on the lips of his main character a sincere and moving utterance to Mary. As early as 1837 in Ludlow, Vermont, Abby Maria Hemenway (who wrote under the pseudonymn of "Josephine Marie") was at work upon a lyric trilogy dealing with Our Lady and St. Joseph. Of its first volume, *Mary of Nazareth,* in seven books, she wrote that she had "appropriated every coveted relic or tradition handed down by historian, Christian or pagan, from the archives of the Latin Church, Hebrew, or Greek"—a touching tribute from a New England Protestant. Edgar Allan Poe's *Hymn* to Mary has been among his most usually quoted poems. Father Tabb's genuinely beautiful lyrics are miniatures of the Virgin. But perhaps the most significant Mary-poem yet written in the New World— "among the greatest, perhaps the greatest in American literature," remarks Alfred Noyes—is the "Prayer to the Virgin of Chartres," written by that "outwardly skeptical and sophistocated" New England Puritan, Henry Adams. The poem was found after his death in a little wallet of special papers, and his niece reports that it had been shown by him to only one friend and "one can understand that he did not care to publish it during his lifetime, for he never wished to lift the veil." The poem is unmistakable proof of its author's painful awareness of what had been lost to the world by its refusal to accept the *Light* that is Christ, and he identifies himself with the past centuries of the faithful praying "the lost prayers of Christendom":

Gracious Lady:—
    Simple, as when I asked your aid before;
      Humble as when I prayed for grace in vain
    Seven hundred years ago; weak, weary, sore
      In heart and hope, I ask your help again.

    You, who remember all, remember me;
      An English scholar of a Norman name,
    I was a thousand who then crossed the sea
      To wrangle in the Paris schools for fame.

    When your Byzantine portal was still young
      I prayed there with my master Abailard;
    When Ave Maris Stella was first sung,
      I helped to sing it here with Saint Bernard.

    When Blanche set up your gorgeous Rose of France
      I stood among the servants of the Queen;
    And when Saint Louis made his penitence,
      I followed barefoot where the King had been.

Then, in devastating contrast follow the ten stanzas of the "Prayer to the Dynamo," and the habitants of the atomic age can keenly appreciate his complaint of surprise at this,

        . . . . the last
    Of the strange prayers Humanity has wailed.

But at its close he is still at the Virgin's feet—

    A curious prayer, dear lady! is it not?
      Strangely unlike the prayers I prayed to you!
    Stranger because you find me at this spot,
      Here, at your feet, asking your help anew.

And the poem closes with that glorious apotheosis—some of the supremest lines ever written to the Virgin Mother—lines of which America can justly be proud:

    But years, or ages, or eternity,
      Will find me still in thought before your throne,
    Pondering the mystery of Maternity,
      Soul within Soul,—Mother and Child in One!

    Help me to see! not with my mimic sight—
      With yours! which carried radiance, like the sun,
    Giving the rays you saw with—light in light—
      Tying all suns and stars and worlds in one.

Help me to know! not with my mocking art—
    With you, who knew yourself unbound by laws;
Gave God your strength, your life, your sight, your heart,
    And took from him the Thought that Is—the Cause.

Help me to feel! not with my insect sense,—
    With yours that felt all life alive in you;
Infinite heart beating at your expense;
    Infinite passion breathing the breath you drew!

Help me to bear! not my own baby load,
    But yours; who bore the failure of the light,
The strength, the knowledge and the thought of God,—
    The futile folly of the Infinite!

From Canada the voice of Marjorie Pickthall pierces to the deep pitifulness of Mary, in her popular "Mary Shepherdess":

All the little sighing souls born of dust's despair,
They who fed on bitter bread when the world was bare,
Frighted of the glory gates and the starry stair.

Crying in the ivy-bloom, fingering at the pane,
Grieving in the hollow dark, lone along the rain,—
Mary—Mary Shepherdess gathers them again.

If I had a little maid to turn my tears away,
If I had a little lad to lead me when I'm grey,
All to Mary Shepherdess they'd fold their hands and pray.

Most auspicious for the future of Marian poetry is the ever growing choir of her poets today, and her songs are sung quite as fittingly in the modern pattern and idiom as in the carefully measured quatrains of Prudentius in the fourth century. That the lyrically gifted among an anointed priesthood, or souls lineal to Roswitha and Teresa of Avila in the cloisters, should contribute their special motif to this chorus of praise is not to be wondered at; but that these should be equalled by, even in many instances surpassed by the secular voice, gives one pause for thought. From bullet-sprinkled beachheads, from fox-holes in perilous mountain passes, from life-rafts on the ocean, and from a bomb-ridden sky a poignant voice has risen in lyric cries to Mary "Queen of Horizons," "Most Blessed Lantern," "Hope of the Half-defeated," "Star of the Sea." Never since the beginning of time has her beauty been sung in more diverse and scattered places. And these powerful poems remain to us as prayers which we might pray to gain a long lasting peace—

> Is this called Peace?
> Our arms prevailed.
> The guns are stilled.
> We did not love
> The men we killed,
> And, thus, we failed.
> We had no shame.
> We cast the stone.
> The Christ who came
> With a great throng
> Went on alone.
> Whatever Pardon
> May be sent
> We shut out
> With our intent.
> Mother, pray for us.
>
> Pray, untainted Virgin—
> Pity what
> You cannot bless
> And beseech
> The kind Trinity
> To prevent
> Our wickedness,
> Lest sweet mercy flee,
> Oh, too far,
> Beyond our reach.
>
> . . . .
>
> Most blessed Lantern
> give us light.
>
> . . . .
>
> Star of the Sea,
> Pray for us.
>
> *From "Star of the Sea" by Richard Webb Sullivan*

The present collection of Marian poetry has been gathered from the literature of the most ancient times to that of the present day. It attempts to be representative, not exhaustive. As was inevitable in a work of this nature, most of the poems are poems originally written in English, yet translations from other languages have been included whenever suitable ones were available or could be made. The selections are for the most part lyrics, either in their own right, or by virtue of their extraction from longer poems which it would have been impossible or superfluous to include. A few hymns, mainly from the *Roman Breviary* have been used. Though a hymn *may* be a good poem, ordinarily it is not, because of the exigencies of the musical pattern to which the poet must conform his text, and the perhaps occasional, or stereotyped, sentiment he is expected to express. However, as regards the Latin hymns of the *Breviary,* one can be quite sure that they are almost always poems in their own right, despite the fact that some of their native freshness and spontaneity may escape in translation.

The bounds of the anthology are broad and gracious ones. Disparity of creed has not been allowed in any way to limit the selections. All—of the great family of God—stand together, and though the individual poets may be in belief worlds asunder, they are here seen to retain one distinctive bond of union: the lyric exaltation of God's Mother. And since this is a *subject* anthology, each poem chosen serves in one manner or another to illuminate some one of the multiple and varied facets of that subject, namely, the personality and life of the Virgin Mary.

Nor has an artificial unity been imposed on the collection; the method of arrangement is strictly chronological. Each singer stands in his own age, singing his song to Mary, and his song must be judged by the manner and standards of literary taste of his respective age.

That excerpts from the sacred writings of the Old Testament initiate the poems of this book should need no defense. The Church, though fully conscious that these passages, notably those of the *Sapiential Books,* in their first and direct sense apply to the Eternal Word of God, the Uncreated Wisdom, has, nevertheless, in her liturgy from the earliest times applied them to Mary, since in a derived sense they aptly express her place and position in the economy of the Eternal Plan. She was no *afterthought* of God but was in the Divine Mind from the beginning.

The gathering of these Mary-songs has been an inspiring and a heartening experience and one filled with singular surprises, especially when quite unexpectedly one came upon his native flowers within an alien garden. As theme for poets the Virgin Mother of God has been irresistible. Truly, her praise has been hymned in every land and by every type of singer—and from the most ancient years. There is indeed a subtle prophetic meaning in the words of Sister Ignatius, who originally closed her poem on "Our Lady of the Libraries" with the arresting lines—

> She storms their cities from within:
> When scholars dream it not,
> A thousand muted tomes will burst
> With her *Magnificat!*

SISTER M. THÉRÈSE

Feast of Our Lady of Mount Carmel
July 16, 1946

ACKNOWLEDGMENTS

For permission to reprint copyright poems in this anthology the editor wishes to acknowledge the courtesy of the following:

GEORGE ALLEN AND UNWIN, LTD., London: For "Cadgwith III," "Our Lady of France," and "Our Lady of the May" from *The Poetical Works of Lionel Johnson* (copyright 1926) by Lionel Johnson and "Epiphany," "The Name," and "After the Annunciation" from *Poems* (copyright 1940) by Eileen Duggan (Canadian rights).

THE AMERICA PRESS, New York: For "Mary's Assumption" and "Chant of Departure" from *Mint by Night* (copyright 1938) by Alfred Barrett, S.J.

B. G. BELL AND SONS, LTD., London: For "The Child's Purchase" and "Regina Coeli" from *Poems* (copyright 1928) by Coventry Patmore.

ERNEST BENN, LTD., London: For selections from *The Greek Anthology* (copyright 1929) translated by Shane Leslie.

BROWNE AND NOLAN, LTD., London: For selection from *Christ Unconquered* by Arthur Little.

BRUCE HUMPHRIES, INC., Boston: For "Madonna: 1936" from *Canticle and Other Poems* (copyright 1936) by John Louis Bonn, S.J.

BURNS OATES AND WASHBOURNE, LTD., London: For "The Two Mothers" from *Verses in Peace and War* by Shane Leslie (Canadian rights); and for the arrangement with the Newman Book Shop, Westminster, Maryland, for "Assumpta Maria," "Lines for a Drawing of Our Lady of the Night," and "The After Woman" from *The Collected Poems of Francis Thompson*.

FRAY ANGELICO CHAVEZ, Santa Fe: For "Mulier Amicta Sole" from *Clothed with the Sun* (copyright 1939) and "Lady of Lidice," "Sea-Birds," "Lady of Peace," and "Mary" from *Eleven Lady-Lyrics* (copyright 1946) by Fray Angelico Chavez.

xl

THE CLARENDON PRESS, Oxford: For "Our Lady" from *The Shorter Poems of Robert Bridges* (copyright 1931) by Robert Bridges.

COWARD MCCANN, INC., New York: For "To Our Lady, the Ark of the Covenants" from *Weep and Prepare* (copyright 1940) by Raymond E. F. Larsson.

ANDREW DAKERS, London: For "Lady-Day in Harvest" from *Saints in Sussex* (copyright 1927) by Sheila Kaye-Smith (Canadian rights).

J. M. DENT AND CO., Toronto: For "Et Verbum Caro Factum Est," "Oriens ex Alto," "Assumpta Est Maria," and "Mater Coronata" from *The Rosary in Terza Rima* (copyright 1941) by Sister Maura.

THE DITCHLING PRESS, LTD., and the Dominican Fathers, Sussex: For "The Akathistos Hymn" translated by Vincent McNabb, O.P.

DODD, MEAD AND CO., New York: For "The Immaculate Conception," "The Annunciation," and "The Assumption" from *The Poetry of Father Tabb* (copyright 1928); and "Mary and Gabriel" from *The Collected Poems of Rupert Brooke* (copyright 1915) by Rupert Brooke.

DOUBLEDAY, DORAN AND CO., INC., Garden City: For "A Blue Valentine" from *The Collected Poems of Joyce Kilmer* (copyright 1942) by Joyce Kilmer.

E. P. DUTTON AND CO., New York: For "Lady Day in Harvest" from *Saints in Sussex* (copyright 1927) by Sheila Kaye-Smith.

FABER AND FABER, LTD., London: For "Part IV of 'The Dry Salvages'" from *Four Quartets* (copyright 1943) by T. S. Eliot (Canadian rights), and "Dialogue Between Mary and Gabriel" from *For the Time Being—A Christmas Oratorio* (copyright 1944) by W. H. Auden (Canadian rights).

THE HARBOR PRESS and Mr. Louis How, New York: For the selection from *The Divine Comedy of Dante* (copyright 1940) translated by Louis How.

HARCOURT, BRACE AND CO., INC., New York: For "Part IV of 'The Dry Salvages'" from *Four Quartets* (copyright 1943) by T. S. Eliot.

JAMES M. HAYES, Washington, D. C.: For "Our Lady of the Skies" from *Arrows of Desire* (copyright 1928) by James M. Hayes.

HENRY HOLT AND CO., New York: For "The Virgin's Slumber Song" from *My Ireland* (copyright 1918) by Francis Carlin.

HERDER BOOK CO., St. Louis: For selections from *The Mirror of the*

Blessed Virgin and the Psalter of Our Lady (copyright 1932) by St. Bonaventure, translated by Sister Mary Emmanuel, O.S.B.

HOLLIS AND CARTER, LTD., London: For "To the Mother of Christ, the Son of Man" from *Last Poems* (copyright 1923) by Alice Meynell.

HOUGHTON, MIFFLIN CO., New York: For "Five Carols for Christmas-Tide" from *Happy Ending* (copyright 1909) by Louise Imogen Guiney; and "Prayer to the Virgin of Chartres" from *Letters to a Niece* (copyright 1920) by Henry Adams.

MARY KING, Adelaide: For "Mary of Bethlehem" from *Mary of Bethlehem and Other Poems* (copyright 1944) by Mary King.

ALFRED A. KNOPF, INC., New York: For "Cradle Song" from *Verses* (copyright 1922) by Adelaide Crapsey.

LOKER RALEY, INC., New York: For "Ode to the Virgin" from *Madrigals and Odes from Petrarch* (copyright 1940) translated by Helen Lee Peabody.

LONGMANS, GREEN AND CO., New York: For "Invocatio ad Mariam," "Prologue to the Prioress's Tale," "Invocation" and "The Prioress's Tale" from *The Canterbury Tales* (copyright 1943) by Geoffrey Chaucer, done into modern English by Frank Ernest Hill; "The Shed" and "The Spinner" from *The Rime of the Rood and Other Poems* (copyright 1928) by Charles L. O'Donnell, and "Preference" from *God's Ambuscade* (copyright 1935) by Daniel Sargent.

THE MACMILLAN COMPANY, New York: For "Epiphany," "The Name," and "After the Annunciation" from *Poems* (copyright 1940) by Eileen Duggan; "Mater Dei" from *Collected Poems* (copyright 1930) by Katherine Tynan; "Last Antiphon: to Mary" from *Exile in the Stars* (coyright 1945) by James J. Donohue; "To the Lighted Lady Window" from *Citadels* (copyright 1926) by Marguerite Wilkinson; "To the Queen of Dolors" and "Our Lady of the Refugees" from *Initiate the Heart* (copyright 1946) by Sister Mary Maura, S.S.N.D.; selections from *Song for a Listener* (copyright 1936) by Leonard Feeney; "I Send Our Lady" from *Give Joan a Sword* (copyright 1944) by Sister M. Thérèse; "The Assumption" from *The Mysteries of the Rosary* (copyright 1932) by John Gilland Brunini; and "Cradle Song" and "Fourth Station" from *The Collected Poems* (copyright 1932) by Padraic Colum.

MACMILLAN AND CO., LTD., and Miss Pamela Hinkson, London: For "Mater Dei" from *Collected Poems of Katherine Tynan Hinkson* (copyright 1930) by Katherine Tynan Hinkson (Canadian rights).

ACKNOWLEDGMENTS

SISTER M. MADELEVA, Notre Dame: For "A Nun Speaks to Mary," "Of Wounds" and "Motif for Mary's Dolors" from *A Question of Lovers and other Poems* (copyright 1935) by Sister M. Madeleva.

MCCLELLAND AND STEWART, LTD., Toronto: For "Mary Shepherdess" from *The Lamp of Poor Souls* (copyright 1927) by Marjorie L. C. Pickthall.

THE MONASTINE PRESS, New York: For "Ave, Vita Nostra" from *Crags* (copyright 1938) by Clifford J. Laube.

BENJAMIN FRANCIS MUSSER, Atlantic City: For "Der Heilige Mantel von Aachen" and "The Holy Land of Walsingham" from *The Bird Below the Waves* (copyright 1938) by Benjamin Musser.

NATIONAL CATHOLIC WELFARE CONFERENCE, Washington: For "Ex Maria Virgine" from *N.C.W.C. Christmas Supplement* (copyright 1944) by Norbert Engels.

NEW DIRECTIONS PRESS, Norfolk: For "The Blessed Virgin Mary Compared to a Window" and "The Evening of the Visitation" from *Thirty Poems* (copyright 1944) by Thomas Merton.

THE NEWMAN BOOK SHOP, Westminster Md.: For "Assumpta Maria," "Lines for a Drawing of Our Lady of the Night," and "The After Woman" from *The Collected Poems of Francis Thompson* (copyright 1947) by Francis Thompson; and "Romance VIII" from *The Complete Works of St. John of the Cross,* translated by E. Allison Peers.

W. W. NORTON AND Co., New York: For "On the Death of Mary" from *Translations from the Poetry of Rainer Maria Rilke* (copyright 1938) by Rainer Maria Rilke, translated by Herter Norton.

OXFORD UNIVERSITY PRESS and the Hopkins Family, London: For "The Blessed Virgin Compared to the Air We Breathe" and "The May Magnificat" from *The Poems of Gerard Manley Hopkins* (copyright 1930) by Gerard Manley Hopkins.

THE OXFORD UNIVERSITY PRESS, London, and Anne W. Douglas, Denver: For the "Alma Redemptoris Mater," "Ave, Regina Coelorum," "Regina Coeli" and "Salve Regina" from the *Monastic Diurnal,* translated by Canon Douglas.

OXFORD UNIVERSITY PRESS, New York: For three stanzas from *The Pearl* (copyright 1932) translated into modern verse by Stanley Perkins Chase.

PANTHEON BOOKS, INC., New York: For "Our Lady Help of Christians," and "Fourth Station" from *Coronal* (copyright 1943) by Paul Claudel, translated by Sister Mary David, S.S.N.D.; and

xliii

"The Passion of Our Lady" from *God Speaks* (copyright 1945) by Paul Péguy, translated by Julian Green.

A. D. PETERS, literary agent for Hilaire Belloc, London, and Hilaire Belloc and Sheed and Ward, Inc., New York: For "Our Lord and Our Lady," "Ballade to Our Lady of Czestochowa," and "In a Boat" from *Sonnets and Verse* (copyright 1942) by Hilaire Belloc.

RANDOM HOUSE, New York: For "Dialogue Between Mary and Gabriel" from *For the Time Being—A Christmas Oratorio* (copyright 1944) by W. H. Auden.

REMINGTON BOOK STORES, Baltimore: For "His Mother in Her Hood of Blue" from *Spicewood* (copyright 1921) by Lizette Woodworth Reese.

CHARLES SCRIBNER'S SONS, New York: For "The Two Mothers" from *Verses in Peace and War* by Shane Leslie.

SHEED AND WARD, INC., New York: For "Christmas" and "Vigil of the Assumption" from *Hymns to the Church* (copyright 1942) by Gertrude von Le Fort, translated by Margaret Chanler; "Litany to Our Lady" and "The Reed" from *The Flowering Tree* (copyright 1945) by Caryll Houselander; "Mary" and "Joy's Peak" from *Time's Wall Asunder* (copyright 1939) by Roibéard Ó Faracháin; and "A Brave-Hearted Maid" and a selection from "The Christ" from *Word-Hoard* (copyright 1940) by Margaret Williams.

SMALL MAYNARD AND COMPANY, Boston: For "A Christmas Eve Choral" from *April Airs* (copyright 1916) by Bliss Carman.

ANSELM M. TOWNSEND, O.P. Chicago: For *"La Prière de Nostre Dame,"* from *Chaucer's Hymn to the Blessed Virgin* (copyright 1935) done in modern English by Anselm M. Townsend, O.P.

THE VIKING PRESS, New York: For "The Gentlest Lady" from *The Portable Dorothy Parker* (copyright 1928, 1944) by Dorothy Parker.

MARY COCHRANE VOJÁČEK, London: For "Mary Was Watching" from *Czechoslovak Xmas Carols,* arranged by Vilém Tauský and Sheila Lennox Robertson.

LORNA GILL WALSH, literary executrix of Thomas Walsh, New York: For "La Preciosa" from *The Pilgrim Kings* (copyright 1915) by Thomas Walsh.

A. P. WATT AND SON, London, and Sheed and Ward, Inc., New York, and to the executrix of the late Mr. G. K. Chesterton: For "The Black Virgin," "Regina Angelorum," and "The Return of Eve" from *The Queen of Seven Swords* (copyright 1926) by G. K. Chesterton.

I also owe thanks to the editors of the following magazines for their kind permission to quote poems which first appeared on their pages:

AMERICA, New York: For "Queen of Horizons" by Joseph Dever; "The Annunciation" by Margaret Devereaux Conway; "Madonna: 1936" by John Louis Bonn; "A Nun to Mary, Virgin" by Sister Mary St. Virginia; "Family Portrait" by Leonard Feeney; "Madonna of the Exiles" by James Edward Tobin; "Heart for All Her Children" by Albert J. Hebert, Jr., and "Cause of Our Joy" by Sister Maris Stella.

AVE MARIA, Notre Dame: For "Madonna of the Empty Arms" by Maurice Francis Egan; and the translations from Saint Ephrem and Nerses by W. H. Kent, C.S.C.

CARMINA, Ireland: For "Joseph Mary Plunkett" by Wilfrid Meynell.

THE CATHOLIC WORLD, New York: For "Philippine Madonna" by Louise Crenshaw Ray; "A Gaelic Christmas" and "Christmas Eve" by Liam Clancy; and "Le Repos En Egypte" by Agnes Repplier.

THE COMMONWEAL, New York: For "Lines for a Feast of Our Lady" by Sister Maris Stella; "Mediatrix of Grace" by Francis Burke; and "And in Her Morning" by Jessica Powers.

THE MAGNIFICAT, Manchester: For "Notre Dame des Petits" by Louis Mercier; and "Assumpta Est Maria" by Liam Brophy.

POET LORE, Boston: For "Our Lady of Good Voyage" by Lucy A. K. Adee.

THE SIGN, Union City: For "Shrine in Nazareth" by Sister Mary St. Virginia.

SPIRIT, New York: For "Our Lady of the Libraries" by Sister M. Ignatius; "The Vision of St. Bernard" by M. Whitcomb Hess; "Petition for a Miracle" by David Morton; "The Cloud of Carmel" by Jessica Powers; "No More Destructive Flame" by Francis X. Connolly; "Ox-Bone Madonna" and "Lady of O" by James J. Galvin; "Ox-Bone Madonna," "Annunciation" and "Our Lady's Labor" by John Duffy; "To Mary at the Thirteenth Station" by Raymond F. Roseliep; "Madonna of the Dons" by Arthur MacGillvray; "Cry from the Battlefield" by Robert Menth; "New Testament: Revised Edition" by Sister Mary

Catherine; and Sonnets IV and XIII from "The Stations of the Cross" by William A. Donaghy.

THE TIDINGS, Los Angeles: For "Cradle Song" and "The Loan of a Stall" by John Duff.

For individual poems, poems heretofore unpublished, and translations made expressly for the anthology, I am deeply grateful to the following poets and translators:

WILLIAM J. BRELL, P.S.M., Milwaukee, Wis.: For the translation of Ruth Schaumann's "Der Vierte Station."

JOHN GILLAND BRUNINI, New York: For "To Mary at Christmas."

EDWIN BUERS, S.D.S., Jordan Seminary, Menominee, Michigan: For the translation of Ruth Schaumann's sonnet, "Mariae Tempelgang."

JAMES J. GALVIN, C.SS.R., Esopus, N. Y.; For "Morning Star," and "Madonna's Lullaby," translation from the Italian of St. Alphonsus Ligouri.

JOSEPH JOEL KEITH, Los Angeles, Cal.: For "Immaculate Palm," "Though She Slumbers" and "She Walks."

SISTER MAURA, Mount St. Vincent College, Halifax, Nova Scotia: For the translation of "O Gloriosa Virginum" of Fortunatus; "Te Redemptoris Dominique Nostri," *Hymn for Lauds* for the Feast of Our Lady Help of Christians, and "Plaude festivo, pia gens, honore," *Hymn for Lauds* for the Feast of Our Lady of Good Counsel.

RAYMOND F. ROSELIEP, Dubuque, Iowa: For "Lady of Letters," "Where Do I Love You, Lovely Maid?" "Symphony in Blue" and the translations of the *Laudes Beatae Mariae Virginis,* "Sentisne Virgo Nobilis" from Hymn XI of the *Cathemerinon* of Prudentius, "Salve, Sancta Parens" from the *Carmen Paschale* of Sedulius, "Ardet pugna ferox" of Pope Leo XIII, the Inscription of Pope Eugenius III, and the "Omnis expertem maculae Mariam," *Hymn for Second Vespers* for the Feast of Our Lady of Lourdes.

CORNELIA OTIS SKINNER, New York: For "To the Sistine Madonna."

HENRY SORG, S.D.S., Salvatorian Seminary, St. Nazianz, Wis.: For the translation from the Old French of "Li Loenge Nostre Dame" from a Parisian manuscript of the thirteenth century.

RICHARD WEBB SULLIVAN, Caribou, Maine: For his original version of "Star of the Sea."

ACKNOWLEDGMENTS

MARGARET WILLIAMS, R.C.S.J., Manhattanville College of the Sacred
Heart, New York: For the translation of lines 71–104, and 301–
407 from *The Christ* by Cynewulf.

It is now my pleasure to thank in a special way those who throughout the making of this book have so generously shared with me
themselves—their lyrical gifts, their encouragement and constant
support. It is difficult to define the debt of gratitude I owe to the
Very Reverend Edwin Buers, S.D.S., of Jordan Seminary, Menominee,
Michigan, for the gracious counsel and wise criticism that have done
more than ever can be told to bring the anthology closer to my ideal.
Nor can a simple thanks ever compass the kindness of the Reverend
Raymond F. Roseliep, Loras College, Dubuque, Iowa, who had the
complete text of the *Laudes Beatae Mariae Virginis* photostated for
me from the copy in the rare book room of the Newberry Library,
Chicago, and then translated so generous a portion of its one hun-
dred and fifty quatrains for inclusion in the anthology. I am also
deeply indebted to him for the final typing of the Biographical
Index. To Doctor John Pick, of Marquette University, Milwaukee,
for his invaluable critical help with the MS., I shall be always grateful. I also owe thanks to Sister M. Madeleva, of St. Mary's College,
Holy Cross, Indiana, and Sister Maura, Mount St. Vincent College,
Halifax, Nova Scotia, for their expert criticism; to Reverend Arthur
MacGillvray, S.J., College of the Holy Cross, Worcester, Massachusetts, for his kind assistance in obtaining and checking certain
elusive biographical data; and to Dr. Anton C. Pegis, of the Pontifical
Institute of Medieval Studies, Toronto, Canada, and Doctors James
M. Purcell, and Victor M. Hamm, of Marquette University, Mil-
waukee, for their many helpful suggestions.

There remains my filial duty of thanking Reverend Mother Ot-
tilia, Sor. D.S., my Provincial Superior, who allowed me time from
my teaching duties in which to complete this book, and who supported me with motherly understanding and solicitude. To my
brother, Reverend Theophane Lentfoehr, S.D.S., of Divine Savior
Seminary, Lanham, Maryland, I shall always be grateful for keeping
the book constantly in his prayers.

S. M. T.

PART ONE

"IN THE BEGINNING OF HIS WAYS"

The Virgin in Prophecy, and in texts of Sacred
Scripture assigned to her by appropriation in the Liturgy of the Church.

MOSES

I will put enmities
Between thee and the woman,
And thy seed and her seed:
She shall crush thy head,
And thou shalt lie in wait for her heel.

Genesis III, 15

DAVID

The queen stood on thy right hand,
in gilded clothing;
surrounded with variety.

Hearken, O daughter, and see,
and incline thy ear:
and forget thy people and thy father's house

And the king shall greatly desire thy beauty;
for he is the Lord thy God,
and him they shall adore.

And the daughters of Tyre with gifts,
yea, all the rich among the people,
shall entreat thy countenance.

3

All the glory of the king's daughter is within
in golden borders,
clothed round about with varieties.

After her shall virgins be brought to the king:
Her neighbors shall be brought to thee.

They shall be brought with gladness and rejoicing:
they shall be brought into the temple of the king.

Psalm XLIV, 10–16

SOLOMON

The Lord possessed me in the beginning of his ways,
before he made any thing from the beginning.

I was set up from eternity,
and of old before the earth was made.

The depths were not as yet,
and I was already conceived,
neither had the fountains of waters as yet sprung out.

The mountains with their huge bulk had not as yet been established,
before the hills I was brought forth:

He had not yet made the earth,
nor the rivers, nor the poles of the world.

When he prepared the heavens I was present:
when with a certain law and compass he enclosed the depths:

When he established the sky above,
and poised the fountains of waters:

4

When he compassed the sea with its bounds,
and set a law to the waters that they should not pass their limits,
when he balanced the foundations of the earth:

I was with him forming all things:
and was delighted every day,
playing before him at all times;

Playing in the world.

Proverbs VIII, 22–31

CANTICLE OF CANTICLES

 I am the flower of the field,
 and the lily of the valleys.

 As the lily among thorns,
 so is my love among the daughters.
 . . . .

 My dove in the clefts of the rock,
 in the hollow place of the wall,
 shew me thy face,
 let thy voice sound in my ears;
 for thy voice is sweet,
 and thy face comely.

Canticle of Canticles II, 1, 2, 14

Thou art beautiful, O my love,
sweet and comely as Jerusalem:
terrible as an army set in array.

. . . .

One is my dove,
my perfect one is but one,
she is the only one of her mother,
the chosen of her that bore her.
The daughters saw her,
and declared her most blessed:
The queens praised her.

Who is she that cometh forth as the morning rising,
fair as the moon, bright as the sun,
terrible as an army set in array?

Canticle of Canticles VI, 3, 8, 9

UNKNOWN ALEXANDRIAN JEW

For she is a vapour
of the power of God,
and a certain pure emanation
of the glory of the almighty God,
and therefore no defiled thing
cometh into her.

For she is the brightness of eternal light;
and the unspotted mirror of God's majesty,
and the image of his goodness.

Wisdom VII, 25–26

JESUS SON OF SIRACH

I am the mother of fair love,
and of fear, and of knowledge,
and of holy hope.

In me is all grace of the way
and of truth,
in me is all hope of life,
and of virtue.

Come over to me, all ye that desire me,
and be filled with my fruits.

For my spirit is sweet above honey,
and my inheritance above honey and the honeycomb.

My memory is unto everlasting generations.

Ecclesiasticus XXIV, 24–28

ISAIAS

Therefore the Lord Himself
shall give you a sign:

Behold a virgin shall conceive,
and bear a son,
and his name shall be called Emmanuel.

He shall eat butter and honey,
that he may know to refuse the evil,
and to choose the good.

Isaias VII, 14–15

PUBLIUS VERGILIUS MARO

(B.C. 70–19)

THE SIBYLLINE PROPHECY

(From the *Fourth Eclogue*)

Muses of Sicily, loftier be our song!
Not to all do humble pastorals and fields give joy;
Thus if we sing of groves, let them be lofty as the Consul's
  rank.
For now we reach the final epoch foretold by Cumae's Sibyl;
A new cycle among the ages comes to birth;
The virgin, Astraea, returns; the Saturnian age of peace is re-
  newed,
For a new order of generation is sent down from the high
  heavens!
Thou, chaste Lucina, be propitious to the boy new-born,
Through whom the Iron Age will reach its end
And the Golden Age will spread over the entire world;
So may the reign of Apollo begin!

From the Latin by Thomas Walsh

PART TWO

"DOORWAY OF THE KING"

The Early Ages of Faith

LUKE THE EVANGELIST

MARY AND GABRIEL

And in the sixth month, the angel Gabriel was sent from God into a city of Galilee, called Nazareth, to a virgin espoused to a man whose name was Joseph, of the house of David; and the virgin's name was Mary. And the angel being come in said unto her:

>Hail, full of grace,
>the Lord is with thee:
>Blessed art thou among women!

Who having heard, was troubled at his saying, and thought within herself what manner of salutation this should be. And the angel said to her:

>Fear not, Mary,
>for thou hast found grace with God.
>
>Behold thou shalt conceive in thy womb,
>and shalt bring forth a son;
>and thou shalt call his name Jesus.
>
>He shall be great,
>and shall be called the Son of the most High;
>and the Lord God shall give unto him
>the throne of David his father;
>and he shall reign in the house of Jacob forever.
>And of his kingdom there shall be no end.

And Mary said to the angel:

> How shall this be done,
> Because I know not man?

And the angel answering said to her:

> The Holy Ghost shall come upon thee,
> and the power of the most High shall overshadow thee.
> And therefore also the Holy which shall be born of thee
> shall be called the Son of God.

> And behold thy cousin Elizabeth,
> she also hath conceived a son in her old age;
> and this is the sixth month with her
> that is called barren:

> Because no word shall be impossible with God.

And Mary said:

> Behold the handmaid of the Lord;
> be it done to me according to thy word.

And the angel departed from her.

Luke I, 26–38

MARY AND ELIZABETH

And Mary rising up in those days, went into the hill country with haste into a city of Juda. And she entered into the house of Zachary, and saluted Elizabeth. And it came to pass that when Elizabeth heard the salutation of Mary, the infant leaped in her womb. And Elizabeth was filled with the Holy Ghost: And she cried with a loud voice, and said:

Blessed art thou among women,
and blessed is the fruit of thy womb.

And whence is this to me,
that the mother of my Lord should come to me?

For behold,
as soon as the voice of thy salutation sounded in my ears,
the infant in my womb leaped for joy.

And blessed art thou that hast believed,
because those things shall be accomplished
That were spoken to thee by the Lord.

Luke I, 39–45

MARY
THE MAGNIFICAT

And Mary said:

My soul doth magnify the Lord,
and my spirit hath rejoiced in God my Savior.

Because he hath regarded the humility of his handmaid;
for behold from henceforth all generations
shall call me blessed.

Because he that is mighty, hath done great things to me;
and holy is his name.

And his mercy is from generation unto generations,
to them that fear him.

13

He hath shewed might in his arm;
he hath scattered the proud in the conceit of their heart.

He hath put down the mighty from their seat,
and hath exalted the humble.

He hath filled the hungry with good things;
and the rich he hath sent empty away.

He hath received Israel his servant,
being mindful of his mercy.

As he spoke to our fathers,
to Abraham and to his seed forever.

Luke I, 46–55

MARY AND SIMEON

And Simeon blessed them, and said to Mary his mother:

Behold this *child* is set for the fall,
and for the resurrection of many in Israel,
and for a sign which shall be contradicted;

And thy own soul a sword shall pierce,
that out of many hearts,
thoughts may be revealed.

Luke II, 34–35

JOHN THE EVANGELIST

A WOMAN CLOTHED WITH THE SUN

And a great sign appeared in heaven:

A woman clothed with the sun,
and the moon under her feet,
and on her head a crown of twelve stars:

And being with child, she cried travailing in birth,
and was in pain to be delivered.

. . . .

And she brought forth a man child,
who was to rule all nations with an iron rod:
and her son was taken up to God,
and to his throne.

. . . .

And I heard a loud voice in heaven, saying:

Now is come salvation, and strength,
and the kingdom of our God,
and the power of his Christ.

Apocalypse XII, 1, 2, 5, 10

SAINT EPHREM

(C. 310–373)

VIRGIN TRULY FULL OF WONDER

(From the *Christmas Hymn*)

Virgin truly full of wonder
Bringing forth God's Son to save us!
My poor lips are all too worthless
And I may not sing thy brightness.

15

Cherubim with faces fourfold
With such brightness are not hallowed;
Seraphim six wings outstretching
Are not glorièd above thee!
Priests, rejoice in her, the blest one
Bearing our great Priest and Victim,
Freeing you from sacrifices.
He Himself, become our Victim,
Reconciles us with the Father.
Mary now for us becometh
As the heavens where God abideth;
For His everlasting Godhead
Deigns to make in her His dwelling;
Made a little Child to lift us,
While His nature never changeth;
In her womb the robe He weaveth
Clad in which He comes to save us;
Wonder that no tongue can utter,
See, her Son the Virgin beareth!
Lo, she gives her milk to feed Him,
Food to Him Who feedeth all things;
See, her tender knees support Him,
Him whose power upholdeth all things!
Still a maid and still a mother,
What is there we may not call her?
Fair in soul, in body holy;
Pure her mind and clear her judgment,
And her thoughts exceeding perfect,
She is chaste and she is prudent,
Fair in form and full of beauty.
Hark, with love and gladness glowing
Mary sweetly sings before Him:
"Whence this gift to one so lowly?
That I should conceive and bear Him—
One so little, One so mighty!
All in me, who dwells in all things!
In the hour when Gabriel sought me,
From a servant freed He made me;

Lo, the handmaid of Thy Godhead
Made the mother of Thy manhood!
Thou my Son and Thou my Maker!
Shall I ope these milky fountains,
Giving drink to Thee the Fountain?
Whence is this that I should feed Thee,
Feeding all things from Thy table?"

From the Syriac by W. H. Kent, C.S.C.

AURELIUS CLEMENS PRUDENTIUS
(348–413)

O NOBLE VIRGIN
(Hymn XI of the *Cathemerinon*, verses 53–60)

Sentisne, virgo nobilis,
Matura per fastidia
Pudoris intactum decus
Honore partus crescere?

O quanta rerum gaudia
Alvus pudica continet,
Ex qua novellum saeculum
Procedit et lux aurea!

Know thou, O Virgin, noble-blest,
That through the timeless tunneled glooms
The blinding beauty of thy soul
With childbirth splendor flames and blooms?

17

What joys are fountained for the world
Within thy womb's well, deep and white,
   Whence streams a new-created age
And golden light, and Golden Light!

From the Latin by Raymond F. Roseliep

VENANTIUS FORTUNATUS
(530–609)

O GLORY OF VIRGINS
(*O gloriosa virginum*)

Where troops of virgins follow the Lamb
Through the streets of the golden city,
Who is she walks in the lily throng
Clothed with the sun,
Her mantle flowing like an azure wave
To the jewel pavement?
High in her arms for all to adore
She holds a Man-Child.
She leads the mystic song that swells **and soars**
Like the noise of many waters,
With the voice of her own *Magnificat*.
The glory of virgins is she, a maiden mother.
O Mary, where your Jesus leads, you follow,
The first of pearl-pure human souls.
The prize that reckless Eve has tossed away,
You stretch a generous hand to give again,
And draw the earth's sad exiles
To their promised land of joy.
O doorway of the mighty King!
O radiant threshold of His light!
Life-giving Virgin!
Nations redeemed praise you with jubilation.

Jesus, Son of Mary,
Father and loving Spirit,
Glory to You forever and ever. Amen.

From the Latin by Sister Maura

CAELIUS SEDULIUS

(FIFTH CENTURY)

HAIL, MAIDEN ROOT

(Carmen Paschale II, verses 63–69)

Salve, sancta parens, enixa puerpera regem,
Qui caelum terramque tenet per saecula, cuius
  Nomen et aeterno complectens omnia gyro
Imperium sine fine manet; quae ventre beato
  Gaudia matris habens cum virginitatis honore
Nec primam similem visa es nec habere sequentem:
Sola sine exemplo placuisti femina Christo.

Hail, Maiden Root! whence lithely mounts a kingly Flowering,
That since our time unwound has petaled world and heaven
 with spring;
Whose word, whose whispered name sends life rebounding
  through earth's wheel,
While thy most envied vestal womb makes centuries rock and
  reel;
Though virgin still, thou hast the rapture every mother knows,
Thou more-than-root, thou stem and sap for One Eternal Rose—
Christ-gladness with no equal, and His everlasting snows.

From the Latin by Raymond F. Roseliep

19

WEDDĀSÊ MĀRYĀM

And now we will write the praises of our Lady, and Mother of God, the Virgin Mary, to whom prayer and petition shall be offered, by the children of Baptism, world without end.

Thou shalt be named the Beloved One, O thou blessèd among women. Thou art that second Chamber which is called the Holy of Holies . . .

Thou art the pure chest of gold in which was laid up the manna, that bread which came down from heaven, and the Giver of life to all the world.

Thou art that candlestick of gold which didst bear the shining Lamp, all times a light to the world . . .

Thou art that golden censer which bore the coals of blessèd fire, which He who shall forgive us our sins and do away transgression took of thee.

Thou art the sweet-smelling flower that sprang up from the root of Jesse.

The rod of Aaron, that budded though unplanted, and unwatered, such art thou, O Mother of Christ . . .

Thou art truly the glory of our race, and the petitioner for life to our souls.

Thou art the ladder seen by Jacob which reached from earth to heaven, and by which the angels of God were ascending and descending.

Thou art the wood which Moses saw in the flame of fire, when the wood was not consumed.

Thou art that field in which seed was not sown, and yet living Fruit came forth from thee.

Thou art the treasure which Joseph purchased, and found therein the precious Pearl, Our Savior Jesus Christ.

Rejoice, O Mother of God, thou joy of angels,

Rejoice, O pure one, foretold by prophets.

O Virgin, O Holy, O Mother of the Lord. Rightly art thou called, she who hath wondrously borne the King. A mystery abode on thee for our salvation. Let us keep silence, for we cannot express it aright, on account of the dignity of the benefactor . . .

Where is the tongue that shall be able to utter what should be said of thee, O Virgin Mother of the Word of the Father? Thou hast become the throne of the King whom the cherubim do bear. We will call thee Blessèd, and will remember thy name to all generations, O fair Dove, Mother of Our Lord Jesus Christ . . .

Great things and marvellous shall they speak concerning thee, O thou City of God; for thou hast been the dwelling-place of the Word of the Father.

All the kings of the earth shall come to thy light, and the people to thy brightness, O Virgin Mary.

Rejoice, O thou intellectual Garden, wherein Christ the Second Adam made His abode . . .

Rejoice, O thou pure Star, adorned with all the beauty of praise.

Rejoice, O Bush, which the fire of His Deity did not consume.

Let us sanctify Mary as the Mother of God, because in the city of David Our Lord and Savior Jesus Christ was born of her.

From the Ethiopian by Sir E. A. Wallis Budge

ENNODIUS

(474–521)

HOW OF THE VIRGIN MOTHER SHALL I SING?

(From *Hymnus Sanctae Mariae*)

How of the Virgin Mother shall I sing?
What utter worthily in Mary's praise?
Her Son must give, adorn, draw out my theme;
And what the Gate, or shut, or open lists,
Herself suggest. Here words should marvels be.

Why order seek, where nature's self is lost?
Our very safety is our powerlessness.

The Virgin, dwelling all alone, conceived
A Son, His body by the Spirit formed.
O prodigy! within her blessed womb
That which the tongue of Gabriel spoke was seed,
Whence sprung the Word Divine in flesh conceived.
As Mother's Offspring, He is all our own:
As Father's, He is God brought nigh to us,
Of Parents twain perfect and only Son;
Of her who bore, and Him who reigns supreme.
No greater is He than His own poor slaves;
Nor than the world's Creator is He less.
She, called the Fountain Sealed, receives Him in,
And self-same Fountain Sealed, gives forth His limbs.
Her own true Offspring leaves the sacred womb,
The seal unbroken, and inviolate.
Mother and Virgin, Jesus born of thee
Is guardian of thine intact purity.

ANONYMOUS

THE MOTHER OF GOD

(From the *Horologium*)

Lady Mary, blissful Dame,
What shall be thy proper name?
Heaven? Forasmuch as He,
Sun of Justice, dawned in thee.
Paradise? Because thy bower
Grew the Everlasting Flower.
Maid? Because, withouten stain,
Virgin aye thou dost remain.

Is it *Mother Undefiled?*
Seeing that the holy Child,
Whom thy spotless arms did bear,
God and Lord is everywhere.
Him, upon Him, prithee, call,
For to save us one and all.

From the Greek by G. R. Woodward

MAID, OUT OF THINE UNQUARRIED
MOUNTAIN-LAND

(The *Heirmos* to Ode IX, at Lauds)

Maid, out of thine unquarried mountain-land
Came Christ, the Corner-stone, unhewn by hand,
Which lined two sundered natures. Hence on high
Thee, God's own Mother, we would magnify.

From the Greek by G. R. Woodward

THE AKATHISTOS HYMN

(C. 626)

(Ode to our Blessed Lady written on the occasion of the deliverance of
Constantinople from the barbarians. A.D. 626.)

Tropárion
He Who was bodiless, having heard the bidding secretly
in his soul, went with haste to Joseph's dwelling and said to
the Unwedded One:

23

He who in his condescension boweth the
heavens down is housed unchanged and
whole within thee.
I see him take the form of a servant; and
wondering I cry to thee:

HAIL! BRIDE UNBRIDED.

I.

Kontákion

To thee, unconquered Queen, I thy city from danger freed
an offering of thanks inscribe. O Forth-bringer of God! Yet
for thy unconquerable might free me from all hurt that I
may sing to thee:

HAIL! BRIDE UNBRIDED.

Oîkos

An angel chieftain was sent from Heaven to greet the Forth-
bringer of God with Hail! Then seeing thee, O Lord, take
flesh he is wonder-wrapt, and standing crieth out with no lips
of flesh to her:

Hail! by whom true hap has dawned.
Hail! by whom mishap has waned.
Hail! sinful Adam's recalling.
Hail! Eve's tears redeeming.
Hail! height untrodden by thoughts of men.
Hail! depth unscanned by angels' ken.
Hail! for the kingly throne thou art.
Hail! for who beareth all thou bearest?
Hail! O star that bore the Sun.
Hail! of God enfleshed the womb.
Hail! through whom things made are all new made.
Hail! through whom becomes a Babe their Maker.
Hail! through whom the Maker is adored.

HAIL! BRIDE UNBRIDED.

24

II.

Kontákion

The holy one seeing herself in chastity said greatly daring unto Gabriel: Thy dark saying seems hard to my mind. What birth of a seedless begetting dost thou name? Crying out:

ALLELUIA.

Oikos

The Virgin yearning to know the knowledge unknowable made clamour to the servitor: from a maiden womb how may a Child be born? tell me. To whom he said, fearing, yet crying out:

Hail! initiate of God's unspeakable counsel.
Hail! keeper of things best kept by silence.
Hail! of Christ's wonders the beginning.
Hail! of his mysteries the head.
Hail! heavenward Ladder by which God came down.
Hail! earthly Bridge carrying the earth-born unto heaven.
Hail! of the Angels much sung marvel.
Hail! of the demons much dirged wounding.
Hail! who unspeakably hast the Light forth-brought.
Hail! who the HOW to none has taught.
Hail! wisdom of the wise outsoaring.
Hail! light on faithful minds outpouring.

HAIL! BRIDE UNBRIDED.

III.

Kontákion

Then the power from on high overshadowed unto begetting the Maid untouched; and he showed her fruitful womb as a meadow sweet to all who sought to reap salvation, as thus he sang:

ALLELUIA.

Oikos

Then the Maid of the God-bearing womb hastened unto Elizabeth; whose babe, knowing straightway her greeting, re-

joiced and with stirrings as if with song cried out to God's
forth-bringer:

Hail! vine of an unwithering Shoot.
Hail! yielder of untainted Fruit.
Hail! thou whom this man-loving Husband-man hast
  tended.
Hail! thou who unto life hast brought him who bringeth
  death to life.
Hail! field with mercies harvest-rich
Hail! board with load of pities spread.
Hail! flower-strewn meadow.
Hail! thou who the soul's safe anchorage preparest.
Hail! grateful incense-cloud of prayer.
Hail! the whole world's offering of peace.
Hail! God's goodness unto men.
Hail! man's trustfulness in God.

HAIL! BRIDE UNBRIDED.

IV.

Kontákion

Looking on thee, O Unwedded One, and dreading a hidden
wedlock, O Sinless One, the chaste Joseph was riven in mind
with a storm of doubts; but having learned that the begetting
was of the Holy Ghost, said:

ALLELUIA.

Oĩkos

The shepherds heard the angels extolling the Christ coming in the flesh; and running as to a shepherd they see him as
a Lamb unspotted being fed on Mary's breast, to whom they
carolled, saying:

Hail! Mother both of Lamb and Shepherd.
Hail! fold of rational sheep.
Hail! against unseen foes defending.
Hail! the heavenly gateways opening.
Hail! for the heavens with earth rejoice.
Hail! for things earthly with things heavenly chorus.

26

Hail! of Apostles never-silent mouthpiece.
Hail! of the Martyrs strength undaunted.
Hail! of Faith the firm foundation.
Hail! of Grace the shining token.
Hail! by whom hell is despoiled.
Hail! by whom we are clothed with glory.

HAIL! BRIDE UNBRIDED.

V.

Kontákion

The Magi, having seen the God-heralding star, followed its shining, and helped by it as by a lantern they sought by its aid the mighty King, and having reached the Unreachable they rejoiced, crying out to thee:

ALLELUIA.

Oîkos

The children of the Chaldees seeing in the virgin hands him whose hands made men, and knowing him as Lord even though he had taken the form of a servant, hastened to worship with their gifts, and cried out to her who is blessed:

Hail! Mother of the unsetting Star.
Hail! Splendour of the Mystic Day.
Hail! thou who hast quenched the fire of error.
Hail! thou who enlightenest the initiates of the Triune.
Hail! who from his seat hast driven the foe of man.
Hail! thou who hast shown to us Christ the merciful lover of men.
Hail! thou who hast redeemed us from pagan rites.
Hail! thou who rescuest us from works of mire.
Hail! thou who hast quenched the cult of fire.
Hail! thou who savest us from passion's flame.
Hail! leading the faithful in ways of self-control.
Hail! Joy of all Generations.

HAIL! BRIDE UNBRIDED.

27

VI.

Kontákion

The Magi being made heralds God-inspired went back to Babylon, having done thy bidding; unto every one they preached thee as Christ and left Herod as if he were raving, unable to sing:

ALLELUIA.

Oïkos

Having shed in Egypt the beams of thy truth thou didst chase the darkness of untruth; for its idols, O Savior, unable to meet thy strength, fell down; and as many as were freed from them cried out to God's forth-bringer:

Hail! thou who raisest mankind up.
Hail! thou who castest demons down.
Hail! thou who the cheat of lies hast trodden 'neath thy feet.
Hail! thou who the fraud of idols hast reproved.
Hail! sea the mystic Pharaoh drowning.
Hail! rock refreshing such as for life are thirsting.
Hail! pillar of fire in darkness guiding.
Hail! shade of the world wider than a cloud.
Hail! unfailing manna-food.
Hail! server of hallowing delights.
Hail! land of promise.
Hail! from whom flow milk and honey.
HAIL! BRIDE UNBRIDED.

VII.

Kontákion

Unto Simeon about to leave this deceitful world wert thou brought as a Babe; but to him wast thou known as the infinite God; wherefore marvelling at thy unspeakable wisdom he cried out:

ALLELUIA.

Oïkos

Thus did he show himself as the new Creature when he, the Creator, revealed himself to us who were made by him;

28

and, blossoming from a seedless womb he kept its unsullied purity, so that we the wonder knowing might hymn her and cry out:

Hail! flower unfading.
Hail! crown of chastity.
Hail! flashing token of resurrection.
Hail! mirror of the life of Angels.
Hail! tree of glorious fruit to feed the faithful.
Hail! wood of grateful shade where many shelter.
Hail! womb bearing the Guide of all who stray.
Hail! forth-bringing the Redeemer of all bondsfolk.
Hail! tireless pleader with the Just Judge.
Hail! help-bringer to sinners many.
Hail! cloak of those bare of hopes.
Hail! love outrunning all desire.

HAIL! BRIDE UNBRIDED.

VIII.

Kontákion

Seeing this Pilgrim Babe let us be pilgrims in this world by fixing our hearts in Heaven. To this end did the God of Heaven appear on earth as a lowly man, because he wished to draw heavenward all those who cry to him:

ALLELUIA.

Oîkos

Wholly in the things below yet not wholly absent from the things above was the infinite Word; a divine condescension, not a place-changing, was the child-bearing of this God-filled Virgin who hears these words:

Hail! who didst comprehend the incomprehensible.
Hail! gate of hallowed mystery.
Hail! word hidden from unbelievers.
Hail! unhidden glory of believers.
Hail! chariot most holy of the One above the Cherubim.

29

Hail! dwelling-place most glorious of the One above the
Seraphim.
Hail! who hast welded into one things opposite.
Hail! who hast woven maidenhood with motherhood.
Hail! by whom was loosed our sin.
Hail! by whom was opened Paradise.
Hail! Key of Christ's Kingdom.
Hail! hope of eternal boons.

HAIL! BRIDE UNBRIDED.

IX.

Kontákion

All angel-kind marvelled at thy great work of flesh-taking;
they saw the inaccessible God accessible to all as a man, dwelling with us and hearing from all:

ALLELUIA.

Oíkos

Men the most eloquent we see become as dumb fishes before
thee, O Forth-bringer; helpless to say in what way thou, being
still a maid, wert able to bring forth. But we, marvelling at
the mystery, cry out in faith:

Hail! casket of God's wisdom.
Hail! treasury of his providence.
Hail! undoing the wisdom of the wise.
Hail! making babble of men's eloquence.
Hail! for the deep thinkers are made foolish.
Hail! for the makers of myths have failed.
Hail! thou who rendest the word-webs of Athens.
Hail! thou who fillest the nets of the fishers.
Hail! thou who liftest from the deeps of unknowing.
Hail! thou who enlightenest many in knowledge.
Hail! bark for those who seek salvation.
Hail! harbour of this life's seafarers.

HAIL! BRIDE UNBRIDED.

X.

Kontákion

Being minded to save the world, the Maker of all came willing unto it and, shepherd because God, to us and for us did he appear a man; and having called like unto like, as God he hears:

ALLELUIA.

Oîkos

Unto all maidens and unto all who fly to thee thou art a wall, O maiden Forth-bringer; the Maker of heaven and earth has prepared thee unto this, dwelling in thy womb and teaching all to sing unto Thee:

Hail! pillar of purity.

Hail! gate of safety.

Hail! beginning of spiritual new-making.

Hail! leader of godly living.

Hail! thou who didst bring to a new life those who in sin were born.

Hail! thou who healest the minds of mentally stricken.

Hail! thou who castest down the corrupter of minds.

Hail! thou who didst bring forth the Sower of Holiness.

Hail! maiden bride-chamber.

Hail! thou who joinest to their Lord the faithful.

Hail! fair nursing-mother of virgins.

Hail! bridesmaid of holy souls.

HAIL! BRIDE UNBRIDED.

XI.

Kontákion

No hymn that seeks to weave into one thy many mercies is worthy of thee; were we to bring thee, O holy King, odes many as the sea sand we should do nothing worthy of what thou hast given to us who sing to thee:

ALLELUIA.

Oîkos

We see the Blessed Virgin as a lamp of living light shining upon those in darkness; she enkindleth an unearthly light to lead all unto divine knowledge; she, the Radiance that enlighteneth the mind, is praised by our cry:

Hail! ray of the spiritual Sun.
Hail! ray-flash of never-waning light.
Hail! lightning-flash illumining souls.
Hail! thunder-clap frightening foes.
Hail! who sendest forth manifold splendour.
Hail! who wellest forth a many-streamed river.
Hail! who imagest Siloe's pool.
Hail! who cleansest the stain of sin.
Hail! cleansing-vat of the conscience.
Hail! loving-cup brimming with gladness.
Hail! scent of Christ's sweetness.
Hail! life of the mystic feasting.

HAIL! BRIDE UNBRIDED.

XII.

Kontákion

When he who payeth all men's debts was minded the ancient debts to pay, self-exiled he came to them who were exiled from his grace and, tearing up the bond, he heard from all:

ALLELUIA.

Oîkos

All we who psalm thy Son give praise to thee as to the living temple, O God's Forth-bringer; when within thy womb dwelt the Lord who holdest all in his hand, he hallowed, honored thee, and taught all to cry to thee:

Hail! tent of the God and Word.
Hail! holy beyond all holy ones.
Hail! ark gilded by the Holy Ghost.
Hail! unfailing treasure-house of life.
Hail! precious diadem of godly Sovereigns.
Hail! worshipful honour of a worthy priesthood.
Hail! the Church's unassailable tower.

Hail! of the Kingdom indestructible wall.

Hail! whereby war-trophies are set up.

Hail! whereby foes are stricken.

Hail! my body's healing.

Hail! my soul's saving.

HAIL! BRIDE UNBRIDED.

Kontákion

O Mother whom all must hymn, O thou who hast brought forth the Word most holy beyond all the holiest, take our present offering, keep all from every hurt, and deliver from all wrath to come those who cry to thee:

ALLELUIA.

From the Greek by Vincent McNabb, O.P.

EPIGRAMS

(From the *Greek Anthology*)

TO THE MOST HOLY MOTHER OF GOD

I, 31

Queen,
thou holdest in thine arms
the all-ruling Son of God,
Child of thine,
Dread of the Angels.
Make Him merciful
in His counsels toward men.
Protect and guard the whole world
from woe.

From the Greek by Shane Leslie

33

ON THE ANNUNCIATION

I, 44

Hail, blissfulest maiden,
full of Grace and stainless bride!
Thou shalt receive a Son without father,
God's Embryo within thy womb.

From the Greek by Shane Leslie

ON OUR LADY OF BLACHERNAE

I, 120

If thou seekest the dread throne of God on earth,
marvel at sight of the Virgin's temple.
For she beareth God in her arms
to this place's glory.
They who are set to be rulers upon earth
believe that their sceptres here retain victory.
Here the sleepless Patriarch
averts many a cosmic cataclysm.
When the barbarians were attacking the city,
they saw her leading the army in the field,
and straightway bent their unbending necks.

From the Greek by Shane Leslie

CONSTANTINE OF RHODES

(SEVENTH CENTURY)

BEFORE THE IKON OF THE MOTHER OF GOD

(From the *Greek Anthology*, XV, 16)

If any would portray thee,
The Mother and the Maid,
He must, in lieu of color,
Call in the stars for aid,

For luminaries only
  Could limn thee, Gate of Light;
But these are not submissive
  To laws of mortal wight.

Howbeit, so far as Nature
  And rules of art permit,
By our poor brush thy beauty
  Is here outlined and writ.

From the Greek by G. R. Woodward

SAINT COSMAS
(D. 760)

THE PURIFICATION

(From the *Menaion*)

Sion, thy bridal-bower prepare
To harbor Christ thy monarch there;
And greet thou Mary maid, for why
She is the gateway to the sky,
And eke, as it is plainly shown,
Is made a cherubimic throne.
The King of Glory she doth seat,
A cloud of light this virgin sweet,
That bears the Son in flesh from far
That as before the Morning-Star.
Him in his arms took Simeon old.
And testified to all, 'Behold
The Savior of the world,' he saith,
'This Bairn is Lord of life and death.'

35

THE GAELIC LITANY TO OUR LADY

O Great Mary.

O Mary, greatest of Maries.

O Greatest of Women.

O Queen of Angels.

O Mistress of the Heavens.

O Woman full and replete with the grace of the Holy
Ghost.

O Blessed and Most Blessed.

O Mother of Eternal Glory.

O Mother of the heavenly and earthly Church.

O Mother of Love and Indulgence.

O Mother of the Golden Heights.

O Honor of the Sky.

O Sign of Tranquillity.

O Gate of Heaven.

O Golden Casket.

O Couch of Love and Mercy.

O Temple of Divinity.

O Beauty of Virgins.

O Mistress of the Tribes.

O Fountain of the Parterres.

O Cleansing of the Sins.

O Purifying of Souls.

O Mother of Orphans.

O Breast of the Infants.

O Solace of the Wretched.

O Star of the Sea.

O Handmaid of the Lord.

O Mother of Christ.

O Resort of the Lord.

O Graceful like the Dove.

O Serene like the Moon.

O Resplendent like the Sun.

O Cancelling Eve's disgrace.
O Regeneration of Life.
O Beauty of Women.
O Leader of the Virgins.
O Enclosed Garden.
O Closely Locked Fountain.
O Mother of God.
O Perpetual Virgin.
O Holy Virgin.
O Prudent Virgin.
O Serene Virgin.
O Chaste Virgin.
O Temple of the Living God.
O Royal Throne of the Eternal King.
O Sanctuary of the Holy Ghost.
O Virgin of the Root of Jesse.
O Cedar of Mount Lebanon.
O Cypress of Mount Sion.
O Crimson Rose of the Land of Jacob.
O Blooming like the Palm Tree.
O Fruitful like the Olive Tree.
O Glorious Son-bearer.
O Light of Nazareth.
O Glory of Jerusalem.
O Beauty of the World.
O Noblest-Born of the Christian Flock.
O Queen of Life.
O Ladder of Heaven.

Translated by Eugene O'Curry

A BRAVE-HEARTED MAID *

Be glad in heart,   grow great before the Lord
for thy comfort,   and build up glory;
hold thy hoard locked,   bind fast thy thought
in thine own mind.   Many a thing is unknown.
True comrades sometimes   fall away, tired,
word-promises grow faint;   so fares this world,
going swiftly in showers,   shaping its destiny.
There is one faith,   one living Lord,
one Baptism,   one Father everlasting,
one Lord of peoples   who made the world,
its good things and joys.   Its glory grew
through this passing earth,   stood for a long time
hidden in gloom,   under a dark helm,
well screened by trees,   overshadowed by darkness,
till a brave-hearted maid   grew up among mankind.
There it pleased Him   who shaped all life,
the Holy Ghost,   to dwell in her treasure-house—
bright on her breast   shone the radiant Child
who was the beginning   of all light.

From the Old English by Margaret Williams

CYNEWULF

(C.750–C.825)

A MAIDEN RING-ADORNED

(From *The Christ*)

Young was the woman,
a stainless maiden,   whom He chose for Mother,
and without man   was that wonder wrought,
that the young bride   brought forth her Bairn.

* One of the earliest extant poems to Our Lady in the English language.

Never was it so   before or since
in the wide world,   such a Child-bearing;
secret was it kept,   God's mystery.
All ghostly grace   goes throughout earth's realm,
there are many things   become enlightened
through Life's Beginner   love of long ago
which had lain dim   in dark shadows,
far-seeing prophets' songs,   ere the Powerful One came,
which make wide the path   of each voice uplifted
of those who with all heart   will to praise
their Maker's name   in wise manner.

. . . . , . .

Lo, joy of women   among wondrous hosts,
woman fairest   through the earth's wideness
of whom sea-side dwellers   have ever heard—
teach us the secret   coming down from the skies,
how that conception   was wrought in thee,
and the bearing of thy Bairn.   Yet it never befell thee
in the manner of others   to know man.
Never in truth   has it been told
in the course of ages   that such came to pass
as thou, grace-gifted,   gained for thyself;
nor do we hope   that again such will happen
in times to come.   True faith, above others,
dwelt with honor in thee.   Now the Lord of glory
thou bearest in thy bosom,   and no blight has befallen
thy mighty maidenhood.   So each child of man,
bringing forth in pain,   sows his sorrows
and afterwards reaps them.   Then said the blessed Maid,
ever filled with majesty,   Sancta Maria,
"what is this marvel   at which you are wondering,
and so grieving   moan your sorrows,
sons of Jerusalem   and its fair daughters?
You crave to know   how I kept my maidenhood
in all chastity,   yet became the mother
of the Maker's great Son?   That is a secret
kept from men,   but Christ unveiled it

39

in the precious daughter   of David's seed
who has wiped out   the sin of Eve,
undone the curse,   and has now made glorious
the lot of women,   through worlds to come
amid angel joy   in the high places,
with the Truth-Father   forever dwelling.

. . . .

Lo, thou the glory   of the great earth,
purest of women   over all the world
of all who have been   since time began,
how right it is   that all voices,
all heroes on earth,   hail thee, and say
with blithe mood   that thou art the bride
of the Noblest One,   the sky's King.
So too the highest   in the heavens,
Christ's thanes,   cry out and sing
that thou art Lady   by thy holy might
of the glorious armies,   of the race of men
living under the heavens,   and of all hell-dwellers.
For thou alone   of all mankind
thought gloriously   in thy strong mind
that thou would bring to thy Maker   thy maidenhood,
give it, sinless.   Not again
will such another   come of men
a maiden ring-adorned   who will thus send
heaven-homeward   with ever pure heart
her bright treasure.   So the Lord of triumphs
bade His high messenger   fly hither
from His strong glory,   and say to thee
that His might should speed thee,   and thou shouldst bear
The Lord's Son,   coming soon
in mercy to men,   and thou, Maria,
for ever and ever   be held unstained.

And we have heard more: that long ago
a truth-fast Prophet   said of old

in the days gone by he,   Isaias,*
that he was led   from the place of this life
into homes everlasting   where he saw all.
The wisest seer   gazed over that land
until he beheld   a brilliant throng
stationed there.   Shining it was,
a mighty gateway   with golden treasure,
bound with bright bands.   It seemed to him
that there was no man   who might prevail
to ever undo   that fast-bound portal,
or to unlock the cloister   of those city-gates,
until God's angel   to his glad thought
unwrapped the mystery   and spoke these words:
"This I tell thee,   in truth it will be done.
God Himself,   by the might of His Ghost,
will prevail to pass through   these golden gates,
and through the shut locks   will seek the earth.
And after His passing   they will stand forever
always the same,   so fast closed
that no other   save God the Savior
may ever after   prevail to unlock them."

    Now is fulfilled   what the wise one once
with his own eyes   gazed upon.
Thou art the Walldoor;   through thee the Lord Wielder
made His way out,   alone on the earth.
Even so He kept thee,   almighty Christ,
girt with His power,   clean and chosen.
And in the after years   the Lord of Angels,
Keeper of Life,   locked thee with His key,
ever spotless   and set apart.
Show us now that mercy   that the angel,
God's tidingbearer,   Gabriel brought thee.
We dwellers in cities   pray thee thus
to make known to thy folk   that fair comfort,
thy Son Himself.   Then may we dare

* A mistake for Ezekiel. cf. Ez. 44, 1–2, and the second Lesson of Matins for Wednesday of the first week in Advent.

41

with one heart   to hope for all things,
as we gaze now   at the Bairn on thy breast.
Plead for us now   with words of power,
that He will not let us   linger too long
in this death den,   to do evil things,
but that He may bear us   past the Father's boundaries,
where we, sorrowless,   may ever after
dwell in glory   with the God of Hosts.

From the Old English by Margaret Williams

ANONYMOUS

INSCRIPTION ON AN ANCIENT BELL

The rose when shaken fragrance shed around,
The bell when struck pours forth melodious sound;
The heart of Mary, moved by earnest prayer,
Will scatter grace and sweetness everywhere.

From the Latin by Fr. Bridgett

JOHN MAUROPUS
(D. 1060)

OUR LADY OF THE PASSION

O Lady of the Passion, dost thou weep?
   What help can we then through our tears survey,
If such as thou a cause for wailing keep?
   What help, what hope, for us, sweet Lady, say?

"Good man, it doth befit thine heart to lay
  More courage next it, having seen me so.
All other hearts find other balm today,—
  The whole world's Consolation is my woe!"

From the Greek by Elizabeth Barrett Browning

ANONYMOUS
(NINTH CENTURY)

AVE MARIS STELLA

Star of ocean fairest,
Mother, God who barest,
Virgin thou immortal
Heaven's blissful portal.

Ave thou receivest,
Gabriel's word believest,
Change to peace and gladness
Eva's name of sadness.

Loose the bonds of terror,
Lighten blinded error,
All our ills repressing,
Pray for every blessing.

Mother's care displaying
Offer him thy praying
Who, when born our Brother
Chose thee for his Mother.

Virgin all-excelling,
Gentle past our telling,
Pardoned sinners render
Gentle, chaste, and tender.

In pure paths direct us,
On our way protect us,
Till, on Jesus gazing,
We shall join thy praising.

Father, Son eternal,
Holy Ghost supernal,
With one praise we bless thee,
Three in One confess thee.

HERMANUS CONTRACTUS

(1013–1054)

ALMA REDEMPTORIS MATER

Gracious Mother of our Redeemer, for ever abiding
Heaven's gateway, and star of ocean, O succour the people,
Who, though falling, strive to rise again.
Thou Maiden who barest thy holy Creator, to the wonder of
  all nature;
Ever Virgin, after, as before thou receivest that Ave
From the mouth of Gabriel; have compassion on us sinners.

From the Latin by Winfred Douglas

SALVE REGINA

Mary, we hail thee, Mother and Queen compassionate;
Mary, our comfort, life and hope, we hail thee.
To thee we exiles, children of Eve, lift our crying—
To thee we are sighing, as mournful and weeping, we pass
  through this vale of sorrow.

44

Turn thou therefore, O our intercessor, those thine eyes of pity
and loving-kindness upon us sinners.

Hereafter, when our earthly exile shall be ended, shew us Jesus,
the blessed fruit of thy womb.

O gentle, O tender, O gracious Virgin Mary.

From the Latin by Winfred Douglas

NERSES
(1098–1173)

THE ANNUNCIATION

Mary, Mother of our Maker,
Daughter sprung from kingly David,
Bearing for us the New Adam,
Ancient Adam's race renewing.
God's true Mother we confess thee;
Hail, as God, the Child thou bearest;
With the angel's words we greet thee,
Echoing his note of gladness.
Dwelling-place of Light, be gladsome;
Temple, where the true Sun dwelleth;
Throne of God, rejoice, that bearest
Him, the Word of the Almighty.
Heaven, exalted o'er the heavens
Than the cherubim far higher;
From the soaring seraph's pinion
Is thy wondrous mystery hidden.
Home of Him that none may compass;
Hostel, where the Sun finds resting;
Dwelling of the Fire of Glory,
Where the Word finds fleshly clothing.
Seers of old in figures saw thee;
Moses' Bush which flames consumed not
Great Isaias' Virgin bearing,

And Ezechiel's fastened Portal.
Daniel's great Stone-bearing Mountain;
Solomon's fair Hill of Incense;
Fountain sealed for him that keeps it;
Garden closed for him that plants it.
Gideon in the Fleece beheld thee;
David saw the Rain descending;
And Micheas, Bethlehem's glory
Saw, and said, 'from thence he cometh.'
Noah's Ark, the true, the living;
Tent of Abraham, our father;
Ark of Covenant and Mercy;
Lamp, where wondrous light is burning.
God's own Garden, fair with blossoms;
Spikenard of the Spirit's sweetness;
Valley, where the lily bloometh;
Fountain whence the four streams issue;
Censer of the sweetest incense
Where the fourfold spices mingle,
Whence amid the saints in glory,
Like sweet smoke thy prayer ascendeth,
Lo, we pray thee, Life's own Mother,
From the stain of sin to cleanse us,
By thy prayer to God our Maker—
Unto whom the praise and glory.

From the Armenian by W. H. Kent, C.S.C.

ANONYMOUS
(TWELFTH CENTURY)

AVE REGINA COELORUM

Queen of the heavens, we hail thee,
Hail thee, Lady of all the Angels;
Thou the dawn, the door of morning

Whence the world's true light is risen:
Joy to thee, O Virgin glorious,
Beautiful beyond all other;
Hail and farewell, O most gracious,
Intercede for us always to Jesus.

From the Latin by Winfred Douglas

ADAM OF SAINT VICTOR

(TWELFTH CENTURY)

HAIL, MOTHER OF THE SAVIOR

(Salve Mater Salvatoris)

Hail to thee, our Savior's mother!
Vessel, honoured o'er all other!
    Chosen vessel of God's grace!
Vessel, known before creation!
Noble vessel, whose formation
    'Neath the All-wise hand took place!

Hail, the world's own mother holy!
Sprung from thorns, but thornless throughly!
    Flower a thornbrake's glory born!
We the thornbrake are, surrounded
With sin's thorns, and by them wounded,
    But thou art without a thorn.

Closed gate! fount through gardens pouring!
Storehouse, precious spikenard storing!
    Store of unguents sweet to smell!
Cinnamon's sweet-scented reed,
Incense, balsam, myrrh, indeed
    Thou in fragrance dost excel!

47

Hail, fair type of maiden grace;
Mediatrix of man's race,
   Of salvation brought to bed;
Continence's myrtle-tree,
Rose of love and clemency,
Nard whence sweetest scents are shed.

Lowliest of valleys thou,
Soil that never felt the plough,
   Which to God himself gave birth;
Meadow-flower, lily fair,
Which the valley, peerless, bare,
   Christ of thee was born on earth.

O thou paradise in heaven,
Lebanon no axe hath riven,
   Breathing sweetness all around;
Virgin whiteness, beauty's brightness,
Finest flavors, sweetest savours,
   Plenteously in thee abound.

Thou the wise king's throne appearest,
Which in shape and substance fairest,
   'Mongst all thrones hath ever been:
Chastity in ivory's whiteness,
Charity in red gold's brightness,
Shadowed forth, therein are seen.

Peerless is the palm thou bearest,
Peerless thou on earth appearest,
   And in heaven amongst the blest;
As the praise of all man's race,
Thee peculiar virtues grace,
   Given to thee above the rest.

As the sun outshines the moon,
   And the moon each twinkling star,
Mary is than every one
   Of God's creatures worthier far.

Light, that no eclipse can know,
    Is her virgin chastity;
Heat, which ne'er will cease to glow,
    Her love's deathless constancy.

*(As the venerable Adam was saluting the Blessed Virgin Mary
in the following stanza, he was himself in return saluted and
thanked by her.)*

MOTHER OF FAIR LOVE, WE NAME THEE,
FAMED TRICLINIUM WE PROCLAIM THEE,
    WHICH THE TRINITY ALL SHARE;
Though thou dost a special dwelling
For the majesty excelling
    Of the Incarnate Word prepare.

Mary, Star o'er ocean glowing,
Rival none in honour knowing,
Foremost in precedence going
    'Mongst all ranks around God's throne;
Placed in highest heaven, commend us
To thine Offspring to befriend us,
And from fear of foes defend us,
    Lest by guile we be o'er thrown.

Safe, in battle-line extended,
May we be by thee defended;
May foes' force and shrewdness blended
Bow before thy virtues splendid,
    And their craft 'neath thy foresight.
Christ the Word, God's generation,
Guard Thy mother's congregation;
Pardon guilt, grant free salvation,
And with the illumination
    Of Thy Glory makes us bright. Amen.

                From the Latin by Digby S. Wrangham

EUGENIUS III

(D. 1153)

DEDICATION

(Inscription on an architrave—sole remnant of the ancient portico of Eugenius III (1145)—in the Basilica of St. Mary Major, Rome.)

Tertius Eugenius Romanus Papa benignus
Obtulit hoc munus, Virgo Maria, tibi,
Quae Mater Christi fieri merito meruisti,
Salva perpetua Virginitate tibi.
Es Via, Vita, Salus, totius Gloria Mundi,
Da veniam culpis, Virginitatis Honos.

Eugenius, thy son, who guards the Rock,
  Carves here thy name upon this niche, O Queen:
Who art Christ's Mother by Love's meriting,
  Yet still a virgin with a virgin's mien.
O Road and Compass, Shield and Dawn-star of the world,
  Keep sinners in thy maiden mantle gently furled.

From the Latin by Raymond F. Roseliep

WALTHER VON DER VOGELWEIDE

(C. 1160–1230)

MARIA BRIGHT

Maria bright, our precious lady good,
Free me of sin, I pray thee, by thy motherhood!
Thou cleansing stream of mercy, make me new.
A sweet flower from thy noble bosom grew.
He is thy God, thy father and thy child.
For us sinners hast thou born him to the world.

He whose height and depth and breadth is measureless,
Thy little body did conceive in bliss.
What miracle can be compared to this?
Didst bear a happy burden, oh maiden undefiled!

From the Medieval German by Ian G. Colvin

ANONYMOUS

(THIRTEENTH CENTURY)

PRAISE OF MARY

(From a Parisian manuscript, *Li Loenge Nostre Dame*)

I

Bountiful in charity
River of humility,
Brightness when the dusk descends;
Often have I joyed in sin;
Out of my adversity
Lady, you have lifted me
Weak in will to make amends;
All my ways are evil ways,
On my cot I lie today
In painful weeping;
Lean down to succor me
Mother of Pity.

III

Rose of a day in May,
Lure from its evil way
My heart that slumbers;
Your fragrance must be nigh
Or of my wounds I die,
Wounds without number.

51

Queen of the saving port
Whither my ship is set,
Beauty beyond dismay,
Haste to the comforting
Of those who call to you
With a heart's ardor.

V

Never can I repay
Though all I have be yours;
I was ill-counseled;
Virgin Mother of a King,
Eyes that could dimly see
Sin has now closed for me.
Lady, devise a way,
You who watch over us,
That I be waked, and so
Alerted to my death;
That thus prepared I may
Pray here before you.

VI

Heart filled with holy joy,
Chamber of noble fruit,
Great, and most powerful;
None who has leaned upon
So great a refuge
Has failed to come to good;
He whom sin tempts and tries
Runs without light or rest
From dawn to evening;
Death has but little care
Whom it surprises;
Lady, make right my way.

52

IX

Beauty ineffable,
Goodness incomparable,
Your loving help I seek;
In my deed and my thought
Often I took delight
In dark deception;
One must not find his joy
In the sharp thorn of sin—
It returns bittterness.
By frequent sinfulness
One is brought near to death
Swift, unprovidedly.

X

A garden filled with flowers
Of every fragrance,
Your Son has made of you.
Tower of Battle,
Be refuge to our need,
Balm to the languishing,
Weary and pensive;
Death is uncertainty—
For help I come to you
That I may seek the right.
Among my enemies
Is no true refuge.

XV

Fountain of living Faith!
Oriflamme of the King!
Rally us round you!

Quench in my soul the thirst
That burns within it
Truly to fight for God.
Well must I pray you:
To bring us safe to Him
Who hid Himself in you.
Barter not, Lady mine,
When so great prize is had
For the mere asking.

From the Old French by Henry Sorg, S.D.S.

ROBERT GROSSETESTE

(1175?-1253)

A LITTLE SONG

Mary, maiden, mild and free,
Chamber of the Trinity,
A little while now list to me,
   As greeting I thee give;
What though my heart unclean may be,
   My offering yet receive.

Thou art the Queen of Paradise,
Of heaven, of earth, of all that is;
Thou bare in thee the King of bliss
   Without a spot or stain;
Thou didst put right what was amiss,
   What man had lost, regain.

The gentle dove of Noë thou art,
The branch of olive-tree that brought,
In token that a peace was wrought,
   And man to God was dear:
Sweet Lady, be my fort,
   When the last fight draws near!

Thou art the sling, thy Son the stone
That David at Goliath flung;
Eke Aaron's rod, whence blossom sprung,
    Though bare it was and dry:
'Tis known to all, who've looked upon
    Thy childbirth wondrous high.

In thee has God become a child,
The wretched foe in thee is foiled;
That unicorn that was so wild
    Is thrown by woman chaste;
Him hast thou tamed, and forced to yield,
    With milk from virgin breast.

Like as the sun full clear doth pass
Without a break through shining glass,
Thy Maidenhood unblemished was
    For bearing of thy Lord;
Now, sweetest comfort of our race,
    To sinners be thou good!

Take, Lady dear, this little song
That out of sinful heart hath come!
Against the fiend now make me strong,
    Guide well my wandering soul:
And, though I once have done thee wrong,
    Forgive, and make me whole.

From the Latin by William de Shoreham;
Modernized by F. M. Capes.

GOTTFRIED VON STRASBURG

(C. 1210)

TO MARY

Thou lily-leaf, thou roseal-bud,
Thou Queen in city of our God,
    Wherein ne'er trod
Maid like to thee, most high.
Thou balm that every pain allays,
Thou joy in harsh and bitter ways,
    Honour and praise
    Be thine eternally.
When that thy purest breast became
The living Godhead's shrine,
As rays of sun through glass will flame,
Thou, in thy virginal chaste frame,
Most sweetly didst proclaim
Christ's indwelling divine.

Thou violet-field, thou valley-rose,
Thou bloom of budded hedge-rows,
    Thou heart's repose,
Who makest heaven glad;
Thou bright and orient-beaming morn,
Thou truest friend in lives forlorn—
    Of thee is born
    Jesus, the Living Bread,
That many darkened hearts and cold
Consumed and kindled be
In love's enchantments manifold,
And through love's potency consoled;
Thence be there told
For ever praise of thee.

Thou blossom-gleam on clover-lea,
Thou burgeoned spray of aloe-tree,
    Thou bounteous sea,
Whereon we gladly float;

Thou sheltering roof of all delight,
Inviolated by the night;
    Thou chamber bright,
    Whose splendour endeth not;
Thou helpful and thou mighty tower,
Before the face of hell—
When Satan comes in storm and power
With princes of the evil hour,
When passions rage and tempests lower,
Thou dost all terrors quell.

From the German by E. M. Sweetman

SAINT BONAVENTURE
(1221–1274)
PSALTER OF THE BLESSED VIRGIN MARY

PSALM I

Blessed is the man, O Virgin Mary,
who loves thy name;
thy grace will comfort his soul.

He will be refreshed as by fountains of water;
thou wilt produce in him the fruits of justice.

Blessed art thou among women;
by the faith of thy holy heart.

By the beauty of thy body thou surpassest all women;
by the excellence of thy sanctity
thou surpassest all angels and archangels.

Thy mercy and thy grace are preached everywhere;
God has blessed the works of thy hands.

PSALM XI

Save me, O Mother of fair love:
fount of clemency and sweetness of piety.

Thou alone makest the circuit of the earth;
that thou mayst help those that call upon thee.

Beautiful are thy ways;
and thy paths are peaceful.

In thee shine forth the beauty of chastity,
the light of justice,
and the splendor of truth.

Thou art clothed with the sunrays as with a vesture:
resplendent with a shining twelve-starred crown.

PSALM XVIII

The heavens declare thy glory;
and the fragrance of thine unguents is spread abroad
among the nations.

Sigh ye unto her, ye lost sinners:
and she will lead you to the harbour of pardon.

In hymns and canticles knock at her heart:
and she will rain down upon you the grace of her sweetness.

Glorify her, ye just, before the throne of God:
for by the fruit of her womb you have worked justice.

Praise ye her, ye heaven of heavens:
and the whole earth will glorify her name.

PSALM LV

Have mercy on me, O Lady,
for my enemies have trodden upon me every day:
all their thoughts are turned to evil against me.

Stir up fury, and be mindful of war:
and pour out thy anger upon them.

Renew wonders and change marvellous things:
let us feel the help of thine arm.

Glorify thy name upon us:
that we may know that thy mercy is forever.

Distill upon us the drops of thy sweetness:
For thou art the cupbearer of the sweetness of grace.

PSALM LVIII

Deliver me from mine enemies, O Lady of the world:
arise to meet me, O Queen of piety.

The purest gold is thy ornament:
the sardine stone and the topaz are thy diadem.

The jasper and the amethyst are in thy right hand:
the beryl and the chrysolite in thy left.

The hyacinths are on thy breast;
shining carbuncles are the jewels of thy bracelets.

Myrrh, frankincense, and balsam are on thy hands:
the sapphire and the emerald on thy fingers.

PSALM LXXXI

God is in the congregation of Jews:
from whom, as a rose, has come forth the Mother of God.

Wipe away my stains, O Lady:
thou who art ever resplendent in purity.

Make the fountain of life flow into my mouth:
Whence the living waters take their rise and flow forth.

All yet who thirst, come to her:
she will willingly give you to drink from her fountain.

He who drinketh from her,
Will spring forth unto life everlasting:
and he will never thirst.

From the Latin by Sister M. Emmanuel

ANONYMOUS
(THIRTEENTH CENTURY)

SALUTATIONS: TO MARY, VIRGIN

(Laudes Beatae Mariae Virginis)

PSALM I

Hail! Mother-Maid, unmatched since time was born,
Found worthy to bear Fruit without our seed:
Give quenchless hearts the manna of God's Law
That, brimming, they may quicken homeward with Godspeed.

PSALM III

Hail! mirror of the Lady Chastity:
Loved be the womb whence stepped a Boy to earth,
Who lived and loved, then wore the rigid shroud
Of death, yet rising, pledged to death immortal birth.

PSALM VI

Hail! door of life for cankering renegades:
Unloose thy lock against the frightful gloom;
Before the sulfurous lash of voices kills,
Swing wide as dawns are wide, expose the bright Peace Room!

PSALM VII

Hail! virgin-daybreak of man's swarthy hope,
By reason of thy mercy's sunfast nod:
Touch eyes surveying through a charry glass
That they may see the skies uncloud the face of God.

PSALM VIII

Hail! towering Queen, fixed starway of our joy:
Bear praise to kingly Christ Who yielded much
Of love by holding back the clash of night
From outlaw sons that least avow His sceptre's touch.

PSALM IX

Hail! throne of grace, majestic crib for Christ,
Deemed ready for the Spirit's fertile flame:
Commute to thy most regal Heir our song
Of thee—ah, mother still with virgin ways and name!

PSALM X

Hail! mountain-pass, where wanderers must cross
To find the thicket where a Ram was slain:
Dispense the peace of sun-capped altitudes
To prodigals returning in the scarlet rain.

PSALM XI

Hail! Mother of our Lord, so close to call:
Deep in our shoulder grooves let snugly cleave
The yoke of thy sweet Christ's Beatitudes,
That we may serve as bondsmen, freed from Mother Eve.

PSALM XIII

Hail! templed place of undreamed purity,
Throne-room of Spirit, very throne of God:
Admit the castoff, penniless of grace,
That he may tramp thy palaced heavens, Mary-shod.

PSALM XIV

Hail! royal housling for the Strong-of-hand:
Praised be thy doors God sundered with His breath,
Then lived and died, and rose to shatter through
The very gates of hell and never-ending death.

PSALM XVI

Hail! city of the Sun, whose Orb is Love;
Desired before the rivered years had run:
Lead us with safety through thy whitened streets
That Love irradiate our souls, being their Sun!

PSALM XXII

Hail! lilied rod of Jesse, bloom of grace
Uncopied by the lilies' white or gold:
Be thou a shepherd staff to chide and soothe,
By whose proved strength the Herdsman prods us to His fold.

PSALM XXIII

Hail! land of glory, land untilled, yet lush
With dews of grace distilled by Spirit blaze:
Let thy most subtle-flavored Fruit upon
The tongue of ancient Adam-sons point new, sweet ways!

PSALM XXVIII

Hail! Mother, truly Mother of Godkind,
Through whom we reach to Christ a brother's hands:
May we search out the whitest of His flock,
Bring lambs of innocence, as He the Lamb commands.

PSALM XXXV

Hail! ark of grace, warm shelter for the Christ,
Prized vessel of the oceans, richly staffed:
Smoothing the ruffled waters, be our hope
Each time we merge the anchor of our wavering raft.

PSALM XLI

Hail! spring where streams of envied richness flow—
Where waters of the Son spill down their trails:
Slake thirsting ones who crave fresh sinew from
The Fount that never dries, the Fount that never fails.

PSALM LI

Hail! urn of ointment that will cool and cleanse
The stain and injury to Adam's race:
Tilting thy treasury toward earthen hearts,
Fill up the ruddy vessels with thy unguent grace.

PSALM LX

Hail! light that spears the shadowed enemy
And all who take the footway of the blind:
Descend as one keen-headed javelin
And lance the clouds without, and those within the mind.

PSALM LXII

Hail! food of savory ingredients,
Made sweet by honey flowing from the Rock:
Dole lustihood unto these hungering,
Who watch and wait the lading of the empty crock.

PSALM LXVIII

Hail! fluid star above the ocean's breast,
Whose rain of light directs the punctual sun:
Dispel the dark that clogs the sea-path of
The soul, and beacon forth a route till years are done.

PSALM LXXI

Hail! wool for lambkin, moistened virgin-fleece,
That, shuttled, formed the garment of a King:
Reflect the longings of each child from earth
To the bright place where heaven's children crowd and sing.

PSALM LXXIX

Hail! dawn of faith, high noon of hope, star-chain
Of love that girds all humankind to truth:
Stamp blindness on the eyes of those who clutch
The serpent's veering sun in days of age or youth.

PSALM LXXXIII

Hail! tabernacle kept for Deity,
In whose gold lodge the noble Christhead dwells:
Unpart the veils that screen our view so we
May see the Red Cross Knight of heaven's citadels.

PSALM LXXXIX

Hail! queenly lighthouse, blazing on the shore
For those who brave a hurricaning sea:
Keep drilling through the night's great mines until
We sight the port of the Almighty Trinity.

PSALM CI

Hail! nest for Christ the Sparrow who has winged
From God and thee to pour His singing down,
To touch His feathers to our guilty stains:
Speed thanks to Him who swept death's yoke from every town.

From the Latin by Raymond F. Roseliep

JACAPONE DA TODI
(1228–1306)

STABAT MATER

By the cross of expiation
The Mother stood, and kept her station,
Weeping for her Son and Lord:

With the nails his hands were riven;
Through her heart the sword was driven,
  Simeon's dread, predicted sword.

Oh, that blessed one grief-laden,
Blessed Mother, blessed Maiden,
  Mother of the All-holy One;
Oh, that silent, ceaseless mourning,
Oh, those dim eyes never turning
  From that wondrous, suffering Son.

Who is he of nature human
Tearless that could watch that Woman?
  Hear unmoved that Mother's moan?
Who, unchanged in shape and colour,
Who could mark that Mother's dolour,
  Weeping with her Son alone?

For his people's sins the All-holy
There she saw, a victim lowly,
  Bleed in torments, bleed and die:
Saw the Lord's Anointed taken;
Saw her Child in death forsaken;
  Heard his last expiring cry.

Fount of love and sacred sorrow,
Mother, may my spirit borrow
  Sadness from thy holy woe;
May it love—on fire within me—
Christ, my God, till great love win me
  Grace to please him here below.

Those five wounds of Jesus smitten,
Mother, in my heart be written
  Deeply as in thine they be;
Thou my Savior's cross who bearest,
Thou thy Son's rebuke who sharest,
  Let me share them both with thee.

In the passion of my maker
Be my sinful soul partaker;
 Let me weep till death with thee:
Unto me this boon be given,
By thy side, like thee bereaven,
 To stand beneath the atoning tree.

Virgin holiest, Virgin purest,
Of that anguish thou endurest
 Make me bear with thee my part;
Of his passion bear the token
In a spirit bowed and broken,
 Bear his death within my heart.

May his wounds both wound and heal me;
His blood enkindle, cleanse, anneal me;
 Be his cross my hope and stay:
Virgin, when the mountains quiver,
From that flame which burns for ever,
 Shield me on the judgment-day.

Christ, when he that shaped me calls me,
When advancing death appals me,
 Through her prayer the storm make calm:
When to dust my dust returneth
Save a soul to thee that yearneth;
 Grant it thou the crown and palm.

From the Latin by A. de Vere

66

DANTE ALIGHIERI

(1265–1321)

SAINT BERNARD'S PRAYER TO OUR LADY

(From the *Paradiso*, XXXIII)

O virgin mother, daughter of thy Son,
  More humble than all creatures and more high,
  Goal unto which the eternal plan has run,
Thou art she who did so greatly dignify
  Man's nature, that no feeling of disdain
  Was in his Maker at being made thereby.
Within thy womb was love kindled again,
  Through whose heat there hath sprung to bloom this flower
  Within the peace that ever shall remain.
Charity's torch ablaze like noonday's hour
  Art thou to us. And down where mortals throng,
  Thou art a living spring whence hope doth shower.
Lady, thou art so great, so very strong,
  That who'd have grace, nor seeks thine aid to find,
  Attempts a wingless flight where wings belong.
Not only those requesting help, thy kind
  Solace assists, but oftentimes of free
  Liberality it leaves requests behind.
Mercy is in thee, pity is in thee,
  In thee is lavishness, in thee the whole
  Goodness that in created things can be.
Now, this man who has, from the lowest bowl,
  Seen, up to this point, throughout all creation,
  The lives of all the spirits, soul by soul,
Begs by thy grace such strength of elevation
  That he may lift his eyes till they've aspired
  Still higher toward the Ultimate Salvation.
And I, for mine own vision never fired
  More than for his, proffer thee every prayer,—
  And pray they be not less than is required,—
That every cloud mortality must wear
  Thou strip him clean of by thy prayers thereto,
  That of the Highest Bliss he be aware.

Queen, who canst what thou wilt, I pray thee too,
  Keep his affections wholesomely awake,
  After his sight of that supernal view.
Protect him from each human urge and ache.
  Behold how Beatrice and many tiers
  Of saints clasp hands to thee, for my prayers' sake.

From the Italian by Louis How

FRANCESCO PETRARCH

(1304–1374)

ODE TO THE VIRGIN

Fair Virgin,
  Vestured with the sun!
Bright shining one,
  Star-crowned:
Who such sweet ultimate favor found
  From all eternity
With the great primal Sun
  That from the height
He stooped in thee to hide the light
  Of His Divinity:
  Now shall my love upraise
  New measures in thy praise,
Though to begin without thy aid were vain
  And without His,
Who, joined with thee in love, shall ever reign.
  The I invoke who never turned deaf ear
When ardent faith called to thee without fear.
  Virgin, if our poor misery,
    Our trafficking with pain,
  In thy deep heart stir pity,
    Incline to me again;

Once more on thy sure succour now I lean,
Though of base clay am I
   And thou be Heaven's queen.

   O Virgin wise,
     Of prudent virgins blest,
   Foremost and best
     Beyond compare,
With shining lamp most clear,
   Bright shield of the oppressed,
     With thee we know
Not mere escape from evil fortune's blow
     Or bitter death;
   But triumph o'er the foe—
Thou who dost cool this flame
Which, blazing among mortals, love we name.
   Virgin, turn thou thine eyes,
   Sad eyes that watched beside
The piteous body of thy Son that died,
     Unto my dubious state;
Thy counsel now I seek,
     Disconsolate.

   Pure Virgin, without stain,
     God's daughter meet,
   And by conception sweet
     His mother too,
Thou, a keen brightness to our dark world sent,
   Art high Heaven's ornament.
     Through thee alone,
O lofty window gleaming with heavenly light,
   Came God's Son and thine own,
To save us mortals from our desperate plight.
   Among all dusty toilers of the earth,
     Virgin most blessed,
Chosen wert thou, pure gold without alloy,
To turn Eve's sorrow into joy.
   O make me of God's grace to worthy be,

Thou who art crowned in heaven eternally.
  Virgin most holy, filled with every grace,
Who the sure path of true humility did'st trace
  To the bright heavens where my prayers ascend,
Thou did'st achieve the much-desired end
    That springs from fairest root.
  Of Justice and of Piety art thou
    The ripened fruit.
  Three sweetest names unite
    In thee alone,
Mother and spouse and daughter, all in one.
    O Virgin glorious,
  Sweet spouse of our high King
    Who gloriously reigns,
    Who freed us from our chains,
By His most sacred wounds—His love's unerring dart,
  O soften thou my heart.

  Virgin, in all this world unparalleled,
    Heaven enamoured is
    Of thy pure bliss.
O thou, the living temple of high God,
  Who thy virginity did fruitful make,
Most joyful for thy sake,
    In spite of inner strife,
    Is all my life.
  Virgin most pious, sweet,
    In whom all graces meet,
  My spirit flows to thee,
    Praying that thou wilt bend
The twisted fragments of my broken life
  Unto a perfect end.

  O Virgin, bathed in ever-living light,
Bright star of our tempestuous dark sea,
    Thou faithful guide
  To mariners that trust in thee,

Behold in what dread tempest I am tossed,
    Rudderless and alone,
  Fearing myself for lost.
With sinful soul I still in thee confide.
  Virgin, I pray
Let not our common enemy deride
    My bitter woe.
  Remember that for man's sin
God took upon Himself our human flesh,
  To thy sweet virgin cloister entering in.

  Virgin, how many tears have I not shed,
What prayers have I not offered and in vain!
  Sorrow and loss and fear of future pain,
    All these have compassed me
Since my first breath I drew by Arno's side;
    My searchings far and wide,
My acts, my words and mortal beauty have undone
      me quite.
  Virgin, sacred of soul,
    Do not delay,
    For who can say
That I approach not to life's end.
  And the long swiftly flowing years,
  Swift as an arrow's dart,
  Filled to the brim with bitter loss and tears,
  Have left no other trace
Than a sure death which looks me in the face.
  Virgin, she whom I mourn is now dry dust,
Who, living, caused me full a thousand woes,
    But of my bitter throes
    She knew not one,
Else had she honor lost, and I had been undone.
  But thou, O heavenly Lady fair,
    Our Goddess rare,
  (If to speak thus of thee is meet)
Virgin of delicate high sentiment,
    Thou see'st all.

Others have failed to end my misery;
But now through thy great power can be wrought
  Health to my soul, and honor unto thee.

Virgin, with whom my hope is most secure,
  In need my refuge sure,
    Let not thy gaze
  Rest on unworthy me.
    But rather see
Him who in likeness to Himself did raise
 My fallen nature base,
  Enduing it with grace;
Else might my eyes of error take their fill.
  Medusa-like
 My heart would turn to stone
And evil humors on the air distill.
  O Virgin, thou of pious, saintly tears,
Rid then my soul of cowardly fears,
  That my last hours devout may be,
Not mixed as heretofore with earthly mire,
  But tinged with heavenly fire.

Virgin, with human heart devoid of pride,
  Humanity thou too did'st take
  By primal Love's decree.
With contrite heart I pray you pity me.
  I that so faithful proved
To mortal lady, greatly, vainly loved,
  So gentle art thou, shall I not love thee?
If from my sad and miserable state
  By thy sweet hands I rise,
Virgin, I consecrate to thee
  All my most treasured enterprise.
    My dear imaginings,
My language and my thoughts, my pen, my heart,
    My tears and sighs;
Be thou my guide to Heaven, nor fail to weigh
  Celestial desires when I pray.

72

The day approaches now, so swift time flies,
  Virgin, uniquely one,
    Of my last end.
Pierced is my heart with thought of death;
  Now to thy Son, true Man, true God, commend
My parting soul, that He may give release,
  Receiving my last breath in peace.

From the Italian by Helen Lee Peabody

GIOVANNI BOCCACCIO

(1313–1375)

THE QUEEN OF THE ANGELS

Queen of the Angels, Mary, thou whose smile
  Adorns the heavens with their brightest ray;
  Calm star that o'er the sea directs the way
Of wandering barks unto their homing isle;
By all the glory, Virgin without guile,
  Relieve me of my grievous woes, I pray!
  Protect me, save me from the snares that stay
Beyond to misdirect me and defile!

I trust in thee with that same trust of old,
  Fixed in the ancient love and reverence
Which now I tell as I have always told.
  Guide thou my journey, strengthen my pretense
To reach with thee at last the blessed fold
  Thy Son prepares His flock in recompense.

From the Italian by Thomas Walsh

ANONYMOUS

(FOURTEENTH CENTURY)

REGINA COELI

O Queen of heaven, be joyful, alleluia:
Because he whom so meetly thou barest, alleluia,
Hath arisen, as he promised, alleluia:
Pray for us to the Father, alleluia.

From the Latin by Winfred Douglas

EYSTEINN OF ASGRÍMSSON

(D. 1361)

AUTHOR'S ENTREATY FOR HIS LAY

(From *Lilya*)

Thee, May * and Mother, I entreat
That, by thine intercession sweet,
From out my mouth a truthful lore
In verses smoothly wrought may pour;
That, from my lips both soft and bright,
As if in glowing gold bedight,
The words proclaimed of old may ring;
To God that gift I needs must bring.

This Mary is our Mother bright,
With honour decked, a Flower of might,
And bloometh like a ruddy rose,
Which by a living fountain grows;
A fragrant Root of lowliness;
A Ray of the Spirit's holiness;
She loves but God and who are good;
In virtue is she like to God.

* *May* is the true Middle-English form of *maid*, *maiden*, or *virgin*.

74

Thou, Mary, art our Mother bright;
Thou, Mary, art with honour dight;
Thou, Mary, beamest bright with love—
O Mary, baleful sin remove;
O Mary, by our faults and fears,
O Mary, heed our flowing tears;
O Mary, our great afflictions calm;
Pour, Mary, o'er our wounds thy balm.

With loving kindness, Mary deign
My heart to fill, as I would fain,
That, if I might still farther bring
My lay, thy praise therein should ring;
But, higher praise, in verses made
On Christ's dear Mother could ne'er be said,
Than, that thou art by God alone,
O May, in purity outshone.

From the Icelandic by Eirik Magnusson

ANONYMOUS

(FOURTEENTH CENTURY)

THE QUEEN OF COURTESY

(The Pearl, stanzas 36–38)

"Blissful," said I, "can this be true—
And else forgive me that I spake—
Art thou the queen of heavens blue,
Honoured where'er sun's light doth break?
From Mary's virgin flower there grew
A Child, and grace did there awake.
Must not some greater worth endue

75

One who from her the crown would take?
   And for her matchless sweetness' sake
   We call her Phoenix of Araby,
   After that bird of spotless make,
   Like to the Queen of Courtesy."

"Courteous Queen!"—as suppliant would,
She knelt to ground and veiled her face—
"Pattern of Mother—and Maidenhood!
Blessed Beginner of every grace!"
Rising, a while she silent stood,
Then said to me, "Of those who chase
And seize their prey a multitude,
But usurpers none, are within this place.
   That Empress's domains embrace
   Earth, Heaven, Hell; and yet will she
   None disinherit or abase,
   For she is Queen of Courtesy.

"The Kingdom's Court where God's Self is,
This nature has in its very frame:
That every one who gains ingress
Is queen or king in deed and name
Of all the realm; none dispossess
The others, but their wealth acclaim;
And each would wish (vain such access!)
The others' crown worth five the same.
   But my Lady, from whom Jesus came,
   High over all hath empery,
   Nor any here account it blame,
   For she is Queen of Courtesy.

Translated into Modern English by Stanley Perkins Chase

ALEXANDER BARCLAY

(1475–1552)

BALLADE TO OUR LADY

(From the Dedication of *The Ship of Fools*)

O Mother Mary, Flower of all womankind,
In beauty passing every earthly creature,
In whom the fiend no thought of sin could find;
O blessed Mother remaining Maiden pure.
O shining Lamp in light passing nature,
Most clear Crystal by clean virginity,
O holy Mother, and virgin most demure,
Direct our life in this tempestuous sea.

O Well of mercy, O godly Graft of grace,
Bright as the moon, and Port of Paradise,
In whom Christ Jesu chose His dwelling place,
Chose as the Son, O Rose, passing all price,
Planted in Anne without consent of vice;
O noble Fruit sprung of a barren tree,
Direct our life in this tempestuous sea.

O Cedar tree growing in Libany,
O Rod of Jesse, and Spouse of Solomon,
O Well of water lasting eternally,
O Garden closed, O Fleece of Gideon,
O City of God, and sempiternal Throne
Of God, elect for thy humility,
To thee I call, O Lady, hear my moan,
Direct our life in this tempestuous sea.

O Mary, Mirror clear and immaculate,
O Tower of David with pinnacles without peer,
O pleasant Olive with virtue decorate,
Pillar of faith while thou wast living here.
O heavenly Star, of gardens, Fountain clear,
O pleasant Lily most godly in beauty,

77

All compassed round with the sharp thorn and briar,
Direct our life in this tempestuous sea.

. . . .

O Queen, deliver us from captivity,
On thee we call, in thee our comfort is,
That by thy prayer to the high Trinity
All shall be pardoned that we have done amiss;
Since thou art in eternal joy and bliss,
Our Mediatrix before the Deity,
Our hope is sure that thou wilt never miss
Our life to guide in this tempestuous sea.

. . . .

Thou art the Star, blazing with beames bright
Above this world's dark waves so violent,
Clearing the dark of sin with thy bright light,
Man's Mediatrix with God omnipotent;
Wherefore, to thee, O Lady, I present
This simple book, though it unworthy be,
But poor and simple, and much ineloquent,
Rudely composed in this tempestuous sea.

PART THREE

"MY THOUGHT WAS ON A MAID SO BRIGHT"

Medieval Mary-Songs

ANONYMOUS

LULLABY

(THIRTEENTH CENTURY)

Dormi, Jesu, mater ridet
Quae tam dulcem somnum videt,
Dormi, Jesu blandule.
Si non dormis mater plorat,
Inter fila cantans orat:
Blande veni somnule.

Slumber, Jesu, lightly dreaming,
On Thee mother's smile is streaming,
Slumber, Jesu, fair-haired son.
Mother grieves if Thou art stirring;
Song spins to her wheel's soft whirring:
"Sandman steal Thee, little One!"

From the Latin by Raymond F. Roseliep

I SAW A MAIDEN

I saw a maiden sit and sing,
She lulled a little child, a sweet lording;
  Lullay, mine Liking, my dear Son, mine Sweeting,
  Lullay, my dear Heart, mine own dear Darling.

81

That very lord is He that made all things
Of all lords He is Lord, King of kings.
 Lullay, mine Liking, my dear Son, mine Sweeting,
 Lullay, my dear Heart, mine own dear Darling.

There was mickle melody at that Childës birth,
All that were in heaven's bliss, they made mickle mirth.
 Lullay, mine Liking, my dear Son, mine Sweeting,
 Lullay, my dear Heart, mine own dear Darling.

Angels bright they sang that night and saiden to that Child,
"Blessed be Thou, and so be she that is both meek and mild."
 Lullay, mine Liking, my dear Son, mine Sweeting,
 Lullay, my dear Heart, mine own dear Darling.

Pray we now to that Child, and to His mother dear,
Grant them His Blessing that now maken cheer.
 Lullay, mine Liking, my dear Son, mine Sweeting,
 Lullay, my dear Heart, mine own dear Darling.

ROSA MYSTICA

There is no rose of such virtue
As is the rose that bare Jesu:
Alleluia!

For in that rose containèd was
Heaven and earth in little space:
Res Miranda!

By that rose we well may see
There be One God in Persons Three:
Pares Forma!

The angels sang, the shepherds too:
Gloria in excelsis Deo!
Gaudeamus!

Leave we all this worldly mirth
And follow we this joyful birth:
Transeamus!

OF ONE THAT IS SO FAIR AND BRIGHT

Of one that is so fair and bright
Velut maris stella,
Brighter than the day is light
Parens et puella.
I cry to thee to turn to me;
Lady, pray thy Son for me,
Tam pia.
That I may come to thee,
Maria.

In sorrow, counsel thou art best,
Felix fecundata:
For all the weary thou art rest,
Mater honorata:
Beseech Him in thy mildest mood,
Who for us did shed His Blood
In Cruce
That we may come to Him
In luce.

All this world was forlorn,
Eva peccatrice.
Till Our Savior Lord was born
De te genetrice;

83

With thy Ave sin went away,
Dark night went and in came day
Salutis.
The well of healing sprang from thee,
Virtutis.

Lady, flower of everything,
Rosa sine spina,
Thou bore Jesus, Heaven's King,
Gratia Divina.
Of all I say thou bore the prize,
Lady, Queen of Paradise
Electa:
Maiden mild, Mother
Es effecta.

Well He knows He is thy Son,
Ventre quem portasti:
He will not refuse thy boon,
Parvum quem lactasti:
So courteous and so good He is,
He hath brought us to our bliss
Superni,
Who hast shut up the dark foul pit
Inferni.

CRADLE SONG OF THE VIRGIN

Jesu, my sweet Son dear,
On a poor bed Thou liest here,
That grieves me sore:
Thy cradle is as a bier,
Ox and ass Thy fellows here,
Weep may I therefore.

Jesu, sweet Son, be not wrath
Though I have neither clout nor cloth
Round Thee to fold;
I have no clout Thee to nest,
But lay Thy feet to my breast
And keep Thee from the cold.

O JESU PARVULE

I saw a sweet and silly sight
A blissful bride, a blossom bright
That mourning made and mirth among—
A maiden mother, meek and mild,
In cradle kept a knavë child
That softly slept; she sat and sang—
"Lullay lullow, lully lullay, lully, lully,
   lully, lully,
    Lullow, lully, lullay,
   My bairn sleep softly now."

MY THOUGHT WAS ON A MAID SO BRIGHT

As I lay upon a night
My thought was on a maid so bright
That men name Mary, full of might,
   Redemptoris Mater.

To her came Gabriel with light
And said, "Hail be thou, blessed wight!
To be named now art thou dight
   Redemptoris Mater."

At that word that lady bright
Anon conceived God full of might,
Then men wist well that she hight
Redemptoris Mater.

Right as the sun shines through glass
So Jesu in his mother was
And therefore wist men that she was
Redemptoris Mater.

Now is born that babe of bliss,
And queen of heaven his mother is,
And therefore think I that she is
Redemptoris Mater.

When Jesu on the road was pight
Mary was doleful of that sight;
Until she saw him rise upright,
Redemptoris Mater.

Jesu, that sittest in heavenly light
Grant us to come before thy sight
With that maid that is so bright,
Redemptoris Mater.

I SING OF A MAIDEN

I sing of a maiden that
    Matchless is,
King of all Kings is her son
    I wis.

He came all so still
    Where his mother was
As dew in April
    That falleth on grass.

86

He came all so still
　　To his mother's bower
As dew in April
　　That falleth on shower.

He came all so still
　　Where his mother lay
As dew in April
　　That falleth on spray.

Mother and maiden
　　Was ne'er none but she
Well may such a lady
　　God's Mother be.

CAROL: THE FIVE JOYS OF THE VIRGIN

Mary, for the love of thee
Blithe and glad may we be,
And I shall sing as ye may see,
　　Sua quinque gaudia.

The first Joy was sent to thee
When Gabriel greeted thee
And said Hail Mary in chastity,
　　Officiaris gravida.

The second Joy was full good
When Christ took both flesh and blood
Without sorrow and changing of mood,
　　Enixa est puerpera.

The third Joy was of great might
When Jesu was on the Rood dight,
Dead and buried in all men's sight,
　　Surrexit die tertia.

The fourth Joy was without aye
When Jesu to Hell took the way
And with him come great array,
Ad coeli palacia.

The fifth Joy was on Holy Thursday
Unto Heaven He took the way,
God and man, and so He is for aye,
Ascendit super sidera.

FAIR MAIDEN, WHO IS THIS BAIRN?

(FIFTEENTH CENTURY)

Mater, ora Filium,
ut post hoc exilium
nobis donet gaudium
beatorum omnium!

Fair maiden, who is this Bairn,
That thou bearest on thine arm?
Sir, it is a King's Son,
That in heaven above doth wone.

Man to father hath he none,
But himself is God alone;
Of a maid he would be born,
To save mankind that was forlorn.

The kings brought him presents,
Gold and myrrh and frankincense,
To my Son, full of might,
King of kings and Lord of right.

Fair maiden, pray for us
Unto thy Son, sweet Jesus,
That he will grant us of his grace
In heaven high to have a place!

NUNC GAUDET MARIA

(FIFTEENTH CENTURY)

Mary is a lady bright,
She hath a son of mickle might,
Over all this world she is light,
   Bona natalicia.

Mary is so fair of face,
And her son so full of grace,
In Heaven (may) He make us a place,
   Cum sua potencia.

Mary is so fair and bright,
And her son so full of might,
Over all this world He is light,
   Bona voluntaria.

Mary is both good and kind,
Ever on us she hath mind,
That the fiend shall us not bind.
   Cum sua malicia.

Mary is queen of everything,
And her son a lovely king;
God grant us all (a) good ending,
   Regnat Dei gracia.

89

THIS OTHER NIGHT

This other night I saw a sight,
  A star as bright as day,
And ever among a Maiden sung:
  'By by, Baby, lullay.
This virgin clear, withouten peer,
  Unto her Son 'gan say:
'My Son, my Lord, my Father dear,
  Why liest thou in hay?
Methink be right, that king and knight
  Should lie in rich array;
Yet, nevertheless, I will not cess
  To sing, By by, lullay.'

This Babe full fain answered again,
  And thus, methought, he said:
'I am a King, above all thing,
  In hay if I be laid:
For us shall see that kingès three
  Shall come on twelve-day;
For this behest give me your breast,
  And sing, By, Baby, lullay.'

'In fay I say, withouten nay,
  Thou art my Darling dear;
I shall thee keep while thou dost sleep,
  And make thee goodè cheer:
And all thy will I will fulfill,
  Thou wottest it well, in fay;
Yet more than this, I will thee kiss
  And sing, By, Baby, lullay.'

'My Mother sweet, when I have sleep,
  Then, take me up at loft
Upon your knee, that ye set me
  And handle me full soft:

And in your arm lap me right warm,
　　And keep a-night a-day;
And if I weep and cannot sleep,
　　Sing, By, Baby, lullay.'

'My Son, my Lord, my Father dear,
　　Sith all is at thy will,
I pray thee, Son, grant me a boon,
　　If it be right and skyll,
That child, or man, or may, or can,
　　Be merry on this day,
To bliss them bring; and I shall sing,
　　By by, Baby, lullay.'

'My Mother sheen, of Heaven Queen,
　　Your asking shall I speed;
So that this mirth displease me not
　　In word, neither in deed;
Sing what ye will, so that ye fulfill
　　My ten commandments aye;
You for to please let them not cease
　　To sing, Baby, lullay.'

This other night I saw a sight,
　　A star as bright as day,
And ever among a Maiden sung,
　　'By by, Baby, lullay.

THE ANNUNCIATION

(SIXTEENTH CENTURY)

(Es ging unsere liebe Fraue)

Our Lady went forth pondering
Upon a high and holy thing—
The way into her cell she took
And prayed from out her little book.

There on its shining page she read
What of God's Mother Scripture said;
The angel Gabriel waiting near,
Caught by her beauty bright and clear,
Slipped in through the close-fastened door
And greeting, knelt upon the floor.
But what was that above her head?
A lovely Dove with wings outspread—
The Holy Ghost came like a prayer
Within the little maiden there.
She carried God beneath her heart
Without a touch of pain or smart;
She carried Him till Christmas morn
When Jesus Christ the Lord was born.

From the German

MARY PASSES

(Maria durch 'nen Dornenwald ging)

Mary went through the thorn-wood wild;
Mary went through the thorn-wood wild
That had borne no blossom for seven years.

What did she carry beneath her heart?
Without a pang—a little child
She carried gently beneath her heart.

And on the thorn-boughs roses stood
As she carried the sweet child through the wood;
Upon the thorn-boughs roses stood.

From the German

MARY WAS WATCHING

(Chtic, Aby Spal)

Mary was watching tenderly
Her little son;
Softly the mother sang to sleep
Her darling one.
Sleep, lovely child, be now at rest,
Thou son of Light,
Sleep, pretty fledgling in thy nest,
All through the night!

Mary has spread your manger bed;
Sleep little Dove,
God's creatures all draw near to praise;
Crown of my love.
Sleep, little Pearl, Creator Lord,
Our homage take,
Bees bring you honey from their hoard,
When you awake.

From the Czechoslovakian by Mary Cochrane Vojácek

MARY'S VISION

"Are you asleep, Mother?"
"I am not, indeed, my son."
"How is that, Mother?"
"Because of a vision I have of thee."
"What vision is that, Mother?"

93

"There came a slim dark man on a slender black
    steed,
A sharp lance in his left hand,
Which pierced thy right side,
Letting thy sacred blood pour down upon thee."
"True is that vision, Mother."

From the Gaelic by Eleanor Hull

PART FOUR

"MARY IS A FLOWER FIELD"

From Chaucer to Donne

GEOFFREY CHAUCER

(1340–1400)

LA PRIÈRE DE NOSTRE DAME

(The A.B.C.)

Almighty and all merciable queen
  To whom that all this world fleeth for succour
  To have release of sin, of sorrow and of teene,
  Glorious Virgin, of every flower the flower,
  To thee I flee, confounded in error.
  Help and relieve me, thou mighty lady fair,
  Have pity on my perilous langour,
  Vanquished me hath my cruel adversaire.

Bounty so fixt hath in thine heart his tent
  That well I know thou wilt my succour be.
  Thou canst not him refuse that with a good intent
  Asketh thine help. Thine heart is aye so free.
  Thou art largesse of true felicity,
  Haven of refuge, of quiet and of rest.
  See how the thievès seven chase after me.
  Help, lady bright, unto my ship distressed.

Comfort is none but in you, lady dear.
  For, lo, my sin and confusion,
  Which ought not in thy presence to appear,
  Upon me lay a heavy accusation
  Of very truth and desperation:
  And, as by right, they might indeed sustain
  That I were worthy my damnation,
  Save for thy mercy, blissful Heaven's queen.

97

Doubt is there none, thou queen of misericorde,
  That thou art cause of grace and mercy here.
  God vouchsafed through thee with us to accord.
  For, truly, Christ's own blissful mother dear,
  Were now the bow bent in such manner,
  As it were first, of justice and of ire,
  The righteous God would of no mercy hear
  But, through thee have we grace, as we desire.

Ever hath mine hope of refuge been in thee.
  For, heretofore, full oft, in many a wise,
  Hast thou to misericorde receivèd me.
  But, mercy, lady, at the grand assize
  When we shall come before the high justice!
  So little fruit shall then in me be found
  That, but thou ere that day shall me chastise,
  Justly indeed my deeds will me confound.

Fleeing, I fly for succour to thy tent
  Me for to hide from tempests full of dread,
  Beseeching thee that thou thee not absent
  Though I be wicked. Still help me in this need.
  All have I been a beast in will and deed.
  Yet, lady, do thou clothe me with thy grace.
  Thine enemy and mine—lady take heed—
  Unto my death all apt is me to chase.

Glorious maid and mother, which that never
  Were bitter, neither in the earth nor sea,
  But full of sweetness and of mercy ever,
  Help that my Father be not wroth with me.
  Speak thou, for Him I dare not see,
  So have I done on earth, alas, the while,
  That, truly, if thou not my succour be,
  To stinke eternal, He will my ghost exile.

He vouchsafed, tell Him, according to His will,
  Become a man, to have our alliance

And, with His Precious Blood, He wrote the bill,
Upon the Cross, as general acquitance
To every penitent in full credence:
And, therefore, lady bright, thou for us pray
Then shalt thou both restrain all His grievance
And make our foe to fall short of his prey.

I know it well, thou wilt be our succour:
Thou art so full of bounty, for certain.
For, when a soul hath fallen in error
Thy pity goeth and healeth him again.
Then makest thou his peace with his Sovereign
And bringest him out of the crooked street.
Whoso thee loveth he shall not love in vain:
That shall he find, as life shall him permit.

Kalends illuminate were they
That in this world were lighted with thy name:
And whoso goes to thee the rightful way
He has no fear that he in soul be lame.
Now, queen of comfort, since thou art that same
To whom I make resort for my medicine,
Let not my foe my wound again inflame
My cure into thy hand I all resign.

Lady, thy sorrow can I not portray
Under the Cross, nor His grievance penance
But for your both's pains I do you pray
Let not our ancient foe repeat his vaunts
That he hath in his records of mischance
Convicted those ye both have bought so dear.
As I have said before, thou ground of our substance,
Continue on us thy piteous eyes so clear.

Moses that saw the bush of flaming red
Burning of which there ne'er a stick was brenned
Was prophet of thine unspotted maidenhead.
Thou art the bush on which there did descend

99

The Holy Ghost, the which that Moses wende
Had been afire: and this was in figure.
Now, lady, from the fire thou us defend
Which shall in Hell eternally endure.

Noble princess, which never had a peer,
   Certes, if any comfort in us be
   It comes of thee, thou Christ's own mother dear.
   We have no other melody nor glee
   Us to rejoice in our adversity:
   Nor any advocate that will and dare so pray
   For us, and that for little hire as thee
   That helpeth for an Ave-Marie or tweye.

O very light of eyes that now are blind,
   O very joy of labour and distress,
   O treasurer of bounty to mankind,
   Thee whom God chose to mother for humblesse
   From His handmaid He made the mistress
   Of heaven and earth, our prayer up for to beede.
   This world awaiteth ever on thy goodness,
   For never failest thou man in his need.

Purposed I have some time for to enquire
   Wherefore and why the Holy Ghost thee sought
   When Gabriel's voice came to thine ear.
   He not to war with us such a wonder wrought
   But for to save us He so dearly bought.
   Then needeth we no weapon us for to save
   But only, that we did not as we ought
   Do penitence and mercy ask and have.

Queen of comfort, yet when I me bethink
   That I offended have both Him and thee
   And that my soul is worthy for to sink,
   Alas, I, caitiff, whither may I flee?
   Who shall unto thy Son my intermediary be?
   Who but thyself that art true pity's well?

Thou hast more ruth on our adversity
Than in this world there any tongue may tell.

Reform me, mother, and me chastise:
  For certainly my Father's chastening
  That dare I not abide in any wise,
  So fearful is His righteous reckoning.
  Mother, of whom Our Mercy chose to spring
  Be thou my judge and too my soul's good leech.
  For ever in you is pity abounding
  To each that will for pity you beseech.

Sooth it is that God granteth no pity
  Without thee: for God, of His goodness,
  Forgiveth none save that it pleaseth thee.
  He hath thee made the vicar and mistress
  Of all this world and eke the governess
  Of heaven, and He restrains His justice
  After thy will: and therefore in witness
  He hath thee crowned in such a royal wise.

Temple devout, where God hath His dwelling,
  From which the misbelieved deprivèd be,
  To you my soul all penitent I bring.
  Receive me, I can no further flee.
  With thorns envenomous, O heaven's queen,
  From which the earth accursèd was of yore,
  I am so wounded, as ye well may see,
  That I am lost almost, it smarts so sore.

Virgin that art so noble of apparaille
  And leadest us unto the lofty tower
  Of Paradise, me do thou teach and counsaile
  How I may have thy grace and thy succour.
  All have I been in filth and in errour.
  Lady, unto that court thou me adjourn
  That calleth is thy Bench, O freshest flower,
  Therein where mercy ever shall sojourn.

Xristus, thy Son, that in this world alighte
  Upon the Cross to suffer His Passion,
  And eke that Longius his heart pighte
  And made His Heart's own Blood to run adown,
  And all was this for my salvation;
  And I to Him am false and e'en unkind
  And yet He will not my damnation—
  For this I thank you, succour of all mankind.

Ysaac was figure of His death, certain,
  That so far forth his father would obey
  That it be reckoned nothing to be slain;
  Right so thy Son willed as a lamb to die.
  Now, lady full of Mercy, I you pray
  Since He His mercy measured out so large,
  Be ye not sparing; for all we sing and say
  That yet from vengeance ever be our targe.

Zachary thee called the open well
  To wash the sinful soul out of his guilt.
  Therefore this lesson ought I well to tell
  That save thy tender pity we were spilt.
  Now, lady bright, since that thou canst and wilt
  Be to the seed of Adam merciable,
  Bring us to that palace that is built
  For penitents that be to mercy able.
                     Amen.

From the Middle English by Anselm M. Townsend, O.P.

INVOCATION

(From *The Prologue of the Prioress's Tale*)

O mother-maid! O maiden-mother free!
O bush unburned, burning in Moses' sight,
That down didst draw, with thine humility,

The spirit of God within thee to alight,
Out of whose virtue, when His will made bright
Thine heart, the Father's wisdom came to birth—
Now help my tale to honor thee on earth!

Lady, thy goodness and thy shining glory,
Thy virtue and thy great humility,
No learnèd tongue can ever put in story,
For sometimes, lady, ere we pray to thee,
Thou hast foreseen, in thy benignity,
And by thine intercession gett'st us light
That to thy dear Son guides our feet aright.

O blessed queen, so feeble is my wit
To utter thy surpassing worthiness,
I cannot well sustain the weight of it,
But like a child twelve months of age or less,
That scarce a word of two can well express,
So am I now; therefore I pray of you,
Guide well my song that I shall say of you.

*Translated into Modern English by Frank **Ernest** Hill*

THE PRIORESS'S TALE

There was in Asia, in a city great,
Mid Christian folk, a Jewish colony,
Protected by a lord who ruled that state,
For wicked gain and foulest usury,
Hateful to Christ and to His company;
And through the street all men could walk or ride;
For it was free, with both ends open wide.

A little school of Christian people stood
Down at the farther end, in which there were
Children full many come of Christian blood
That studied in that school from year to year
The kind of lessons taught to students there—
Singing, that is to say, and reading too,
Such things as children in their childhood do.

Among these children was a widow's son—
A little chorister but seven years old;
Who day by day to school had always gone;
And any time he might the form behold
Of Jesu's mother, then, as he was schooled,
It was his custom down to kneel and say
His *Ave Marie* as he went his way.

The widow thus her little son had taught
Alway's to worship Christ's own mother dear,
Lady of bliss; and nowise he forgot,
For a good child is quick of eye and ear,
But when I call to mind this story here,
St. Nicholas himself appears to me,
For he when young served Christ so reverently.

This little child, while studying among
The others in the school was soon aware
Of *Alma Redemptoris* being sung
By children that were learning anthems there;
And ever he edged as close as he might dare,
And listened to the singing, word and note,
Until he had the whole first verse by rote.

Nothing he knew of what this Latin said,
Being too tender in his years, and young.
But with a comrade on a day he plead
To explain this song to him in his own tongue,
Or tell him wherefore it was being sung;
To know the words and what was meant by these
Eager and oft he prayed him on bare knees.

104

His comrade was an older boy than he,
And answered thus: "This song, I hear folk say,
Was made about our blissful Lady free,
To hail and give her greeting, and to pray
Her help and grace when we shall pass away.
No more about the matter can I tell;
Singing I learn, but grammar not so well."

"And is this song made then in reverence
Of Christ's dear mother?" cried this innocent;
"Now truly, I will make great diligence
To know it all, ere Christmastide be spent,
Though in my work I suffer punishment
And thrice an hour be beaten for it," said he,
"Yet will I learn it, honoring our Lady."

Each day his fellow taught him privately
While going home, until he knew by rote
The whole, and sang it well and lustily
From word to word, according to the note,
And twice a day the song would pass his throat,
Once when to school and once when home he went;
On Christ's dear mother was his whole intent.

This child passed through the Jewish colony,
As I have said, in going to and fro,
And there full merry would he sing, and cry
"*O Alma Redemptoris;*" for the glow
And sweetness pierced his little spirit so
Of Christ's dear mother, that he could not stay
His song to pray to her along the way.

Satan, that serpent and our ancient foe,
That hath in Jewish heart his hornet's nest,
Swelled up and cried, "Woe, Hebrew people, woe!
In such dishonor do ye dwell at rest?
Must ye endure these accents ye detest,
Hearing this boy that goes with evil cause
To desecrate by song your faith and laws?"

And from that day the wicked Jews conspired
How they might bring this innocent to die,
And to this end a homicide they hired
That had his dwelling in an alley nigh,
And as the little child was going by,
This Jew leapt forth and seized him fast, and slit
His throat, and cast his body in a pit.

Into a privy they his body threw,
Where all these Jews had purged them commonly,
O cursed folk, O Herods born anew,
What shall avail you all your infamy?
Murder will out; yea, this is certainty;
And where God's honor lifteth voice to plead,
Loud cries the blood against your cursèd deed!

O martyr wedded to virginity
Now mayest thou sing indeed, and follow on
After the white celestial Lamb (cried she);
Of thee the great evangelist, St. John
In Patmos wrote, saying of martyrs gone
Before the Lamb, and singing songs all new,
That never women in the flesh they knew!

This widow sat awaiting all the night
Her little child, and yet he cometh not;
So when the day drew once again to light,
Her face all pale with fear and heavy thought
At school and every place about she sought,
Until thus much she learned at length—that he
Was seen last in the Jewish colony.

With mother's pity burning in her breast,
She goes as if she had but half her mind,
To every place where there could be the least
Of likelihood her little child to find;
And ever on Christ's mother meek and kind
She called, and so at length, and long distraught,
Among the cursèd Jews her child she sought.

She asketh and she prayeth piteously
Of all the Jews that dwelt within that place,
To tell her if they saw her child go by,
And they said "No." But Jesu, of His grace,
This impulse gave her in a little space:
That for her little son she stood and cried
Where he within the pit lay close beside.

O mighty God, who let'st Thy praise be called
By mouths of innocents, lo, here Thy might!
This gem of chastity, this emerald
Of martyrdom, this blessèd ruby bright,
There where he lay with throat all gashed and white,
"*O Alma Redemptoris*" clearly sang—
So loud that all the place about him rang.

The Christians on the street, that came and went,
Rushed up with wonder as they heard him sing,
And for the provost hastily they sent;
And he came thither without tarrying,
And Christ be praised that is of heaven the King,
And His dear mother, glory of mankind;
And after that, the Jews he bade them bind.

This little child with piteous lamentation
Was lifted up the while he sang his song,
And, honored by a mighty congregation,
Unto the nearest abbey borne along;
There by the bier his mother swooning hung,
And scarcely could the people that were there
This second Rachel from his body tear.

This provost bade at once that every Jew
With torture and by shameful death should die
That anything about this murder knew;
He would not tolerate such iniquity;
Evil to them where evil ought to lie!
So first he had them dragged behind wild horses,
Then hanged: the judgment which the law enforces.

Upon his bier still lay this innocent
By the chief altar while the mass was said
And after that, the priests and abbot went
With all dispatch to burial of the dead;
But sprinkling holy water on his head,
They heard him speak, at sprinkling of the water,
And sing—"*O Alma Redemptoris Mater!*"

Now this good abbot was a holy man,
As all monks are (or leastwise ought to be!)
And so to conjure this young child began,
And said, "Beloved child, I ask of thee,
By virtue of the Holy Trinity,
Tell me the reason why, though it appear
Thy throat is cut, thou singest still so clear."

"My throat is cut, yea, to the very bone,"
Answered this child, "and following nature's way,
Long time ago I should have died and gone,
But Jesu Christ, as find ye books to say,
Wills that His glory be in mind, and stay,
And so for honor of His mother dear,
Still may I sing *O Alma* loud and clear.

"Always I loved Christ's Mother, well of grace,
My wit and knowledge wholly thus applying,
And when they threw my body in that place,
She came to me and spoke as I was lying,
And bade me sing this song when I was dying,
As ye have heard, and, after I had sung,
I thought she laid a grain upon my tongue.

"Therefore I sing, and sing I must indeed,
In honor of that sainted maiden free,
Till from my tongue ye take away the seed;
And afterwards these words she said to me:
'My little child, I will come back for thee
When from thy tongue the grain at last is taken;
Be not dismayed, thou shalt not be forsaken.'"

This holy monk, this abbot, instantly
Drew out the tongue and took away the grain,
And he gave up his spirit quietly;
And when the abbot saw this wonder plain,
His salt tears trickled down his cheeks like rain,
Face down he fell all flat upon the ground,
And lay there still as he with cords were bound.

And all the convent on the pavement lay
Weeping and praising Christ's own mother dear,
And after that they rose and went away
Taking this blessed martyr from his bier
And made for him a tomb of marble clear,
And in it closed his little body sweet;
Where he is now, pray God we all shall meet!

O Hugh of Lincoln, slain in youth also
By cursèd Jews, as all the world knows well,
For it was but a little time ago,
Pray too for us, sinful and changeable,
That God, in whom abounding mercies dwell,
May multiply His grace on us, and thence
Do to His mother Mary reverence!

Translated into Modern English by Frank Ernest Hill

INVOCATIO AD MARIAM

(From *The Prologue to the Second Nun's Tale*)

And thou that art the flower of virgins all,
Of whom Bernard has such a love to write,
To thee now in beginning first I call!
Comfort of wretched us, help me recite

Thy maiden's death, who, through her merit bright,
Won life eternal, vanquishing with glory
The fiend, as men can read here in her story.

Thou daughter of thy son, mother and maid,
Thou well of mercy, sinful souls' physician,
In whom for goodness God to dwell essayed,
Thou humble, yet enthroned in high position,
So didst thou lift our nature with thy mission
That He that made all nature thus was won
To clothe in flesh and blood His only Son.

Within the blissful cloister of thy side
To man's shape grew the eternal Love and Peace,
Lord of the three-fold universe, and Guide,
Whom earth and heaven and ocean never cease
To praise. Thou, spotless virgin, for a space,
Bore in thee, maiden still in every feature,
He that Creator was of every creature.

In thee are mercy and magnificence,
Goodness and pity in such unity
That thou, that art the sun of excellence,
Not only helpest those that pray to thee,
But often times, in thy benignity,
Freely, before men any help petition,
Thou dost appear, and art their lives' physician.

Help me, thou lovely, meek, and blessèd maid,
Who banished now in bitterness must dwell;
Think on the wife of Canaan, she who said
That dogs would feed upon the crumbs that fell
Down from their master's table. I know well
That I am sinful, wretched son of Eve,
And yet accept my faith, for I believe.

And since all faith, when lacking works, is dead,
So give me now for work both wit and space,

That I from darkness be deliverèd!
O thou that art so fair and full of grace,
Be advocate for me in that high place
Where there is endless singing of "Hosannah!"
Mother of Christ, dear daughter of St. Anna!

And from thy light my soul in prison light,
Where it is troubled by contamination
Of this my body, and the heavy weight
Of earthly lust, and all false inclination;
O heaven of refuge for us, O salvation
Of all souls whom distress and sorrow neighbor,
Help me, for I will now attempt my labor!

Translated into Modern English by Frank Ernest Hill

ROBERT FABYAN
(D. 1513)

DEDICATION OF THE CHRONICLES OF
ENGLAND AND FRANCE

Most Blessed Lady, Comfort to such as call
To thee for help in each necessity,
And what thou aidest may in no wise appal,
But to the best is formed in like degree,
Wherefore, good Lady, I pray it may please thee,
At my beginning my pen so to lead
That by thine aid this work may have good speed.

QUIA AMORE LANGUEO

(The Virgin's Complaint)

Within a chamber of a tower,
As musing on the moon stood I,
A Queen with honour crowned and power
Methought I saw, enthroned on high.
She made her plaint with bitter cry,
For soul of man by sin brought low:
I may not leave mankind to die,
 Quia amore langueo.

I look for love of man my brother,
And plead for him in every guise,
His Mother I, who can no other,
Why should I my dear child despise?
Though he offend me divers wise
Through fleshly frailty falling so,
Yet must I rue until he rise,
 Quia amore langueo.

I wait and bide with longing great;
I love and look till man shall crave;
I plain for pity of his state;
Would he ask grace 'twere his to have:
Call on me, Soul, thee will I save,
Child, bid me come, and I will go;
Thou ne'er didst pray, but I forgave,
 Quia amore langueo.

Mother of Mercy I was made,
For thee who need'st it to illume:
More fain am I to grant its aid
Than thee to ask; why mute in gloom?

When said I nay? tell me to whom?
Ne'er yet, indeed, to friend or foe;
When ye ask not, I weep your doom,
    Quia amore langueo.

O wretch on earth, I look on thee
And see thee trespass day by day,
With sin against my purity,
With pride against my meek array:
My love thee waits, wrath is away;
My love thee calls; from me wilt go?
I prithee, sinner, to me pray.
    Quia amore langueo.

My Son was outlawed for thy sin,
And scourged for trespasses of thine;
It pricks my heart so near my Kin
Should be so used. Ah, son of mine,
Thy Father is the Son benign
My breast hath fed; He loved thee so,
He died for thee; my heart is thine,
    Quia amore langueo.

My Son hath suffered for thy love;
His heart was piercèd with a spear;
To bring thy soul to heaven above
For love of thee so died He here.
Therefore thou art to me most dear,
Since my dear Son hath loved thee so;
Thou ne'er dost pray but I thee hear,
    Quia amore langueo.

My Son hath granted for thy sake
Each grace that I to ask am fain,
For He no vengeance wills to take,
If I for thee crave grace amain:

Then mercy ask, thou shalt obtain,
I with such ruth look on thy woe;
I long for mercy thou shouldst plain,
    Quia amore langueo.

From the Middle English by E. M. Clerke

JOHN LYDGATE
(1370–1451)

THE CHILD JESUS TO MARY THE ROSE

My Father above, beholding the meekness
    As dew on roses doth his balm spread,
Sendeth His Ghost, most sovereign of cleanness,
    Into thy breast, ah, Rose of Womanhood!
    When I for man was born in my manhood—
For which, with roses of heavenly influence,
I me rejoice to play in thy presence.

Benign Mother, who first did enclose
    The blessèd bud that sprang out of Jesse,
Thou of Judah the very perfect Rose,
    Chosen of my Father for thine humility
    Without fading, most cleanest to bear me—
For which with roses of chaste innocence
I me rejoice to play in thy presence.

O Mother! Mother! of mercy most abound,
    Fairest Mother that ever was alive,
Though I for man have many a bloody wound,
    Among them all there be roses five,
    Against whose mercy fiends may not strive;
Mankind to save, best roses of defence,
When they me pray for help in thy presence.

LUIGI PULCI

(1432–1484)

APPEAL FOR ILLUMINATION

(From the *Morgante Maggiore*, Canto I, ii)

And thou, O Virgin, Daughter, Mother, Bride
　　Of the same Lord, who gave to you each key
Of heaven and hell, and everything beside,
　　The day thy Gabriel said "All hail" to thee,
Since to thy servants pity's ne'er denied,
　　With flowing rhymes, a pleasant style and free—
Be to my verses, then, benignly kind,
And to the end illuminate my mind.

From the Italian by George Gordon, Lord Byron

FRANÇOIS VILLON

(1431–1485)

HIS MOTHER'S SERVICE TO OUR LADY

Lady of Heaven and earth, and therewithal
　　Crowned Empress of the nether clefts of Hell,—
I, thy poor Christian, on thy name do call
　　Commending me to thee, with thee to dwell,
　　Albeit in nought I be commendable.
But all mine undeserving may not mar
Such mercies as thy sovereign mercies are;
　　Without the which (as true words testify)
No soul can reach thy Heaven so fair and far.
Even in this faith I choose to live and die.

115

Unto thy Son say thou that I am His.
  And to me graceless make Him gracious.
Sad Mary of Egypt lacked not of that bliss,
    Nor yet the sorrowful clerk Theophilus,
    Whose bitter sins were set aside even thus
Though to the Fiend his bounden service was.
Oh, help me, lest in vain for me should pass
    (Sweet Virgin that shalt have no loss thereby!)
The blessed Host and sacring of the Mass.
  Even in this faith I choose to live and die.

A pitiful woman, shrunk and old,
  I am, and nothing learned in letter-lore.
Within my parish-cloister I behold
    A painted heaven where harps and lutes adore,
    And eke in Hell whose damned folk seethe full sore:
One bringeth fear, the other joy to me.
That joy, great Goddess, make thou mine to be,—
    Thou of whom all must ask it even I;
And that which faith desires, that let it see.
  For in this faith I choose to live and die.

O excellent Virgin Princess! thou didst bear
  King Jesus, the most excellent comforter,
Who even of this our weakness craved a share
    And for our sake stooped to us from on high,
Offering to death His young life sweet and fair.
Such as He is, Our Lord, I Him declare,
  And in this faith I choose to live and die.

From the French by Dante Gabriel Rossetti

GIROLAMO SAVONAROLA

(1452–1498)

O STAR OF GALILEE

(Written during the Great Plague in Florence)

O Star of Galilee,
Shining over earth's dark sea,
Shed thy glorious light on me.

Queen of clemency and love,
Be my advocate above,
And through Christ all sin remove.

When the angel called thee blest,
And with transports filled thy breast,
Thy high Lord became thy guest.

Earth's purest creature thou,
In the heavens exulting now,
With a halo round thy brow.

Beauty beams in every trace
Of the Virgin-Mother's face,
Full of glory and of grace—

A Beacon to the just,
To the sinner hope and trust,
Joy of the angel-host.

Ever-glorified, thy throne
Is where thy blessed Son
Doth reign: through Him alone,

All pestilence shall cease,
And sin and strife decrease,
And the kingdom come of peace.

From the Latin by R. R. Madden

SINCERUS SANNAZARIUS

(1458–1530)

CELESTIAL QUEEN

(From *De Partu Virginis,* Book III)

                              Celestial Queen,
Thou on whom men below and saints above
Their hopes repose; on whom the bannered hosts
Of heaven attend—ten thousand squadrons armed,
Ten thousand cars self-moved, the clarion shrill,
The trumpet's voice—while round in martial pomp,
Orb within orb, the thronging seraphs wheel:
If on thy fane, of snow-white marble reared,
I offer yearly garlands; if I raise
Enduring altars in the hollowed rock
Where Margyllina, lifting her tall head,
Looks down upon the foamy waves beneath—
A sea-mark to the passing sailor's eye;
If, with due reverence to thy name, I pay
The solemn rites, the sacrificial pomp,
When each returning year we celebrate
The wondrous mystery of the Birth Divine—
Do thou assist thy feeble bard, unused
To tasks so great, and wandering on his way:
Guide thou my efforts and inspire my song.

From the Latin by John C. Eustace

118

WILLIAM DUNBAR

(C. 1460–C. 1520)

BALLAD OF OUR LADY

O Empress high, celestial Queen most rare,
  Eternal Princess, Flower immaculate,
Our sovereign Help when we to thee repair—
  Hail, Rose intact; hail Maid inviolate,
  That, with the Father, was predestinate
The Bairn and Maker of us all to bear,
  Untouched with slightest soil of sinful state,
But, Virgin pure, more clear than crystal fair.

O blessed Rose, O Gem of chastity,
  O Well of beauty, of all goodness Store,
O Way of bliss, Flower of virginity,
  O Fount of truth, O Star ne'er darkened o'er—
  Grant sinful me, who live in foulness sore,
To track the steps of perfect charity,
  And to forsake my sins both less and more,
Aye serving him who shed his Blood for me.

O blessed Lady, of all goodness made,
  Since all my hope and trust is in your grace,
By your high sweetness let your Son be prayed,
  To grant me leisure ere I die, and space
  From out my soul all foulness to erase;
And aye to live in virtue pure arrayed,
  From out the fiend's close bondage and embrace—
Now, glorious Lady, of your goodness aid.

For e'en as Phoebus, with his beams so bright,
  Illumines all this earth in longitude,
E'en so, your grace, your beauty and your might
  Adorneth all this world in latitude;
  Therefore to me ye show your gratitude

119

And your magnificence, that day and night
Your grace benign to me of life be food;
And save me from each foul malignant wight.

Modernized by E. M. Clerke

DESIDERIUS ERASMUS
(1467–1536)

VOTIVE ODE

(At Our Lady's Shrine in Walsingham)

Hail, Jesus' Virgin-Mother ever Blest,
Alone of women Mother eke and Maid,
Others to thee their several offerings make;
This one brings gold, that silver, while a third
Bears to thy shrine his gift of costly gems.
For these, each craves his boon—one strength of limb—
One wealth—one, through his spouse's fruitfulness,
The hope a father's pleasing name to bear—
One Nestor's eld would equal. I, poor bard,
Rich in goodwill, but poor in all beside,
Bring thee my verse—nought have I else to bring—
And beg, in quital of this worthless gift,
That greatest meed—a heart that feareth God,
And free for aye from sin's foul tyranny.
                    Erasmus, his vow.

From the Greek by J. T. Walford

120

GIL VINCENTE

(1470–1540)

CANTIGA

White and crimson, cheek and breast,
O Virgin blest!
The pledge of love in Bethlehem
A flower was on the rose-tree's stem,
O Virgin blest!
In Bethlehem in sign of love
The rosebranch raised a rose above,
O Virgin blest!
In the rose came forth a flower—
Jesus, our high Lord of Power—
O Virgin blest!
The Rose of all the rosetree's span,
God in nature and a Man,—
O Virgin blest!

From the Galician-Castilian by Thomas Walsh

ANONYMOUS

HYMN FOR LAUDES
FEAST OF OUR LADY OF GOOD COUNSEL

(C. 1520)

(Plaude festivo, pia gens, honore)

Clap hands with festal joy, O holy people,
And honor the Genestan shrine,
For there the picture of our Lord's great Mother
Shines gracious and serene.
Silent and swift as thought our Lady came,

And by her beauty, ever ancient, ever new,
She charmed the hearts of all
In happy Genazzano.
With her she brought
To the wide region round
Blessing on blessing multiplied:
She healed the sick in body or in mind;
And wafting far
Dark perils to the Roman realm,
She shone as bright and fair as noonday light.
O Virgin, marvel-crowned!
Still do you shine with heavenly radiance.
Bring aid to those in misery;
And, patient with petitioners,
Smile on their urgent prayers.

So, honor, glory, power be to Him
Who, from His dazzling throne in heaven,
Rules the succession of this world's events,
One God in three Persons. Amen.

From the Latin by Sister Maura

(SIXTEENTH CENTURY)

A LAMENT FOR OUR LADY'S SHRINE
AT WALSINGHAM

(In 1538 the shrine was stripped, and at Cromwell's orders the image of
Our Lady was sent by cart to Chelsea, and there publicly burned.)

In the wrecks of Walsingham
Whom should I choose,
But the Queen of Walsingham
To be guide to my muse?

Then, thou Prince of Walsingham,
   Grant me to frame
Bitter plaints to rue thy wrong,
   Bitter woe for thy name.

Bitter was it, oh, to see
   The silly sheep
Murdered by the ravening wolves,
   While the shepherds did sleep.
Bitter was it, oh, to view
   The sacred vine,
While the gardeners played all close,
   Rooted up by the swine.
Bitter, bitter, oh, to behold
   The grass to grow
Where the walls of Walsingham
   So stately did show.

Such were the works of Walsingham,
   While she did stand:
Such are the wrecks as now do show
   Of that holy land.
Level, level with the ground
   The towers do lie,
Which, with their golden glittering tops,
   Pierced once the sky.

Where were gates, no gates are now:
   The ways unknown
Where the press of peers did pass,
   While her fame far was blown.
Owls do shriek, where the sweetest hymns
   Lately were sung:
Toads and serpents hold their dens,
   Where the palmers did throng.

Weep, weep, O Walsingham,
   Whose days are nights:
Blessings turned to blasphemies,

Holy deeds to despites;
Sin is where our Lady sate;
Heaven turned is to hell:
Satan sits where our Lord did sway—
Walsingham, oh, farewell.

SAINT JOHN OF THE CROSS
(1542–1591)

ROMANCE VIII

Then He summoned an archangel,
Blessed Gabriel by name.
To a lowly girl called Mary
The Divine archangel came.

For with her co-operation
This great mystery could be.
With her flesh the Word was clothed
By the Blessed Trinity.

All three Persons worked that wonder,
Though in One alone 'twas done.
In the womb of Blessed Mary
Took her flesh the Incarnate Son.

He that erst had had but Father
Had a Mother likewise then,
And He was conceived in Mary,
As have been no other men.

Hers His flesh and hers His dwelling
Ere His human life began,
Wherefore He is called together
Son of God and Son of Man.

From the Spanish by E. Allison Peers

THE SONG OF MARY THE MOTHER OF CHRIST

Fain would I write, my mind ashamèd is,
My verse doth fear to do the matter wrong:
No earthly music good enough for this,
Not David's harp, nor Hierom's mourning song.
Nor Esaie's lips are worthy once to move,
Though Seraphim's fire hath kindled them with love.

. . .

Then sing, O saints, O holy heavenly choir!
And I shall strive to follow on your song:
This sacred ditty is my chief desire,
My soul to hear this music now doth long.
And longing thus, all wist, there was no din,
They silent stood, to see who should begin.

For none did think him worthy to be one,
And every one to other there gave place:
But bowing knees to Jesus every one,
They him besought for to decide the case.
Who said to me, most fit for this appears
My mother's plaint, and sacred virgin tears.

Straight all agreed. The Virgin ready prest
To do the will of her eternal Son:
With heavenly cheer and most melodious breast,
Her sacred song and ditty thus begun.
Bowing herself unto the glorious throne,
Where Three did sit adorèd all in one.

. . .

And still as they the Virgin singing hear,
In self same time, so echoed all the choir:

. . .

Thou only Son of God, Father of might,
Maker of me and all, the well of grace:
Fountain of love, eternal Son of light,
Became my Son; and falling on her face,
Repeating this full oft (with music sweet)
She did adore and kiss our Savior's feet.

. . . .

O how my cross was ever mixed with sweet!
My pain with joy, mine earth with heavenly bliss!
Who always might adore my Savior's feet,
Embrace my God, my loving infant kiss.
And give him suck Who gives the angels food,
And turn my milk into my Savior's blood.

Sometimes he cast his hand about my neck,
And smiling looked his mother in the face:
Some joy or skill, I found in every beck,
Each day discovered wisdom, love and grace,
I cannot utter what I did espy,
When I beheld his little glorious eye.

. . . .

Till thirty years my Lord at home did dwell,
Joseph and I enjoyed his presence still:
Where I my self abashed am· to tell
How he in all, obeyèd to my will.
How do you think I movèd was to see
The Prince of Angels subject unto me?

. . . .

What should I here his holy life recount,
Which he with me these thirty years did spend?
This story would unto a volume mount,
My song doth to his sacred passion tend.
And all do know his pity needs must pass
Who, of all saints, the Lord and Savior was.

. . . .

ROBERT SOUTHWELL

(C. 1561–1595)

OUR LADY'S SALUTATION

Spell Eva back and Ave shall you find,
  The first began, the last reversed our harms;
An angel's witching words did Eva blind,
  And angel's Ave disenchantes the charms;
Death first by woman's weakness entered in,
In woman's virtue life doth now begin.

O virgin breast! The heavens to thee incline,
  In thee their joy and sovereign they agnize;
Too mean their glory is to match with thyne,
  Whose chaste receite God more than heaven did prize.
Hail fairest heaven, that heaven and earth doth bliss,
Where virtue stars, God, Son of justice is!

With haughty mind to Godhead man aspired,
  And was by pride from place of pleasure chased;
With loving mind our manhood God desired,
  And us by love in greater pleasure placed:
Man laboring to ascend procured our fall,
God yielding to descend cut off our thrall.

HENRY CONSTABLE

(1562–1613)

TO OUR BLESSED LADY

In that, O Queen of Queens, thy birth was free
From guilt, which others do of grace bereave,
When, in their mother's womb, they life receive,

127

God, as His sole-borne daughter, lovèd thee.
To match thee, like thy birth's nobility,
He thee His Spirit for thy spouse did leave,
And so wast linked to all the Trinity.

Cease, then, O Queens, who earthly crowns do wear
To glory in the pomp of worldly things;
If men such high respect unto you bear,
Which daughters, wives, and mothers are of kings,
What honour should unto that Queen be done,
Who had your God for Father, Spouse, and Son!

RICHARD VERSTEGAN (ROWLANDS)
(1548–1636)

OUR LADY'S LULLABY

Upon my lap my Sovereign sits,
    And sucks upon my breast;
Meanwhile His love sustains my life,
    And gives my body rest.
        Sing lullaby, my little Boy,
        Sing lullaby, my life's Joy!

When Thou hast taken Thy repast,
    Repose, my Babe, on me;
So may Thy Mother and Thy nurse
    Thy cradle also be.
        Sing lullaby, my little Boy,
        Sing lullaby, my life's Joy!

I grieve that duty doth not work
  All that my wishing would,
Because I would not be to Thee
  But in the best I should.
     Sing lullaby, my little Boy,
     Sing lullaby, my life's Joy!

Yet as I am, and as I may,
  I must and will be Thine,
Though all too little for Thyself
  Vouchsafing to be mine.
     Sing lullaby, my little Boy,
     Sing lullaby, my life's Joy!

My wits, my words, my deeds, my thoughts,
  And else what is in me,
I rather will not wish to us
  If not in serving Thee.
     Sing lullaby, my little Boy,
     Sing lullaby, my life's Joy!

My Babe, my Bliss, my Child, my Choice
  My Fruit, my Flower and Bud;
My Jesus, and my only Joy,
  The sum of all my good.
     Sing lullaby, my little Boy,
     Sing lullaby, my life's Joy!

My Sweetness, and the Sweetest most
  That heaven could earth deliver;
Soul of my love, Spirit of my life,
  Abide with me for ever.
     Sing lullaby, my little Boy,
     Sing lullaby, my life's Joy!

Live still with me, and be my Love,
  And death will me refrain;
Unless Thou let me die with Thee,
  To live with Thee again.

Sing lullaby, my little Boy,
Sing lullaby, my life's Joy!

Leave now to wail, thou luckless wight,
That wrought'st thy race's woe;
Redress is found, and foiléd is
Thy fruit-alluring foe.
Sing lullaby, my little Boy,
Sing lullaby, my life's Joy!

Thy fruit of Death from Paradise
Made Thee exilèd mourn;
My fruit of Life to Paradise
Makes joyful Thy return.
Sing lullaby, my little Boy,
Sing lullaby, my life's Joy!

Grow up, good Fruit, be nourisht by
These fountains two of me,
That only flow with maiden's-milk,
The only meat for Thee.
Sing lullaby, my little Boy,
Sing lullaby, my life's Joy!

The earth is now a heaven become,
And this base bower of mine
A princely palace unto me
My Son doth make to shine.
Sing lullaby, my little Boy,
Sing lullaby, my life's Joy!

His sight gives clearness to my sight,
When waking I Him see;
And sleeping, His mild countenance
Gives favour unto me.
Sing lullaby, my little Boy,
Sing lullaby, my life's Joy!

When I Him in my arms embrace,
　I feel my heart embraced,
Ev'n by the inward grace of His,
　Which He in me hath placed.
　　　Sing lullaby, my little Boy,
　　　Sing lullaby, my life's Joy!

And when I kiss His loving lips,
　Then His sweet-smelling breath
Doth yield a favour to my soul,
　That feeds Love, Hope, and Faith.
　　　Sing lullaby, my little Boy,
　　　Sing lullaby, my life's Joy!

The shepherds left their keeping sheep,
　For joy to see my Lamb;
How may I more rejoice to see
　Myself to be the Dam.
　　　Sing lullaby, my little Boy,
　　　Sing lullaby, my life's Joy!

Three kings their treasures hither brought
　Of incense, myrrh, and gold,
The heaven's Treasure and the King
　That here they might behold.
　　　Sing lullaby, my little Boy,
　　　Sing lullaby, my life's Joy!

One sort of angel did direct;
　A star did guide the other;
And all the fairest Son to see
　That ever had a mother.
　　　Sing lullaby, my little Boy,
　　　Sing lullaby, my life's Joy!

This sight I see, this Child I have,
　This Infant I embrace,
O endless Comfort of the earth,
　And heaven's eternal Grace.

Sing lullaby, my little Boy,
Sing lullaby, my life's Joy!

Thee Sanctity herself doth serve;
Thee Goodness doth attend;
Thee Blessedness doth wait upon,
And Virtues all commend.
Sing lullaby, my little Boy,
Sing lullaby, my life's Joy!

Great kings and prophets wished have
To see that I possess;
Yet wish I never Thee to see,
If not in thankfulness.
Sing lullaby, my little Boy,
Sing lullaby, my life's Joy!

Let heaven, and earth, and saints, and men,
Assistance give to me,
That all their most occurring aid
Augment my thanks to Thee.
Sing lullaby, my little Boy,
Sing lullaby, my life's Joy!

And let th'ensuing blessed race
Thou wilt succeeding raise,
Join all their praises unto mine
To multiply Thy praise.
Sing lullaby, my little Boy,
Sing lullaby, my life's Joy!

And take my service well in worth,
And Joseph's here with me,
Who of my husband bears the name,
Thy servant for to be.
Sing lullaby, my little Boy,
Sing lullaby, my life's Joy!

ZEREA JACOB

(FIFTEENTH CENTURY)

SALUTATION

Hail, hail to thy blessed name, O Mary. Thy name which is sweeter than all perfumes. Gentle Virgin, may thy love be as a refreshing stream flowing into my soul.

Hail to thy abundant hair, O Mary. O great citadel of God, leave not thy servant in grief so that my enemies say to me: "Where now is the source of all your confidence?"

Hail to thine eyelashes, O Mary. Heavy they were with tears that day thy Jesus was dragged before Pilate and Caiphas. Be my support on the Day of Judgment, my advocate on that great Day of the Lord!

Hail to thine eyes, O Mary. Like the morning stars they stand vigils of the Will of God. Refuge of my soul, in whose undisturbed peace is my consolation for days of sadness. Let the cords of bitterness never enchain my soul.

Hail to thy hands, O Mary. They have touched the fire of Divinity. No need have they of jewelled ornaments. O Elect Dove, keep me pure beneath thy wings!

Hail to thy fingers, O Mary. Lovely were the garments they fashioned in the village of Nazareth. Thou art as gold to poor exiles lost in distant lands. No solicitude is on their lives, for art thou not their Viaticum?

Hail to thy lips, O Mary. Red they are and sweet as the rose, O thou, redolent of holiness and purity, Virgin Mary, star of God to save and shield me from griefs and tears!

Hail to thy mouth, O Mary. Whose lips kissed the fruit of thy bosom, that Divine Infant who was the Father of the Aged.

O sweet Virgin Mary, draw me to thee when sadness bows me down!

Hail to thine Assumption into Heaven, O Mary. Thornless art thou and more fragrant than the rose. Poor and outcast as I am, oh, bestow thy love on me, be a Mother to me!

O Virgin Mary, thus I stammer in my praises. Were the whole globe the surface of my parchment, my utterance would still be unworthy of thee. All the winter rains turned into ink, all the firmament into paper, could never be sufficient to praise thee.

O Virgin, thou art the heaven that enshrines the sun, the field that bears the corn. Refuge of sinners, have pity on me. Give life to me as thou didst to my fathers, and pardon the sins of all my people!

From the Abyssinian by F. Baetman

PART FIVE

"MOST BLESSÈD LANTERN"

The Age of Transition

JOHN DONNE

(1573–1631)

ANNUNCIATION

Salvation to all that will is nigh:
    That All which always is All everywhere;
    Which cannot sin, and yet, all sins must bear;
Which cannot die, yet, cannot choose but die—
Lo, faithful Virgin, yields himself to lie
    In prison in thy womb; and though he there
    Can take no sin, nor thou give, yet, he'll wear
Taken from thence, flesh, which death's force may try.
Ere, by the spheres time was created, thou
    Wast in his mind—which is thy Son and Brother,
    Whom thou conceivest—conceived; yea, thou art now
Thy Maker's Maker, and thy Father's Mother:
Thou hast Light in dark, and shut in little room
Immensity, cloistered in thy dear womb.

BEN JONSON

(1573–1637)

THE GHYRLOND OF THE BLESSED VIRGIN MARIE

Here, are five letters in this blessed Name,
   Which, chang'd, a five-fold mysterie designe,
The *M*. the *M*yrtle, *A*. the *A*lmonds clame,
   R. *R*ose, *I*. *I*vy, *E*. sweet *E*glantine.

These forme thy Ghyrlond. Whereof *Myrtle* green,
   The gladdest ground to all the numbred-five,
Is so implexed, and laid in, between,
   As Love, here studied to keep Grace alive.

The second string is the sweet *Almond* bloome
   Ymounted high upon *Selinis* crest:
As it, alone, (and onely it) had roome,
   To knit thy Crowne, and glorifie the rest.

The third, is from the garden call'd the *Rose*,
   The Eye of flowers, worthy, for his scent,
To top the fairest Lillie, now, that growes,
   With wonder on the thorny regiment.

The fourth is humble *Ivy*, intersert,
   But lowlie laid, as on the earth asleep.
Preserved, in her antique bed of *Vert*,
   No faith's more firme, or flat, then, where't doth creep.

But, that which summes all, is the *Eglantine*,
   Which, of the field is clep'd the sweetest brier,
Inflam'd with ardor to that mystick Shine,
   In *Moses* bush, un-wasted in the fire.

Thus, Love, and Hope, and burning Charitie,
   (Divinest graces) are so entermixt,
With od'rous sweets, and soft humilitie,
   As if they' ador'd the Head, whereon th'are fixt.

These Mysteries do point to three more great,
  On the reverse of this your circling crowne,
All, pouring their full showre of graces downe,
  The glorious *Trinity* in *Union* met.

Daughter, and Mother, and the Spouse of God,
  Alike of kin, to that most blessed *Trine*,
Of Persons, yet in Union (One) divine.
  How are thy gifts, and graces blaz'd abroad!

Most holy, and pure Virgin, blessed Mayd,
  Sweet Tree of Life, King *David's* Strength and Tower,
The House of gold, the Gate of heavens power,
  The Morning-star, whose light our Fal hath stay'd.

Great Queen of Queens, most mild, most meek, most wise.
  Most venerable. Cause of all our joy.
  Whose chearfull look our sadnesse doth destroy,
And art the spotlesse Mirrour to Mans eyes.

The Seat of Sapience, the most lovely Mother,
  And most to be admired of thy Sexe,
  Who mad'st us happy all, in thy reflexe,
By bringing forth God's onely Son, no other.

Thou Throne of glory, beauteous as the Moone,
  The rosie Morning, or the rising Sun,
  Who like a Giant hasts his course to run,
Till he hath reach'd his two-fold point of Noone.

How are thy gifts and graces blaz'd abro'd,
  Through all the lines of this circumference,
  T'imprint in all purg'd hearts this virgin sence,
Of being Daughter, Mother, Spouse of God?

JOHN MILTON

(1608–1674)

BUT TO HIS MOTHER MARY

(From *Paradise Regained*, Book II, 60–108)

But to his mother Mary, when she saw
Others returned from baptism, not her Son,
Nor left at Jordan tidings of him none,
Within her breast though calm, her breast though pure,
Motherly cares and fears got head, and raised
Some troubled thoughts, which she in sighs thus clad:—
   "Oh, what avails me now that honour high,
To have conceived of God, or that salute,
'Hail, highly favoured, among women blest!'
While I to sorrows am no less advanced,
And fears as eminent above the lot
Of other women, by the birth I bore:
In such a season born, when scarce a shed
Could be obtained to shelter him or me
From the bleak air? A stable was our warmth,
A manger his; yet soon enforced to fly
Thence into Egypt, till the murderous king
Were dead, who sought his life, and, missing, filled
With infant blood the streets of Bethlehem.
From Egypt home returned, in Nazareth
Hath been our dwelling many years; his life
Private, unactive, calm, contemplative,
Little suspicious to any king. But now,
Full grown to man, acknowledged, as I hear,
By John the Baptist, and in public shown,
Son owned from Heaven by his Father's voice,
I looked for some great change. To honour? no;
But trouble, as old Simeon plain foretold,
That to the fall and rising he should be
Of many in Israel, and to a sign
Spoken against—that through my very soul
A sword shall pierce. This is my favoured lot,

140

My exaltation to afflictions high!
Afflicted I may be, it seems, and blest!
I will not argue that, nor will repine.
But where delays he now? Some great intent
Conceals him. When twelve years he scarce had seen,
I lost him, but so found as well I saw
He could not lose himself, but went about
His Father's business. What he meant I mused—
Since understand; much more his absence now
Thus long to some great purpose he obscures.
But I to wait with patience am inured;
My heart hath been a storehouse long of things
And sayings laid up, portending strange events."
    Thus Mary, pondering oft, and oft to mind
Recalling what remarkably had passed
Since first her salutation heard, with thoughts
Meekly composed awaited the fulfilling.

RICHARD CRASHAW

(1613–1649)

ON THE GLORIOUS ASSUMPTION OF OUR BLESSED LADY

(The Hymn)

Hark! she is call'd, the parting houre is come
Take thy Farewell, poor world! heav'n must goe home
A piece of heav'nly earth; purer and brighter
Than the chaste stars, whose choice lamps come to light her
While through the crystall orbes, clearer than they
She climbes; and makes a far more milky way.
She's call'd. Hark, how the dear immortall dove
Sighes to his silver mate, rise up, my love!
Rise up, my fair, my spotless one!
The winter's past, the rain is gone.

The Spring is come, the flow'rs appear
No sweets, but thou, are wanting here.
    Come away, my love!
    Come away, my dove! cast off delay,
    The court of heav'n is come
    To wait upon thee home; Come, come away!
    The flow'rs appear,
Or quickly would, wert thou once here.
The spring is come, or if it stay,
'Tis to keep time with thy delay.
The rain is gone, except so much as we
Detain in needful teares to weep the want of thee.
    The winter's past.
    Or if he make lesse haste,
His answer is, why, she does so.
If summer come not, how can winter goe.
    Come away, come away.
The shrill winds chide, the waters weep thy stay;
The fountains murmur; and each loftiest tree
Bowes low'st his heavy top, to look for thee.
    Come away, my love.
    Come away, my dove! cast off delay,
    The court of heav'n is come
    To wait upon thee home; Come, come away!
She's call'd again. And will she goe?
When heav'n bids come, who can say no?
Heav'n calls her, and she must away.
Heav'n will not, and she cannot stay.
Goe then; goe Glorious.
    On the golden wing
Of the bright youth of heav'n, that sings
Under so sweet a Burthen, Goe,
Since thy dread son will have it so.
And while thou goest, our song and we
Will, as we may, reach after thee.
Hail, holy Queen of humble hearts!
We in thy praise will have our parts.

Thy pretious Name shall be
Thy self to us; and we
With holy care will keep it by us.
We to the last
Will hold it fast
And no Assumption shall deny us.
All the sweetest show'res
Of our fairest flow'res
Will we strow upon it.
Though our sweets cannot make
It sweeter, then can take
Themselves new sweetness from it.
Maria, men and Angels sing
Maria, mother of our King.
  Live, rosy princesse, Live. And may the bright
Crown of a most incomparable light
Embrace thy radiant browes. O may the best
Of everlasting joyes bathe thy white breast.
Live, our chast love, the holy mirth
Of heav'n; the humble pride of earth.
Live, crown of women; Queen of men.
Live mistresse of our song. And when
Our weak desires have done their best,
Sweet Angels come, and sing the rest.

ON THE BLESSED VIRGIN'S BASHFULNESS

That on her lap she casts her humble eye,
'Tis the sweet pride of her humility.
The fair star is well fixt, for where, O where
Could she have fixt it on a fairer sphere?

143

'Tis Heaven, 'tis Heaven she sees, Heaven's God
  there lies;
She can see Heaven and ne'er lift up her eyes:
This new Guest to her eyes new laws hath given,
'Twas once, look up, 'tis now, look down, to Heaven.

JOSEPH BEAUMONT

(1616–1699)

PURIFICATION OF THE BLESSED VIRGIN

(S. Luc. II, 24)

May we have leave to ask, illustrious Mother,
  Why thou dost turtles bring
  For thy Son's offering,
And rather giv'st not one lamb for another?

It seems that golden shower which th'other day
  The forward faithful East
  Poured at thy feet, made haste
Through some devout expence to find its way.

O precious poverty, which canst appear
  Richer to holy eyes
  Than any golden prize,
And sweeter art than frankincense and myrrh!

Come then, that silver, which thy turtles wear
  Upon their wings, shall make
  Precious thy gift, and speak
That Son of thine, like them, all pure and fair.

But know that heaven will not be long in debt;
   No; the *Eternal Dove*
   Down from his nest above
Shall come, and on thy Son's dear head shall sit.

Heaven will not have Him ransomed, heaven's law
   Makes no exception
   For lambs, and such a one
Is He: a fairer Lamb heaven never saw.

He must be offered, nor must thou repine:
   Heaven hath a title too,
   As near and sure as thou;
And He is God's Firstborn as well as thine.

He must be offered, or the world is lost:
   The whole world's ransome lies
   In this great sacrifice;
And He will pay its debt, whate'er it cost.

Nor shall these turtles unrepayed be,
   These turtles which today
   Thy love for Him did pay:
Thou ransom'dst Him, and He will ransom thee.

A dear and full redemption will He give
   Thee and the world: this Son,
   And none but this alone
By His own death can make His Mother live.

HENRY VAUGHAN

(1622–1695)

THE KNOT

Bright Queen of Heaven, God's Virgin Spouse,
  The glad world's blessed Maid!
Whose beauty tied life to thy house,
  And brought us saving aid.

Thou are the true Love's-knot; by thee
  God is made our ally;
And man's inferior essence He
  With His did dignify.

For coalescent by that band
  We are His body grown,
Nourished with favours from His hand
  Whom for our Head we own.

And such a knot, what arm dares loose,
  What life, what death can sever?
Which us in Him, and Him in us,
  United keeps for ever.

NAHUM TATE

(1652–1715)

THE BLESSED VIRGIN'S EXPOSTULATION

(When Our Savior at Twelve Years of Age had withdrawn Himself)

Tell me, some pitying angel, quickly say
  Where does my soul's sweet Darling stray,
In tigers', or more cruel Herod's way?
O! rather let his tender foot-steps press
  Unguarded through the wilderness,

Where milder savages resort,
The desert's safer than a tyrant's court.
　Why, fairest object of my love,
Why dost thou from my longing eyes remove?
Was it a waking dream that did foretell
Thy wondrous birth? No vision from above?
I call—He comes not—flattering hopes, farewell.

　Me Judah's daughters once caressed,
　Called me of Mothers the most blest.
Now (fatal change!) of Mothers most distressed!
　How shall my soul its emotions guide,
　How shall I stem the various tide,
Whilst faith and doubt my laboring thoughts divide?
For which of thy dear sight I am beguiled,
I trust the God—but oh! I fear the *child!*

JOHN BYROM

(1692–1763)

THE SALUTATION OF THE BLESSED VIRGIN

(Verses written under a print from a design of Anthony Crypel)

See represented here, in light and shade,
The angel's visit to the blessed maid;—
To Mary, destin'd, when the time should come,
To bear the Savior in her virgin womb;—
Explaining to her the mysterious plan
Of man's redemption—*his becoming man.*

When ev'ry precious wonder had been done,
The virgin then was to conceive a Son;

And to prepare her for the grand event
From God, his Father, Gabriel was sent,
To hail the chosen organ of his birth
Of *God with us,*—of JESUS upon earth.

Unable to express celestial things
Imagination adds expanded wings
To human form exact, and beauteous face;
Which angels have, but with angelic grace,
Free from all grossness and defect; nor seen,
But with a pure chaste eye, divinely keen.

Such Mary's was, whose posture here design'd
The most profound humility of mind;
Modestly asking how the thing could be;
And saying, when informed of God's decree,
*Behold the handmaid of the Lord! His will
Let Him, according to thy word, fulfill.*

What fair instruction may the scene impart
To them who look beyond the painter's art!
Who, in th' angelic message from above,
See the revealing of God's gracious love
To ev'ry soul, that yields itself to all
That pleases Him, whatever may befall!

Whatever circumstances of heav'nly grace
Might be peculiar to the virgin's case,
That holy thing, that saves a soul from sin,
Of God's good Spirit *must be born within:*
For *all salvation is,* upon the whole,
The birth of JESUS *in the human soul.*

SAINT ALPHONSUS DE LIGOURI

(1696–1787)

MADONNA'S LULLABY

When Our Lady sings the heavens
Hush to hear her lark-soft voice
Angels ravished by her beauty
With the listening stars rejoice
While she soothes her Jesu's cry
Gently with this lullaby:

"Rock-a-by my God, my Baby,
Hush now. Close your little eyes.
But your face adream so charms me
That for bliss I agonize:
Though You cannot see me now,
Your gaze enkindles me somehow."

From the Italian by James J. Galvin, C.SS.R.

PART SIX

"LADY, THOU ART A FLAME!"

The Romanticists

J. WOLFGANG VON GOETHE

(1748–1832)

O CHILD OF BEAUTY RARE

O Child of beauty rare—
O Mother, chaste and fair—
How happy seem they both, so far beyond compare.
She in her Infant blest,
And he in conscious rest,
Nestling within the soft warm cradle of her breast.
What joy that sight might bear
To him who sees them there,
If, with a pure and guilt-untroubled eye,
He looked upon the twain, like Joseph standing by.

From the German by E. Aytoun

WILLIAM WORDSWORTH

(1770–1850)

SONNET TO THE VIRGIN

Mother! whose virgin bosom was uncrost
With the least shade of thought to sin allied;
Woman! above all women glorified,
Our tainted nature's solitary boast;
Purer than foam on central ocean tost;

153

Brighter than eastern skies at daybreak strewn
With fancied roses, than the unblemished moon
Before her wane begins on heaven's blue coast:
Thy Image falls to earth. Yet some, I ween,
Not unforgiven the suppliant knee might bend,
As to a visible Power, in which did blend
All that was mixed and reconciled in Thee
Of mother's love with maiden purity,
Of high with low, celestial with terrene!

SAMUEL TAYLOR COLERIDGE

(1772–1834)

A CHRISTMAS CAROL

I

The shepherds went their hasty way,
   And found the lowly stable-shed
Where the Virgin-Mother lay:
   And now they checked their eager tread,
For to the Babe, that at her bosom clung,
A Mother's song the Virgin-Mother sung.

II

They told her how a glorious light,
   Streaming from a heavenly throng,
Around them shone, suspending night!
   While sweeter than a mother's song,
Blest Angels heralded the Savior's birth,
Glory to God on high! and Peace on Earth.

III

She listened to the tale divine,
　　And closer still the Babe she pressed;
And while she cried, the Babe is mine!
　　The milk rushed faster to her breast:
Joy rose within her, like a summer's morn;
Peace, Peace on Earth! the Prince of Peace is born.

IV

Thou Mother of the Prince of Peace,
　　Poor, simple, and of low estate!
That strife should vanish, battle cease,
　　O why should this thy soul elate?
Sweet Music's loudest note, the Poet's story,—
Didst thou ne'er love to hear of fame and glory?

V

And is not War a youthful king,
　　A stately Hero clad in mail?
Beneath his footsteps laurels spring;
　　Him Earth's majestic monarchs hail
Their friend, their playmate! and his bold bright eye
Compels the maiden's love-confessing sigh.

VI

'Tell this in some more courtly scene,
　　To maids and youths in robes of state!
I am a woman poor and mean,
　　And wherefore is my soul elate.
War is a ruffian, all with guilt defiled,
That from the agéd father's tears his child!

VII

'A murderous fiend, by fiends adored,
  He kills the sire and starves the son;
The husband kills, and from her board
  Steals all his widow's toil had won;
Plunders God's world of beauty; rends away
All safety from the night, all comfort from the day.

VIII

'Then wisely is my soul elate,
  That strife should vanish, battle cease:
I'm poor and of a low estate,
  The Mother of the Prince of Peace.
Joy rises in me, like a summer's morn:
Peace, Peace on Earth! The Prince of Peace is born!'

SIR WALTER SCOTT
(1771–1832)

AVE MARIA
(From *The Lady of the Lake*, Canto IV)

Ave, Maria, Maiden mild—
  Listen to a maiden's prayer;
Thou canst hear though from the wild,
  Thou canst save amid despair.
Safe may we sleep beneath thy care,
  Though banished, outcast and reviled—
Maiden, hear a maiden's prayer;
  Mother, hear a suppliant child.
                    Ave, Maria.

Ave, Maria, undefiled—
  The flinty couch we now must share
Shall seem with down of eider piled,
  If thy protection hover there.
The murky cavern's heavy air
  Shall breathe of balm, if thou hast smiled—
Then, Maiden, hear a maiden's prayer;
  Mother, list a suppliant child.
                    Ave, Maria.

Ave, Maria, stainless styled—
  Foul demons of the earth and air,
From this their wonted haunt exiled,
  Shall flee before thy presence fair.
We bow us to our lot of care,
  Beneath thy guidance reconciled—
Hear for a maid a maiden's prayer;
  And for a father hear a child.
                    Ave, Maria.

CHARLES LAMB

(1775–1834)

LINES
ON THE CELEBRATED PICTURE BY
LEONARDO DA VINCI,
CALLED THE VIRGIN OF THE ROCKS

While young John runs to greet
The greater Infant's feet,
The mother standing by, with trembling passion
Of devout admiration,
Beholds the engaging mystic play, and pretty adoration;
Nor knows as yet the full event

Of those so low beginnings,
From whence we date our winnings,
But wonders at the intent
Of those new rites, and what that strange child-worship meant.
But at her side
An angel doth abide,
With such a perfect joy
As no dim doubts alloy,
An intuition,
A glory, an amenity,
Passing the dark condition
Of blind humanity,
As if he surely knew
—All the blest wonders should ensue,
Or he had lately left the upper sphere,
And had read all the sovran schemes and divine riddles there.

MARY LAMB

(1764–1847)

MATERNAL LADY WITH THE VIRGIN GRACE

Maternal lady with the virgin grace,
Heaven-born thy Jesus seemeth sure,
And of a virgin pure.
Lady most perfect, when thy sinless face
Men look upon, they wish to be
A Catholic, Madonna fair, to worship thee.

GEORGE GORDON, LORD BYRON

(1788–1824)

AVE MARIA

(From *Don Juan*, Canto III, cii–ciii)

Ave Maria! blessed be the hour!
The time, the clime, the spot, where I so oft
Have felt that moment in its fullest power
Sink o'er the earth so beautiful and soft,
While swung the deep bell in the distant tower,
Or the faint dying day-hymn stole aloft,
And not a breath crept through the rosy air,
And yet the forest leaves seem'd stirr'd with prayer.

Ave Maria! 'tis the hour of prayer!
Ave Maria! 'tis the hour of love!
Ave Maria! may our spirits dare
Look up to thine and to thy Son's above!
Ave Maria! oh that face so fair!
Those downcast eyes beneath the Almighty Dove—
What though 'tis but a pictured image—strike?—
That painting is no idol, 'tis too like.

PERCY BYSSHE SHELLEY

(1792–1822)

SERAPH OF HEAVEN

(From *Epipsychidion*, lines 21–40)

Seraph of Heaven! too gentle to be human,
Veiling beneath that radiant form of Woman
All that is insupportable in thee
Of light, and love, and immortality!

Sweet Benediction in the eternal Curse!
Veiled Glory of this lampless Universe!
Thou Moon beyond the clouds! Thou living Form
Among the Dead! Thou Star above the Storm!
Thou Wonder, and thou Beauty, and thou Terror!
Thou Harmony of Nature's art! Thou Mirror
In whom, as in the splendour of the Sun,
All shapes look glorious which thou gazest on!
Ay, even the dim words which obscure thee now
Flash, lightning-like, with unaccustomed glow;
I pray thee that thou blot from this sad song
All of its much mortality and wrong,
With those clear drops, which start like sacred dew
From the twin lights thy sweet soul darkens through,
Weeping, till sorrow becomes ecstasy:
Then smile on it, so that it may not die.

PART SEVEN

"THE LADY OF MY DELIGHT"

Nineteenth Century and Modern (European)

HYMN FOR *LAUDES*

FEAST OF OUR LADY, HELP OF CHRISTIANS

(Te Redemptoris Dominique nostri)

We call you Mother of our Lord and Savior,
O beautiful Virgin,
Honor of Christians and
Assuager of distress.
The gates of hell may rage.
The primal enemy may raise his horrid voice
And stir up storms of wrath
Against God's people;
But futile is his savage hate to harm.
Our Lady smiles
Upon pure souls who pray to her
And makes them strong with heavenly fortitude.
By her protecting power,
War's wicked tumult dies away;
A thousand maniples fall or flee,
A thousand cohorts.
She lifts her head
Like a holy tower in Sion,
A stout-walled citadel,
The city of David
Girded with shields and keen-armed soldiery.
Strong with the strength of God's right hand
And dowered with gifts of heaven,

163

The mighty Virgin
Drives hell's attack
Far from her loving household.

O Trinity supremely to be honored,
May we worship You through the eternal years;
In faith may our minds praise You,
And our lips in echoing song. Amen.

From the Latin by Sister Maura

ROBERT STEPHEN HAWKER

(1803–1875)

AISHAH SHECHINAH *

A shape, like folded light, embodied air,
Yet wreathed with flesh, and warm;
All that of Heaven is feminine and fair,
Moulded in visible form.

She stood, the Lady Shechinah of Earth,
A chancel for the sky;—
Where woke, to breath and beauty, God's own birth,
For men to see Him by.

Round her, too pure to mingle with the day,
Light, that was Life, abode;
Folded within her fibres meekly lay
The link of boundless God.

So linked, so blent, that when, with pulse fulfilled,
Moved by that infant Hand,

---

* Symbolic Hebraisms denoting Our Lady as the Pillar of Cloud.

Far, far away, His conscious Godhead thrilled,
And stars might understand.

Lo! where they pause, with intergathering rest,
The Threefold and the One!
And lo! He binds them to her Orient breast,
His Manhood girded on.

The Zone where two glad worlds for ever meet,
Beneath that bosom ran:
Deep in that womb, the conquering Paraclete
Smote Godhead on to man!

Sole scene among the stars; where, yearning, glide
The Threefold and the One:
Her God upon her lap: the Virgin-Bride,
Her awful Child: her Son.

KING ARTHUR'S WAES-HAEL

When the brown bowl is filled for yule, let the dome or upper half be set on; then let the waes-haelers kneel one by one and draw up the wine with their reeds through the two bosses at the rim. Let one breath only be drawn by each of the morice for his waes-hael.

The rounded shape of the bowl for waes-hael was intended to recall the image of a mother's breast; and thus it was meant, with touching simplicity, to blend the thought of our Christmas gladness with the earliest nurture of the child Jesus.

Waes-hael for the knight and the dame!
    O! merry be their dole;
Drink-hael! In Jesu's name
    We fill the tawny bowl;
But cover down the curving crest,
Mould of the Orient Lady's breast.

Waes-hael! yet lift no lid:
    Drain ye the reeds for wine!
Drink-hael! the milk was hid
    That soothed that Babe divine;
Hushed, as this hollow channel flows,
He drew the balsam from the rose.

Waes-hael! thus glowed the breast
    Where a God yearned to cling;
Drink-hael! so Jesus pressed
    Life from its mystic spring;
Then hush, and bend in reverent sigh,
And breathe the thrilling reeds for wine.

Waes-hael! in shadowy scene,
    Lo! Christmas children we;
Drink-hael! behold we lean
    At a far Mother's knee:
To dream, that thus her bosom smiled,
And learn the lip of Bethlehem's child.

ELIZABETH BARRETT BROWNING
(1806–1861)

THE VIRGIN MARY TO THE CHILD JESUS

> But see, the Virgin blest
> Hath laid her babe to rest.
> Milton's *Hymn on the Nativity*

I

Sleep, sleep mine Holy One!
My flesh, my Lord!—what name? I do not know
A name that seemeth not too high or low,
    Too far from me or heaven.

My Jesus, *that* is best! that word being given
By the majestic angel whose command
Was softly as a man's beseeching said,
When I and all the earth appeared to stand
      In the great overflow
Of light celestial from his wings and head.
  Sleep, sleep, my saving One!

II

And art Thou come for saving, baby-browed
And speechless Being—art Thou come for saving?
The palm that grows beside our door is bowed
By treadings of the low wind from the south,
A restless shadow through the chamber waving:
Upon its bough a bird sings in the sun;
But Thou, with that close slumber on thy mouth,
Dost seem of wind and sun already weary.
Art come for saving, O my weary One?

III

Perchance this sleep that shutteth out the dreary
Earth-sounds and motion, opens on Thy soul
      High dreams on fire with God;
High songs that make the pathways where they roll
More bright than stars do theirs; and visions new
Of thine eternal Nature's old abode.
      Suffer this mother's kiss,
      Best thing that earthly is,
To glide the music and the glory through,
Nor narrow in Thy dream the broad upliftings
      Of any seraph wing.
Thus noiseless, thus. Sleep, sleep, my dreaming One!

V

We sate among the stalls at Bethlehem.
The dumb kine from their fodder turning them,

Softened their hornéd faces
To almost human gazes
Toward the newly Born.
The simple shepherds from the star-lit brooks
Brought visionary looks,
As yet in their astonished hearing rung
The strange, sweet angel-tongue:
The magi of the East, in sandals worn,
Knelt reverent, sweeping round,
With long pale beards, their gifts upon the ground,
The incense, myrrh, and gold
These baby hands were impotent to hold.
So, let all earthlies and celestials wait
Upon Thy royal state.
Sleep, sleep, my kingly One!

VI

I am not proud—meek angels ye invest
New meeknesses to hear such utterance rest
On mortal lips,—'I am not proud'—*not proud!*
Albeit in my flesh God sent His Son.
Albeit over Him my head is bowed
As others bow before Him, still mine heart
Bends lower than their knees. O centuries
That roll, in vision, your futurities
My future grace athwart,—
Whose murmurs seem to reach me while I keep
Watch o'er this sleep,—
Say of me as the Heavenly said—'Thou art
The blessedest of women!'—blessedest,
Not holiest, not noblest—no high name,
Whose height misplaced may pierce me like a shame,
When I sit meek in heaven!

VII

For me—for me—
God knows that I am feeble like the rest!—
I often wandered forth, more child than maiden,

168

Among the midnight hills of Galilee,
      Whose summits looked heaven-laden;
Listening to silence as it seemed to be
God's voice, so soft yet strong—so fain to press
Upon my heart as heaven did on the height,
And waken up its shadows by a light,
And show its vileness by a holiness.
Then I knelt down most silent like the night,
      Too self-renounced for fears,
Raising my small face to the boundless blue
Whose stars did mix and tremble in my tears.
God heard *them* falling after—with his dew.

IX

Art Thou a King then? Come His universe,
      Come, crown me Him a King!
Pluck rays from all such stars as never fling
      Their light where fell a curse.
And make a crowning for this kingly brow!—
What is my word?—Each empyreal star
      Sits in a sphere afar
      In shining ambuscade:
      The child-brow, crowned by none,
      Keeps its unchildlike shade.
      Sleep, sleep, my crownless One!

XI

And then the drear sharp tongue of prophecy,
With the dread sense of things which shall be done
Doth smite me inly, like a sword—a sword?—
(*That* 'smites the Shepherd!') then, I think aloud
The words 'despised,'—'rejected,'—every word
Recoiling into darkness as I view
      The darling on my knee.
Bright angels,—move not!—lest ye stir the cloud
Betwixt my soul and His futurity!
I must not die, with mother's work to do,
      And could not live—and see.

XII

It is enough to bear
This image still and fair—
—This holier in sleep,
Than a saint at prayer:
This aspect of a child
Who never sinned or smiled—
This presence in an infant's face:
This sadness most like love,
This love than love more deep,
This weakness like omnipotence,
It is so strong to move!
Awful is this watching place,
Awful what I see from hence—
A king, without regalia,
A God, without the thunder,
A child, without the heart for play;
Ay, a Creator rent asunder
From his first glory and cast away
On His own world, for me alone
To hold in hands created, crying—Son!

XIII

That tear fell not on Thee
Belovèd, yet Thou stirrest in thy slumber!
Thou, stirring not for glad sounds out of number
Which through the vibratory palm trees run
From summer wind and bird,
So quickly hast Thou heard
A tear fall silently?
Wak'st Thou, O loving One?—

LEO XIII

(1810–1903)

WAR CRY: TO MARY

(Ardet pugna ferox; Lucifer ipse, videns)

When warfare blusters at high Lucifer's command,
And writhing monsters fume a course from Acheron's land,
With speed of wind and wing, O loving Mother haste!
Shield for the plagued of soul, sword for the heart laid waste!
Crush with thy virgin foot these cobras of the night,
Erect thy son a tower on the Mary-height
Where he may watch the serpents leave, as stars in flight.

From the Latin by Raymond F. Roseliep

AUBREY DE VERE

(1814–1902)

HYMN FOR THE FEAST OF THE ANNUNCIATION

1

Subsiding from those heavenly wings the air
Lies motionless: yet on that forehead fair
Still hangs a pearly gloom, as if the shade
    Of those departing pinions
      On her brow were stayed.
    Still sits she on that virgin bed
    From which so late she reared her head;
Forward she bends in prayer.
    Her hands upon her breast are crossed;
    Her heart in heavenly vision lost.
    Her silver lids are closing—mark,

171

A tear is trembling on their lashes dark.
　　It falls: to earth that tear is given:
　　That sign an echo finds in Heaven!

2

O joyful Virgin, henceforth blesséd ever
　　Among all nations! cause for joy thou hast.
Not vain henceforth shall prove man's great endeavor;
　　　Henceforth no more His Future
　　　　Shall be but as the Past.
　　　Henceforth wise, good men
　　　Shall toil no more in vain
The seeds of Hope, and Love, and Peace to sow
　　　Among their kind below.
　　Faith, mover of the mountains,
　　　From Earth's o'er-burdened heart
　　The Sinai mount at last shall raise:
　　　The Law hath done its part!
　　Henceforth men shall not gaze
　　On the stars with blank amaze,
And vainly pine for wings to bear them
　　From the tumult of Life's mart.
　　No more self-caused afflictions!
　　　No more self-willed transgressions!
　　But Gladness, Benedictions,
　　　And humbly-toned Confessions;
　　And anthem, and loud hymn
Sent up from earth responsive to the harping Cherubim!

3

Are such the thoughts whose radiant trains are passing,
　　Thrice-hallowed Virgin, through that pure, calm breast,
Which swells to meet them, as the ocean glassing
　　　In its tide-wave those splendours
　　　　That woke it from its rest?
　　　Knowledge with men is stored
　　　　By many a slow degree;

172

But all thy shining lore is poured
  In a gentle stream on thee!
'Tis Hope thy brow doth gird
  With that second, heavenlier bow:
'Tis Love, that, breathing hymns unheard,
  Warms sweetly with faint crimson
    Thy lips, through which they flow!
Thou tastest first the joy of all thy kind:
  Grace first in thee fulfills her earthly mission;
Thy tearful eyes, to outward objects blind,
  Of God and Heaven have deep and full fruition!
    O second Eve!—But she
Said not, "Even as Thy word, so be it unto me!"

4

Mournful, till now, to the o'er-experienced ear,
  Mournful were all the harmonies of earth,
As Autumn's dirge over the dying Year:
    Yea, more than sadness blended
      With melodies of mirth.
  The ocean, murmuring on the shore,
  Breathed inland far a sad "no more":
  The winds but left their midnight cells
  To fill the day with lorn "farewells."
'Tis o'er! The reign of force is o'er:
  The arm of flesh is Lord no longer:
More dear henceforth is peace than war:
  The weak henceforward is the stronger.
Earth's fountains, touched by breath **Divine,**
Gush up, henceforth, in bridal wine!
  Now children (creatures lowly)
    Point upward to the sky:
  Honour henceforth is holy,
    And Virgin Purity!
In star-pierced thickets the night bird
Translates henceforth each rapturous word

That she all day in Heaven hath heard—
Peace, peace! misdoubting Earth, be dumb!
Her Christ His power shall take: His kingdom it shall come!

5

Lo! round her feet celestial flowers are lying!—
　The breath pathetic of those mild perfumes,
Comes it from them, or from her blessed sighing?
　　Lo! silver gleams alternate
　　　With diviner glooms!
　　The air, at every pore alive,
Sings like the golden murmur of the hive.
All round a paradisal light is glowing.
　Down, down the Virgin sinks by slow degrees:
Her tender hands unfold; her tresses flowing
　O'er that declining brow, upon her knees.
　Daughter of God—Mother Elect—low-bent
　She kneels; and adoration is consent.
　　Two beams of light, down-shining from above,
　Fall, on her bosom one, one on her head;
　Between those two great beams on plumes outspread
　　Hovers and gleams the everlasting Dove!

MATER AMABILIS

(Written on hearing that a Catholic Church was to be built at Ambleside,
and dedicated under the title of 'Sta. Maria Amabilia.')

I

A Roman host descended from the height
Of Kirkstone Pass, rock-walled and roofed with cloud:
Slowly they trod: sudden they cried aloud:
The mists had risen—what met their raptured sight?
A golden vale sun-saturate, on the right,

Nor vexed by storm, nor veiled by flying shroud
Slept 'mid green hills: a rainbow o'er it bowed:
Upon the left, a blue lake laughed in light.
For years embosomed in that gracious valley,
At last those warriors found a stainless bliss;
They wreathed its flowers; in skiff, or bannered galley
They clove its lake; its lawns, its woods they ranged;
Parting, a name they gave it—scarcely changed,
That name survives—'Situs Amabilis.'

II

A grateful name, loving and sweet; yet, sweeter
Among our Lady's titles one there is,
One loving more—'Mater Amabilis.'
By it, her destined fane ere long shall greet her;
By it, shall souls sore tried for help entreat her,
When fiercer tempests round them rave and hiss
Than those that shake black tarn, or precipice:
For mountain-girdled church what name were meeter?
Ascend, pure walls. Centuries to come shall hear
From hill to hill again her church-bells ringing,
Her 'Ave, Stella,' cheer the dawn-touched water;
Old men grow young once more, when, tottering near,
They catch the chime of English children singing
Her anthem, 'Salve, Redemptoris Mater.'

FREDERICK WILLIAM FABER
(1814–1865)

OUR LADY IN THE MIDDLE AGES

I looked upon the earth: it was a floor
For noisy pageant and rude bravery—
Wassail, and arms, and chase, among the high,

And burning hearts uncheered among the poor;
And gentleness from every land withdrew.
Methought that beds of whitest lilies grew
All suddenly upon the earth, in bowers;
And gentleness, that wandered like a wind,
And nowhere could meet sanctuary find,
Passed like a dewy breath into the flowers.
Earth heeded not; she still was tributary
To kings and knights, and man's heart well-nigh failed;
Then were the natural charities exhaled
Afresh, from out the blessed love of Mary.

COVENTRY PATMORE

(1823–1896)

THE CHILD'S PURCHASE

(A Prologue)

As a young Child, whose Mother, for a jest,
To his own use a golden coin flings down,
Devises blythe how he may spend it best,
Or on a horse, a bride-cake, or a crown,
Till, wearied with his quest,
Nor liking altogether that nor this,
He gives it back for nothing but a kiss,
Endow'd so I
With golden speech, my choice of toys to buy,
And scanning power and pleasure and renown,
Till each in turn, with looking at, looks vain,
For her mouth's bliss,
To her who gave it give I it again.

Ah, Lady elect,
Whom the Time's scorn has saved from its respect,

Would I had art
For uttering this which sings within my heart!
But, lo,
Thee to admire is all the art I know.
My Mother and God's; Fountain of miracle!
Give me thereby some praise of thee to tell
In such a Song
As may my Guide severe and glad not wrong
Who never spake till thou'dst on him conferr'd
The right, convincing word!
Grant me the steady heat
Of thought wise, splendid, sweet,
Urged by the great, rejoicing wind that rings
With draught of unseen wings,
Making each phrase, for love and for delight,
Twinkle like Sirius on a frosty night!
Aid thou thine own dear fame, thou only Fair,
At whose petition meek
The Heavens themselves decree that, as it were,
They will be weak!

Thou Speaker of all wisdom in a Word,
Thy Lord!
Speaker who thus could'st well afford
Thence to be silent;—ah, what silence that
Which had for prologue thy 'Magnificat?'—
O, Silence full of wonders
More than by Moses in the Mount were heard,
More than were utter'd by the Seven Thunders;
Silence that crowns, unnoted, like the voiceless blue,
The loud world's varying view,
And in its holy heart the sense of all things ponders!
That acceptably I may speak of thee,
Ora pro me!

Key-note and stop
Of the thunder-going chorus of sky-Powers;
Essential drop

Distill'd from worlds of sweetest-savour'd flowers
To anoint with nuptial praise
The Head which for thy Beauty doff'd its rays,
And thee, in His exceeding glad descending, meant,
And Man's new days
Made of His deed the adorning accident!
Vast Nothingness of Self, fair female Twin
Of Fulness, sucking all God's glory in!
(Ah, Mistress mine,
To nothing I have added only sin,
And yet would shine!)
Ora pro me!

 Life's cradle and death's tomb!
To lie within whose womb,
There, with divine self-will infatuate,
Love-captive to the thing He did create,
Thy God did not abhor,
No more
Than Man, in Youth's high spousal-tide,
Abhors at last to touch
The strange lips of his long-procrastinating Bride;
Nay, not the least imagined part as much!
Ora pro me!

 My Lady, yea the Lady of my Lord,
Who didst the first descry
The burning secret of virginity,
We know with what reward!
Prism whereby
Alone we see
Heav'n's light in its triplicity;
Rainbow complex
In bright distinction of all beams of sex,
Shining for aye
In the simultaneous sky,
To One, thy Husband, Father, Son, and Brother,
Spouse blissful, Daughter, Sister, milk-sweet Mother:
Ora pro me!

178

Mildness, whom God obeys, obeying thyself
Him in thy joyful Saint, nigh lost to sight
In the great gulf
Of his own glory and thy neighbour light;
With whom thou wast as else with husband none
For perfect fruit of inmost amity;
Who felt for thee
Such rapture of refusal that no kiss
Ever seal'd wedlock so conjoint with bliss;
And whose good singular eternally
'Tis now, with nameless peace and vehemence,
To enjoy thy married smile,
That mystery of innocence;
Ora pro me!

Sweet Girlhood without guile,
The extreme of God's creative energy;
Sunshiny Peak of human personality;
The world's sad aspirations' one Success;
Bright Blush, that sav'st our shame from shamelessness;
Chief Stone of stumbling; Sign built in the way
To set the foolish everywhere a-bray;
Hem of God's robe, which all who touch are heal'd;
To which the outside Many honour yield
With a reward and grace
Unguess'd by the unwash'd boor that hails Him to His face,
Spurning the safe, ingratiant courtesy
Of suing Him by thee;
Ora pro me!

Creature of God rather the sole than first;
Knot of the cord
Which binds together all and all unto their Lord;
Suppliant Omnipotence; best to the worst;
Our only Savior from an abstract Christ
And Egypt's brick-kilns, where the lost crowd plods,
Blaspheming its false Gods;
Peace-beaming Star, by which shall come enticed,

Though nought thereof as yet they weet,
Unto thy Babe's small feet,
The Mighty, wand'ring disemparadised,
Like Lucifer, because to thee
They will not bend the knee;
Ora pro me!

Desire of Him whom all things else desire!
Bush aye with Him as He with thee on fire!
Neither in His great Deed nor on His throne—
O, folly of Love, the intense
Last culmination of Intelligence,—
Him seem'd it good that God should be alone!
Basking in unborn laughter of thy lips,
Ere the world was, with absolute delight
His Infinite reposed in thy Finite;
Well-match'd: He, universal being's Spring,
And thou, in whom art gather'd up the ends of everything!
Ora pro me!

In season due, on His sweet-fearful bed,
Rock'd by an earthquake, curtain'd with eclipse,
Thou shar'd'st the rapture of the sharp spear's head,
And thy bliss pale
Wrought for our boon what Eve's did for our bale;
Thereafter, holding a little thy soft breath,
Thou underwent'st the ceremony of death;
And, now, Queen-Wife,
Sitt'st at the right hand of the Lord of Life,
Who, of all bounty, craves for only fee
The glory of hearing it besought with smiles by thee!
Ora pro me!

Mother, who lead'st me still by unknown ways,
Giving the gifts I know not how to ask,
Bless thou the work
Which, done, redeems my many wasted days,
Makes white the murk,

And crowns the few which thou wilt not dispraise,
When clear my Songs of Lady's graces rang,
And little guess'd I 'twas of thee I sang!

Vainly, till now, my pray'rs would thee compel
To fire my verse with thy shy fame, too long
Shunning world-blazon of well-ponder'd song;
But doubtful smiles, at last, 'mid thy denials lurk;
From which I spell,
'Humility and greatness grace the task
Which he who does it deems impossible!'

REGINA COELI

Say, did his sisters wonder what could Joseph see
In a mild, silent little Maid like thee?
And was it awful, in that narrow house,
With God for Babe and Spouse?
Nay, like thy simple, female sort, each one
Apt to find Him in Husband and in Son,
Nothing to thee came strange in this.
Thy wonder was but wondrous bliss:
Wondrous, for, though
True Virgin lives not but does know,
(Howbeit none ever yet confess'd),
That God lies really in her breast,
Of thine He made His special nest!
And so
All mothers worship little feet,
And kiss the very ground they've trod;
But, ah, thy little Baby sweet
Who was indeed thy God!

DANTE GABRIEL ROSSETTI

(1828–1882)

MARY'S GIRLHOOD

This is the blessed Mary, pre-elect
　God's virgin. Gone is a great while, and she
　Dwelt young in Nazareth of Galilee.
Unto God's will she brought devout respect
Profound simplicity of intellect.
　And supreme patience. From her mother's knee
　Faithful and hopeful; wise in charity;
Strong in grave peace; in pity circumspect.

So held she through her girlhood; as it were
　An angel-watered lily, that near God
　　Grows and is quiet. Till, one day at home
She woke in her white bed, and had no fear
　At all—yet wept till sunshine, and felt awed:
　　Because the fulness of the time was come.

AVE

Mother of the Fair Delight,
Thou handmaid perfect in God's sight,
Now sitting fourth beside the Three,
Thyself a Woman-Trinity,
Being a daughter born to God,
Mother of Christ from stall to rood,
And wife unto the Holy Ghost:—
O, when our need is uttermost,

Think that to such as death may strike
Thou once wert sister, sisterlike!
Thou Headstone of Humanity,
Groundstone of the great Mystery,
Fashioned like us, yet more than we.

Mind'st thou not (when June's heavy breath
Warmed the long days in Nazareth,)
That ere thou didst go forth to give
Thy flowers some drink that they might live
One faint night more amid the sands?
Far off the trees were as pale wands
Against the fervid sky: the sea
Sighed further off eternally
As human sorrow sighs in sleep.
Then suddenly the awe grew deep,
As of a day to which all days
Were footsteps in God's secret ways;
Until a folding sense, like prayer,
Which is, as God is, everywhere,
Gathered about thee; and a voice
Spake to thee without any noise,
Being of the silence:—"Hail!" it said,
"Thou that art highly favourèd;
The Lord is with thee here and now;
Blessed among all women thou!"

Ah! knew'st thou of the end, when first
That Babe was on thy bosom nursed?
Or when He tottered round thy knee,
Did thy great sorrow dawn on thee?
And through His boyhood, year by year,
Eating with Him the Passover,
Didst thou discern confusedly
That Holier Sacrament, when He,
The bitter cup about to quaff,
Should break the bread and eat thereof?—

Or came not yet the knowledge even,
Till on some day forecast in Heaven
His feet passed through thy door to press
Upon His Father's business?
Or still was God's high secret kept?
Nay, but I think the whisper crept
Like growth through childhood. Work and play
Things common to the course of day
Awed thee with meanings, unfulfilled;
And all through girlhood, something stilled
Thy senses like the birth of light,
When thou hast trimmed thy lamp at night
Or washed thy garments in the stream;
To whose white bed had come the dream
That He was thine, and thou wast His
Who feeds among the field-lilies.
O solemn shadow of the end
In that wise spirit long contained!
O awful end! and those unsaid
Long years when it was Finishèd.

Mind'st thou not (when the twilight gone
Left darkness in the house of John,)
Between the naked window-bars
That spacious vigil of the stars?
For thou, a watcher even as they
Wouldst rise from where throughout the day
Thou wroughtest raiment for His poor;
And, finding the fixed terms endure
Of day and night which never brought
Sounds of His coming chariot,
Would'st lift through cloud-waste, unexplored,
Those eyes which said, "How long, O Lord?"
Then that disciple whom He loved,
Well heeding, haply would be moved
To ask thy blessing in His Name;
And that one thought in both, the same

Though silent, then would clasp ye round
To weep together—tears long bound,
Sick tears of patience, dumb and slow.
Yet, "Surely I come quickly";—so
He said, from life and death gone home.
Amen! even so, Lord Jesus, come!
But, O! what human tongue can speak
That day when Michael came to break
From the tired spirit, like a veil,
Its covenant with Gabriel,
Endured at length unto the end?
What human thought can apprehend
That mystery of motherhood,
When thy Beloved at length renewed
The sweet communion severèd,
His Left Hand underneath thine head,
And His Right Hand embracing thee?
Lo! He was thine, and this is He!

Soul, is it Faith, or Love, or Hope,
That lets me see her standing up
Where the light of the Throne is bright?
Unto the left, unto the right,
The Cherubim, succinct, conjoint,
Float inward to a golden point,
And from between the Seraphim
The glory issues for a hymn.
O Mary Mother, be not loth
To listen; thou whom the stars clothe,
Who seèst, and mayst not be seen!
Hear us at last, O Mary Queen!
Into our shadow bend thy face,
Bowing thee from the secret place,
O Mary Virgin, full of grace!

CHRISTINA ROSSETTI

(1830–1894)

HERSELF A ROSE WHO BORE THE ROSE

Herself a rose, who bore the Rose,
　　She bore the Rose and felt its thorn.
　　All loveliness new-born
Took on her bosom its repose,
　　And slept and woke there night and morn.

Lily herself, she bore the one
　　Fair Lily; sweeter, whiter, far
　　Than she or others are:
The Sun of Righteousness her Son,
　　She was His morning star.

She gracious, He essential Grace,
　　He was the Fountain, she the rill:
　　Her goodness to fulfil
And gladness, with proportioned pace
　　He led her steps thro' good and ill.

Christ's mirror she of grace and love,
　　Of beauty and of life and death:
　　By hope and love and faith
Transfigured to His likeness, 'Dove,
　　Spouse, Sister, Mother,' Jesus saith.

ROBERT BRIDGES

(1844–1930)

OUR LADY

I

Goddess azure-mantled and aureoled
That standing barefoot upon the moon
  Or throned as a Queen of the earth
  Tranquilly smilest to hold
  The Child-god in thine arms,
Whence thy glory? Art not she
The country maiden of Galilee
Simple in dowerless poverty
Who from humble cradle to grave
  Hadst no thought of this wonder?

  When to man dull of heart
  Dawn'd at length graciously
  Thy might of Motherhood
The starry Truth beam'd on his home;
Then with insight exalted he gave thee
The trappings—Lady—wherewith his art
Delighteth to picture his spirit to sense
  And that grace is immortal.

  Fount of creative Love
  Mother of the Word eternal
  Atoning man with God:
Who set thee apart as a garden enclosed
From Nature's all-producing wilds
To rear the richest fruit o' the Life
Ever continuing out from Him
  Urgent since the beginning.

II

Behold! Man setteth thine image in the
  height of Heaven
And hallowing his untemper'd love
   Crowneth and throneth thee ador'd
   (Tranquilly joyous to hold
   The man-child in thine arms)
God-like apart from conflict to save thee
To guard thy weak caressive beauty
With incontaminate jewels of soul
Courage, patience, and self-devotion:
   All this glory he gave thee.

   Secret and slow is Nature
   Imperceptibly moving
   With surely determinate aim:
To woman it fell to be early in prime
Ready to labour, mould, and cherish
The delicate head of all Production
The wistful late-maturing boy
   Who made Knowing of Being.

   Therefore art thou ador'd
   Mother of God in man
   Naturing nurse of power:
They who adore not thee shall perish
But thou shalt keep thy path of joy
Envied of Angels because the All-father
Call'd thee to mother his nascent Word
   And complete the creation.

GERARD MANLEY HOPKINS
(1844–1889)

THE BLESSED VIRGIN COMPARED TO
THE AIR WE BREATHE

Wild air, world-mothering air,
Nestling me everywhere,
That each eyelash or hair
Girdles; goes home betwixt
The fleeciest, frailest-fixed
Snowflake; that's fairly mixed
With, riddles, and is rife
In every least thing's life;
This needful, never spent,
And nursing element;
My more than meat and drink,
My meal at every wink;
This air, which, by life's law,
My lung must draw and draw
Now but to breathe its praise,
Minds me in many ways
Of her who not only
Gave God's infinity
Dwindled to infancy
Welcome in womb and breast,
Birth, milk, and all the rest
But mothers each new grace
That does now reach our race—
Mary Immaculate,
Merely a woman, yet
Whose presence, power is
Great as no goddess's
Was deemèd, dreamèd; who
This one work has to do—
Let all God's glory through,

God's glory which would go
Through her and from her flow
Off, and no way but so.

I say that we are wound
With mercy round and round
As if with air: the same
Is Mary, more by name.
She, wild web, wondrous robe,
Mantles the guilty globe,
Since God has let dispense
Her prayers his providence:
Nay, more than almoner,
The sweet alms' self is her
And men are meant to share
Her life as life does air.

If I have understood,
She holds high motherhood
Towards all our ghostly good
And plays in grace her part
About man's beating heart,
Laying, like air's fine flood,
The deathdance in his blood;
Yet no part but what will
Be Christ our Savior still.
Of her flesh He took flesh:
He does take fresh and fresh,
Though much the mystery **how**,
Not flesh but spirit now
And makes, O marvellous!
New Nazareths in us,
Where she shall yet conceive
Him, morning, noon, and eve;
New Bethlems, and he born
There, evening, noon, and morn—
Bethlem or Nazareth,

Men here may draw like breath
More Christ and baffle death;
Who, born so, comes to be
New self and nobler me
In each one and each one
More makes, when all is done,
Both God's and Mary's Son.

Again, look overhead
How air is azurèd;
O how! nay do but stand
Where you can lift your hand
Skywards: rich, rich it laps
Round the four fingergaps.
Yet such a sapphire-shot,
Charged, steepèd sky will not
Stain light. Yea, mark you this:
It does no prejudice.
The glass-blue days are those
When every color glows,
Each shape and shadow shows.
Blue be it: this blue heaven
The seven or seven times seven
Hued sunbeam will transmit
Perfect, not alter it.
Or if there does some soft,
On things aloof, aloft,
Bloom breathe, that one breath more
Earth is the fairer for.
Whereas did air not make
This bath of blue and slake
His fire, the sun would shake,
A blear and blinding ball
With blackness bound, and all
The thick stars round him roll
Flashing like flecks of coal,
Quartz-fret, or sparks of salt,
In grimy vasty vault.

So God was god of old:
A mother came to mould
Those limbs like ours which are
What must make our daystar
Much dearer to mankind;
Whose glory bare would blind
Or less would win man's mind.
Through her we may see him
Made sweeter, not made dim,
And her hand leaves his light
Sifted to suit our sight.

Be thou then, O thou dear
Mother, my atmosphere;
My happier world, wherein
To wend and meet no sin;
Above me, round me lie
Fronting my froward eye
With sweet and scarless sky;
Stir in my ears, speak there
Of God's love, O live air,
Of patience, penance, prayer:
World-mothering air, air wild,
Wound with thee, in thee isled,
Fold home, fast fold thy child.

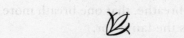

THE MAY MAGNIFICAT

May is Mary's month, and I
Muse at that and wonder why:
  Her feasts follow reason,
  Dated due to season—

Candlemas, Lady Day;
But the Lady Month, May,
    Why fasten that upon her,
    With a feasting in her honour?

Is it only its being brighter
Than the most are must delight her?
    Is it opportunest
    And flowers finds soonest?

Ask of her, the mighty mother:
Her reply puts this other
    Question: What is Spring?—
    Growth in every thing—

Flesh and fleece, fur and feather,
Grass and greenworld all together;
    Star-eyed strawberry-breasted
    Throstle above her nested

Cluster of bugle blue eggs thin
Forms and warms the life within;
    And bird and blossom swell
    In sod or sheath or shell.

All things rising, all things sizing
Mary sees, sympathising
    With that world of good,
    Nature's motherhood.

Their magnifying of each its kind
With delight calls to mind
    How she did in her stored
    Magnify the Lord.

Well but there was more than this:
Spring's universal bliss
    Much, had much to say
    To offering Mary May.

When drop-of-blood-and-foam-dapple
Bloom lights the orchard-apple
    And thicket and thorp are merry
    With silver-surfèd cherry

And azuring-over greybell makes
Wood banks and brakes wash wet like lakes
    And magic cuckoo call
    Caps, clears, and clinches all—

This ecstasy all through mothering earth
Tells Mary her mirth till Christ's birth
    To remember and exultation
    In God who was her salvation.

ALICE MEYNELL
(1847–1922)

TO THE MOTHER OF CHRIST, THE SON OF MAN

    We too (one cried), we too,
We the unready, the perplexed, the cold,
Must shape, the Eternal in our thoughts anew,
    Cherish, possess, enfold.

    Thou sweetly, we in strife.
It is our passion to conceive Him thus
In mind, in sense, within our house of life;
    That seed is locked in us.

    We must affirm our Son
From the ambiguous Nature's difficult speech,
Gather in darkness that resplendent One,
    Close as our grasp can reach.

Nor shall we ever rest
From this our task. An hour sufficed for thee,
Thou innocent! He lingers in the breast
Of our humanity.

WILFRID MEYNELL

(1852–   )

JOSEPH MARY PLUNKETT

(Who signed, as only Joseph Plunkett, the Declaration of the Irish Republic)

Because you left her name unnamed,
Lest some should surely think it shamed,
I, with a bolder pen in rhyme,
Link Joseph Mary all the time.

I think, although you were not due,
She waited at the gate for you;
And wore a sweet celestial pout,
Because her name had been left out.

For this is very She who sings:
"The poor, God filleth with good things,"
And, Rebel She, who dares to say:
"But empty sends the rich away."

195

OSCAR WILDE
(1856–1900)

AVE MARIA, GRATIA PLENA

Was this His coming! I had hoped to see
A scene of wondrous glory, as was told
Of some great God who in a rain of gold
Broke open bars and fell on Danae:
Or a dread vision as when Semele,
Sickening for love and unappeased desire,
Prayed to see God's clear body, and the fire
Caught her brown limbs and slew her utterly.
With such glad dreams I sought this holy place,
And now with wondering eyes and heart I stand
Before this supreme mystery of Love:
Some kneeling girl with passionless pale face,
An angel with a lily in his hand,
And over both the white wings of a Dove.

ANONYMOUS

HYMN FOR SECOND VESPERS

FEAST OF THE APPARITION OF OUR LADY OF LOURDES

LADY OF LOURDES
(*Omnis expertem maculae Mariam*)

Untouched by Adam's curse—our Mary's soul!
Like great bell tones the Pontiff's edict rings—
While every heart on earth re-sounds the word,
And all earth sings.

196

Comely she stands before a shy young girl
Who tells her *Aves,* trembling to await
The bright air broken by a word—"I am
Immaculate!"

O happy cave, majestic rock that felt
Her feet press lightly as they do in dream,
Whence waters brimmed with healing break their source,
And with life, stream.

From every countryside and city square
A troop of pilgrims crowds upon the way:
Some come to kneel in child-eyed wonderment,
Some come to pray.

She dries her children's tears as mothers do,
And pours a draught of grace from prayer-cupped hands,
That each may journey back refreshed and glad
To better lands.

O Virgin, let thy fleet compassion's spark
Light up the murky paths we stumble on;
Give us the warmth of thy embrace when earth's
Cold pain is gone.

All song and glory to our Father rise
And to the Christhead (Mary's Only Son!)
With Their swift Spirit winged with love for Both,
Three-always-One!

From the Latin by Raymond F. Roseliep

FRANCIS THOMPSON

(1859–1907)

ASSUMPTA MARIA

(Thou needst not make new songs, but say the old.—Cowley)

'Mortals, that behold a Woman
 Rising twixt the Moon and Sun;
Who am I the heavens assume? an
 All am I, and I am one.

'Multitudinous ascend I,
 Dreadful as a battle arrayed,
For I bear you whither tend I;
 Ye are I: be undismayed!
I, the Ark that for the graven
 Tables of the Law was made;
Man's own heart was one; one, Heaven;
 Both within my womb were laid.
  For there Anteros with Eros,
   Heaven with man, conjonèd was,—
  Twin-stone of the Law, *Ischyros*,
   Agios Athanatos.

'I, the flesh-girt Paradises
 Gardenered by the Adam new,
Daintied o'er with dear devices
 Which He loveth, for He grew.
I, the boundless strict savannah
 Which God's leaping feet go through;
I, the Heaven whence the Manna,
 Weary Israel, slid on you!
  He the Anteros and Eros
   I the body, He the Cross;
  He upbeareth me, *Ischyros*,
   Agios Athanatos!

'I am Daniel's mystic Mountain,
　　Whence the mighty stone was rolled;
I am the four Rivers' Fountain,
　　Watering Paradise of old;
Cloud down-raining the Just One am,
　　Danae of the Shower of Gold;
I the Hostel of the Sun am;
　　He the Lamb, and I the Fold.
　　　He the Anteros and Eros,
　　　　I the body, He the Cross;
　　　He is fast to me, *Ischyros*,
　　　　Agios Athanatos!

'I, the Presence-hall where Angels
　　Do enwheel their placèd King—
Even my thoughts which, without change else,
　　Cyclic burn and cyclic sing.
To the hollow of heaven transplanted,
　　I a breathing Eden spring,
Where with venom all outpanted
　　Lies the slimed Curse shrivelling.
　　　For the brazen Serpent clear on
　　　　That old fangèd knowledge shone;
　　　I to Wisdom rise, *Ischyron*,
　　　　Agion Athanaton!'

'Then commanded and spake to me
　　He who framed all things that be;
And my Maker entered through me,
　　In my tent His rest took He.
Lo! He standeth, Spouse and Brother,
　　I to Him, and He to me,
Who upraised me where my mother
　　Fell, beneath the apple-tree.
　　　Risen 'twixt Anteros and Eros,
　　　　Blood and Water, Moon and Sun,
　　　He upbears me, He *Ischyros*,
　　　　I bear Him, the *Athanaton!*

199

Where is laid the Lord arisen?
    In the light we walk in gloom;
Though the Sun has burst his prison,
    We know not his biding-room.
Tell us where the Lord sojourneth,
    For we find an empty tomb.
'Whence He sprung, there he returneth,
    Mystic Sun,—the Virgin's Womb.'
        Hidden Sun, His beams so near us,
            Cloud-enpillared as He was
        From of old, there He, *Ischyros*,
            Waits our search, *Athanatos*.

Who is She, in candid vesture,
    Rushing up from out the brine?
Treading with resilient gesture
    Air, and with that Cup divine?
She in us and we in her are,
    Beating God-ward: all that pine,
Lo, a wonder and a terror—
    The Sun hath blushed the Sea to Wine!
        He the Anteros and Eros,
            She the Bride and Spirit; for
        Now the days of promise near us,
            And the Sea shall be no more.

Open wide thy gates, O Virgin,
    That the King may enter thee!
At all gates the clangours gurge in,
    God's paludament lightens, see!
Camp of Angels! Well we even
    Of this thing may doubtful be,—
If thou art assumed to Heaven,
    Or is Heaven assumed to thee!
        Consummatum. Christ the promised,
            Thy maiden realm is won, O Strong!
        Since to such sweet Kingdom comest,
            Remember me, poor Thief of Song!

Cadent fails the stars along:—
Mortals, that behold a woman
Rising 'twixt the Moon and Sun;
Who am I the heavens assume? an
All am I, and I am one.

THE AFTER WOMAN

Daughter of the ancient Eve,
We know the gifts ye gave—and give.
Who knows the gifts which *you* shall give,
Daughter of the newer Eve?
You, if my soul be augur, you
Shall—O what shall you not, Sweet, do?
The celestial traitress play,
And all mankind to bliss betray;
With sacrosanct cajoleries
And starry treachery of your eyes,
Tempt us back to Paradise!
Make heavenly trespass;—ay, press in
Where faint the fledge-foot seraphin,
Blest fool! Be ensign of our wars,
And shame us all to warriors!
Unbanner your bright locks,—advance
Girl, their gilded puissance,
I' the mystic vaward, and draw on
After the lovely gonfalon
Us to out-folly the excess
Of your sweet foolhardiness;
To adventure like intense
Assault against Omnipotence!

Give me song, as She is, new,
Earth should turn in time thereto!
New, and new, and thrice so new,
All old sweets, New Sweet, meant you!
Fair, I had a dream of thee,
When my young heart beat prophecy,
And in apparition elate
Thy little breasts knew waxèd great,
Sister of the Canticle,
And thee for God grown marriageable.

How my desire desired your day,
That, wheeled in rumour on its way,
Shook me thus with presentience! Then
Eden's lopped tree shall shoot again:
For who Christ's eyes shall miss, with those
Eyes for evident nuncios?
Or who be tardy to His call
In your accents augural?
Who shall not feel the Heavens hid
Impend, at tremble of your lid,
And divine advent shine avowed
Under that dim and lucid cloud;
Yea, 'fore the silver apocalypse
Fail, at the unsealing of your lips?
—When to love *you* is (O Christ's Spouse!)
To love the beauty of His house;
Then come the Isaian days; the old
Shall dream; and our young men behold
Vision—yea, the vision of Thabor mount,
Which none to other shall recount,
Because in all men's hearts shall be
The seeing and the prophecy.
For ended is the Mystery Play,
When Christ is life, and you the way;
When Egypt's spoils are Israel's right,
And Day fulfils the married arms of Night.
But here my lips are still.

Until
You and the hour shall be revealed,
This song is sung and sung not, and its words are sealed.

LINES FOR A DRAWING OF OUR LADY
OF THE NIGHT

This, could I paint my inward sight,
This were Our Lady of the Night:

She bears on her front's lucency
The starlight of her purity:

For as the white rays of that star
The union of all colours are,

She sums all virtues that may be
In her sweet light of purity.

The mantle which she holds on high
Is the great mantle of the sky.

Think, O sick toiler, when the night
Comes on thee, sad and infinite,

Think, sometimes, 'tis our own Lady
Spreads her blue mantle over thee,

And folds the earth, a wearied thing,
Beneath its gentle shadowing;

Then rest a little; and in sleep
Forget to weep, forget to weep!

203

KATHERINE TYNAN HINKSON

(1861–1931)

MATER DEI

She looked to east, she looked to west,
    Her eyes, unfathomable, mild,
That saw both worlds, came home to rest,—
    Home to her own sweet child:
God's golden head was at her breast.

What need to look o'er land and sea?
    What could the winged ships bring to her?
What gold or gems of price might be,
    Ivory or miniver,
Since God Himself lay on her knee?

What could th'intense blue heaven keep
    To draw her eyes and thoughts so high?
All heaven was where her Boy did leap,
    Where her foot quietly
Went rocking the dear God asleep.

The angel folk fared up and down
    A Jacob's Ladder hung between
Her quiet chamber and God's Town.
    She saw unawed, serene;
Since God Himself played by her gown.

MAY PROBYN

A CHRISTMAS CAROL

Lacking samite and sable,
Lacking silver and gold,
The Prince Jesus in the poor stable
Slept, and was three hours old.

As doves by the fair water,
Mary, not touched of sin,
Sat by Him,—the King's daughter,
All glorious within.

A lily without one stain, a
Star where no spot hath room—
Ave, gratia plena,
Virgo Virginum.

Clad not in pearl-sewn vesture,
Clad not in cramoisie,
She hath hushed, she hath cradled to rest, her
God the first time on her knee.

Where is one to adore Him?
The ox hath dumbly confessed,
With the ass, meek kneeling before Him,
"Et homo factus est."

Not throned on ivory or cedar,
Not crowned with a Queen's crown,
At her breast it is Mary shall feed her
Maker, from Heaven come down.

The trees in Paradise blossom
Sudden, and its bells chime—
She giveth Him, held to her bosom,
Her immaculate milk the first time.

The night with wings of angels
Was alight, and its snow-packed ways
Sweet made (say the Evangels)
With the noise of their virelays.

Quem vidistis, pastores?
Why go ye feet unshod?
Wot ye within yon door is
Mary, the Mother of God?

No smoke of spice ascending
There—no roses are piled—
But, choicer than all balms blending,
There Mary hath kissed her Child.

LAURENCE HOUSMAN
(1865–   )

GOD'S MOTHER

A garden bower in bower
Grew waiting for God's hour:
Where no man ever trod,
This was the Gate of God.
The first bower was red—
Her lips which 'welcome' said.
The second bower was blue—
Her eyes that let God through.
The third bower was white—
Her soul in God's sight.
Three bowers of love
Won Christ from Heaven above.

O MARY PIERCED WITH SORROW

(From *Song Before Action*)

O Mary, pierced with sorrow
   Remember, reach and save
The soul that goes tomorrow
   Before the God that gave;
As each was born of woman,
   For each, in utter need
True comrade and brave foeman,
Madonna, intercede.

LIONEL JOHNSON

(1867–1902)

CADGWITH

III

Mary Star of the sea!
Look on this little place:
Bless the kind fisher race,
Mary Star of the sea!

Send harvest from the deep,
Mary Star of the Sea!
Mary Star of the Sea!
Let not these women weep.

Mary Star of the Sea!
Give wife and mother joy

In husband and in boy:
Mary Star of the Sea!

With intercession save,
Mary Star of the Sea!
Mary Star of the Sea!
These children of the wave.

Mary Star of the Sea!
Pour peace upon the wild
Waves, make their murmurs mild:
Mary Star of the Sea!

Now in thy mercy pray,
Mary Star of the Sea!
Mary Star of the Sea!
For sailors far away.

Mary Star of the Sea!
Now be thy great prayers said
For all poor seamen dead:
Mary Star of the Sea!

OUR LADY OF FRANCE

Leave we awhile without the turmoil of the town;
Leave we the sullen gloom, the faces full of care:
Stay we awhile and dream, within this place of prayer,
Stay we, and pray, and dream: till in our hearts die
   down
Thoughts of the world, unkind and weary: till Christ
   crown

Laborious day with love. Hark! on the fragrant air,
Music of France, voices of France, fall piercing fair:
Poor France, where Mary's star shines, lest her children
    drown.

Our Lady of France! doest thou in habit here? Behold,
What sullen gloom invests this city strange to thee!
In Seine, and pleasant Loire, thou gloriest from of old;
Thou rulest rich Provence; lovest the Breton sea:
What dost thou far from home? *Nay! here my children*
    fold
Their exiled hands in orison, and long for me.

OUR LADY OF THE MAY

O Flower of flowers, our Lady of the May!
    Thou gavest us the World's one Light of Light:
Under the stars, amid the snows, He lay;
    While Angels, through the Galilean night
        Sang glory and sang peace:
        Nor doth their singing cease,
For thou their Queen and He their King sit crowned
Above the stars, above the bitter snows;
They chaunt to thee the Lily, Him the Rose,
    With white Saints kneeling round.
Gone is cold night: thine now are spring and day:
O Flower of flowers, our Lady of the May!

O Flower of flowers, our Lady of the May!
    Thou gavest us the blessed Christmas mirth:
And now, not snows, but blossoms, light thy way;
    We give thee the fresh flower-time of the earth.
        These early flowers we bring,
        Are angels of the spring,

Spirits of gracious rain and light and dew.
Nothing so like to thee the whole earth yields,
As these pure children of her vales and fields,
    Bright beneath skies of blue.
Hail Holy Queen! their fragrant breathings say:
O Flower of flowers, our Lady of the May!

O Flower of flowers, our Lady of the May!
  Breathe from God's garden of eternal flowers
Blessing, when we thy little children pray:
  Let thy soul's grace steal gently over ours.
    Send on us dew and rain,
    That we may bloom again,
Nor wither in the dry and parching dust.
Lift up our hearts, till with adoring eyes,
O Morning Star! we hail thee in the skies,
    Star of our hope and trust!
Sweet Star, sweet Flower, there bid thy beauty stay:
O Flower of flowers, our Lady of the May!

O Flower of flowers, our Lady of the May!
  Thou leftest lilies rising from thy tomb:
They shone in stately and serene array,
  Immaculate amid death's house of gloom.
    Ah, let thy graces be
    Sown in our dark hearts! We
Would make our hearts gardens for thy dear care:
Watered from wells of Paradise, and sweet
With balm winds flowing from the Mercy Seat,
    And full of heavenly air:
While music ever in thy praise should play,
O Flower of flowers, our Lady of the May!

O Flower of flowers, our Lady of the May!
  Not only for ourselves we plead, God's Flower!
Look on thy blinded children, who still stray,
  Lost in this pleasant land, thy chosen Dower!
    Send us a perfect spring:
    Let faith arise and sing,

And England from her long, cold winter wake.
Mother of Mercy! turn upon her need
Thine eyes of mercy: be there spring indeed:
    So shall thine Angels make
A starrier music, than our hearts can say,
O Flower of flowers, our Lady of the May!

PAUL CLAUDEL
(1868–   )

FOURTH STATION

Mothers who have seen him die—your first child, your only one—
Remember the very last night when all that you could do was
  done:
Thermometers, ice, the water for thirst that it could not slake—
Death coming inch by inch, impossible now to mistake! . . .
Put on his pitiful shoes, clothe him in garments all fresh!
They are coming to take him away, to fold him in earth's brown
  mesh.
My own little son, goodby! God be with you, flesh of my flesh!

The fourth station is Mary's acceptance of all God's will.
At the bend of the street she awaits the Treasure of Poverty's fill.
No more of tears for her eyes, no moisture to ease her throat.
She says no word but looks at Jesus in seamless coat.
She accepts. Again she accepts. The cry
Is firmly repressed in her heart, whose strength has sufficed.
She says no word, but gazes on Jesus Christ.
The Mother looks on her Son, the Church on her Savior;
Like the cry of a soldier at death, her soul leaps out to His side!
She stands erect before God and gives Him her soul to read:
There is naught in her heart that refuses, how deep soever it
  bleed,

No fibre of that pierced heart but gives its utter consent;
And, as God Himself, she is there with her will to present.
She accepts, and looks on this Son that her body has borne.
She says no word, but looks on the crown He has worn . . .

From the French by Sister Mary David, S.S.N.D.

OUR LADY, HELP OF CHRISTIANS

To M. l'Abbé Fontaine

The puny child who knows he can have but little love,
When by chance upon his face he feels a kind glance rove,
Reddens and bravely smiles, determined not to cry.
So in this wicked world the orphans and those passed by,
The penniless, those without joy that learning or humor lends,
As they do without everything, do equally without friends.
The poor are seldom confiding, yet a man can gain their heart.
He has only to treat them kindly, to honor them without art.
Take then this glance, this handclasp, O beggar, but trust me not!
Soon I shall be with my own sort and you will be forgot.
Only of friends more poor need a poor woman not be wary.
Wherefore, my burdened sister, draw near and look upon Mary!
Poor woman, whose husband drinks and whose children are far
    from strong,
When you have no money for rent and death seems delayed too
    long,
Ah, when everything fails you and misery presses you ill,
Come to the church and look on the Mother of God, and be still!
Whatever injustice we bear, though our lot seem worse than all
    other,
Yet when the children are sick, it is harder to be their Mother!
So, uncomplaining and hopeless, look upon her who is there,
Like a poor man finding a poorer, and each at the other stare!

From the French by Sister Mary David, S.S.N.D.

VINCENT MCNABB

(1868–1943)

THE SPOTLESS MAID

Ladye Marye! today
Let me say my own say,
In my own daring way.

Yet if I dare, 'tis He
Must bear the blame, Who thee
So high made—and lowly.

When a fond son doth praise
His mother, what he says
Has it, think yet, two ways?

Fairer than the rose, thou,
O my Mother's white brow!—
Dark is the snow-drift now.

Stars and sun have I seen:
Deep night-gloom have they been
To thy dear eyes' love-sheen.

Men see the silver moon,
And cry, 'A godlike boon!'
God sets it 'neath thy shoon.

Men see the sun, and say,
'A god, it!'—God says, 'Nay,
But Mary's gown, sad grey.'

Once I look on thy light,
My weak eyes, dazed with fright,
Seek the sun, noonday-bright.

For rest;—as, scorched with sun,
Oft for rest my eyes run
Unto earth's green homespun.

How glad all thy kith feel!
For he who sank our weal
Lies wrecked under thy heel.

Ne'er aught of thee or thine
Was the sly foul fiend's shrine;
Thou art all God's—all mine!

All God's, all men's! and thus
It is for us, for us,
He made thee glorious.

Ladye Marye! today
Is fall'n men's feast, for they
Lured thy dear Son thy way.

For us He yearned for earth;
For us He dowered thy birth,
To turn our woe to mirth.

Thy crown is ours. And we
Are thine. And both shall be
Jesu's eternally.

HILAIRE BELLOC

(1870–   )

BALLADE TO OUR LADY OF CZESTOCHOWA

I

Lady and Queen and Mystery manifold
   And very Regent of the untroubled sky,
Whom in a dream St. Hilda did behold
   And heard a woodland music passing by:
   You shall receive me when the clouds are high

With evening and the sheep attain the fold.
This is the faith that I have held and hold,
 And this is that in which I mean to die.

II

Steep are the seas and savaging and cold
 In broken waters terrible to try;
And vast against the winter night the wold,
 And harbourless for any sail to lie.
 But you shall lead me to the lights, and I
Shall hymn you in a harbour story told.
This is the faith that I have held and hold,
 And this is that in which I mean to die.

III

Help of the half-defeated, House of gold,
 Shrine of the Sword, and Tower of Ivory;
Splendour apart, supreme and aureoled,
 The Battler's vision and the World's reply.
 You shall restore me, O my last Ally,
To vengeance and the glories of the bold.
This is the faith that I have held and hold,
 And this is that in which I mean to die.

Envoi

Prince of the degradations bought and sold,
 These verses, written in your crumbling sty,
Proclaim the faith that I have held and hold
 And publish that in which I mean to die.

OUR LORD AND OUR LADY

They warned Our Lady for the Child
  That was Our Blessed Lord,
And She took Him into the desert wild
  Over the camel's ford.

And a long song She sang to Him
  And a short story told:
And She wrapped Him in a woolen cloak
  To keep Him from the cold.

But when Our Lord was grown a man
  The Rich they dragged Him down,
And they crucified Him in Golgotha,
  Out and beyond the town.

They crucified Him on Calvary,
  Upon an April day;
And because He had been Her little Son
  She followed Him all the way.

Our Lady stood beside the cross
  A little space apart,
And when She heard Our Lord cry out
  A sword went through Her heart.

They laid Our Lord in a marble tomb,
  Dead, in a winding sheet,
But Our Lady stands above the world
  With the White Moon at her feet.

IN A BOAT

Lady! Lady!
Upon Heaven-height,
Above the harsh morning
In the mere light.

Above the spindrift
And above the snow,
Where no seas tumble,
And no winds blow.

The twisting tides,
And the perilous sands
Upon all sides
Are in your holy hands.

The wind harries
And the cold kills;
But I see your chapel
Over far hills.

My body is frozen,
My soul is afraid:
Stretch out your hands to me,
Mother and maid.

Mother of Christ,
And Mother of me,
Save me alive
From the howl of the sea.

If you will Mother me
Till I grow old,
I will hang in your chapel
A ship of pure gold.

LOUIS MERCIER
(1870-   )

NOTRE DAME DES PETITS

When the little children die,—
And Death loves the fairest heads—
While on earth their mothers mourn,
Weeping by their tiny beds,

They have cast their cerements
From their limbs and lightly rise,
Leave nightly graveyards grim,
Run direct to Paradise,—

To the Holy City straight,
Trembling for their little shrouds,
Come they, scarce with rosy feet
Touching blue and opal clouds.

Seeing them all naked so
Mary wistful doth recall
Sorrows of earth long ago
When her Jesus, too, was small.

Instantly her slender staff
Satin bobbin doth adorn,
Weaving warp and woof made moist
With the humid breath of morn.

Taking the soft clouds nearby
Cherubs in their angel fun
Cut out pretty robes of mist,
Fit the babies every one.

Soon their robes are fitted on
And the infants romping come,
Mid lilies white and violets blue
To play in their new Heaven-home.

Seeing them all joyful so
Mary smiling doth recall
Joys on earth once long ago
When her Jesus, too, was small.

From the French by Liam Brophy

CHARLES PÉGUY

(1873–1914)

THE PASSION OF OUR LADY

. . . .

For the past three days she had been wandering, and following.
She followed the people.
She followed the events.
She seemed to be following a funeral.
But it was a living man's funeral.—
She followed like a follower.
Like a servant.
Like a weeper at a Roman funeral.—
As if it had been her only occupation.
To weep.—
That is what he had done to his mother.
Since the day when he had begun his mission.—
You saw her everywhere.
With the people and a little apart from the people.
Under the porticoes, under the arcades, in drafty places.
In the temples, in the palaces.
In the streets.
In the yards and in the back-yards.
And she had also gone up to Calvary.
She too had climbed up Calvary.
A very steep hill.

And she did not even feel that she was walking.
She did not even feel that her feet were carrying her.—
She too had gone up *her* Calvary.
She too had gone up and up
In the general confusion, lagging a little behind . . .
She wept and wept under a big linen veil.
A big blue veil.
A little faded.—
She wept as it will never be granted to a woman to weep.
As it will never be asked
Of a woman to weep on this earth.
Never at any time.—
What was very strange was that everyone respected her.
People greatly respect the parents of the condemned.
They even said: *Poor woman.*
And at the same time they struck at her son.
Because man is like that.—
The world is like that.
Men are what they are and you never can change them.
She did not know that, on the contrary, he had come to change
    man.
That he had come to change the world.
She followed and wept.
Everybody respected her.
Everybody pitied her.
They said: *Poor woman.*
Because they weren't perhaps really bad.
They weren't bad at heart.
They fulfilled the Scriptures.—
They honored, respected and admired her grief.
They didn't make her go away, they pushed her back only a little
    with special attentions
Because she was the mother of the condemned.
They thought: It's the family of the condemned.
They even said so in a low voice.
They said it among themselves
With a secret admiration.—
She followed and wept, and didn't understand very well.

But she understood quite well that the government was against
 her boy.
And that is a very bad business.—
She understood that all the governments were together against
 her boy.
The government of the Jews and the government of the Romans.
The government of judges and the government of priests.
The government of soldiers and the government of parsons.
He could never get out of it.
Certainly not.—
What was strange was that all derision was heaped on him.
Not on her at all.—
There was only respect for her.
For her grief.—
They didn't insult her.
On the contrary.
People even refrained from looking at her too much.
All the more to respect her.
So she too had gone up.
Gone up with everybody else.
Up to the very top of the hill.
Without even being aware of it.
Her legs had carried her and she did not even know it.
She too had made the Way of the Cross.
The fourteen stations of the Way of the Cross.
Were there fourteen stations?
Were there really fourteen stations?—
She didn't know for sure.
She couldn't remember.
Yet she had not missed one.
She was sure of that.
But you can always make a mistake.
In moments like that your head swims.
Everybody was against him.
Everybody wanted him to die.
It is strange.
People who are not usually together.
The government and the people.

That was awful luck.
When you have someone for you and someone against you,
   sometimes you can get out of it.
You can scramble out of it.
But he wouldn't.
Certainly he wouldn't.
When you have everyone against you.
But what had he done to everyone?

I'll tell you.
He had saved the world.

From the French by Julian Green

GILBERT KEITH CHESTERTON
(1874–1936)

THE BLACK VIRGIN

One in thy thousand statues we salute thee
On all thy thousand thrones acclaim and claim
Who walk in forest of thy forms and faces
Walk in a forest calling on one name
And, most of all, how this thing may be so
Who know thee not are mystified to know—
That one cries "Here she stands" and one cries "Yonder"
And thou wert home in heaven long ago.

Burn deep in Bethlehem in the golden shadows,
Ride above Rome upon the horns of stone,
From low Lancastrian or South Saxon shelters
Watch through dark years the dower that was thine own:
Ghost of our land, White Lady of Walsinghame,
Shall they not live that call upon thy name
If an old song on a wild wind be blowing
Crying of the holy country whence they came?

Root deep in Chartres the roses blown of glass
Burning above thee in the high vitrailles,
On Cornish crags take for salute of swords
O'er peacock seas the far salute of sails,
Glooming in bronze or gay in painted wood,
A great doll given when the child is good,
Save that She gave the Child who gave the doll,
In whom all dolls are dreams of motherhood.

I have found thee like a little shepherdess
Gay with green ribbons; and passed on to find
Michael called Angel hew the Mother of God
Like one who fills a mountain with a mind:
Molten in silver or gold or garbed in blue,
Or garbed in red where the inner robe burns through,
Of the King's daughter glorious within:
Change thine unchanging light with every hue.

Clothed with the sun or standing on the moon
Crowned with the stars or single, a morning star,
Sunlight and moonlight are thy luminous shadows,
Starlight and twilight thy refractions are,
Lights and half-lights and all lights turn about thee,
But though we dazed can neither see nor doubt thee,
Something remains. Nor can man live without it
Nor can man find it bearable without thee.

There runs a dark thread through the tapestries
That time has woven with all the tints of time
Something not evil but grotesque and groping,
Something not clear; not final; not sublime;
Quaint as dim pattern of primal plant or tree
Or fish, the legless elfins of the sea,
Yet rare as this thine image in ebony
Being most strange in its simplicity.

Rare as the rushing of the wild black swans
The Romans saw; or rocks remote and grim

Where through black clouds the black sheep runs accursed
And through black clouds the Shepherd follows him.
By the black oak of the aeon-buried grove
By the black gems of the miner's treasure-trove
Monsters and freaks and fallen stars and sunken—
Most holy dark, cover our uncouth love.

From thine high rock look down on Africa
The living darkness of devouring green
The loathsome smell of life unquenchable,
Look on low brows and blinking eyes between,
On the dark heart where white folk find no place,
On the dark bodies of an antic race,
On all that fear thy light and love thy shadow,
Turn thou the mercy of thy midnight face.

This also is in thy spectrum; this dark ray;
Beyond the deepening purples of thy Lent
Darker than violet vestment; dark and secret
Clot of old night yet cloud of heaven sent:
As the black moon of some divine eclipse,
As the black sun of the Apocalypse,
As the black flower that blessed Odysseus back
From witchcraft; and he saw again the ships.

In all thy thousand images we salute thee,
Claim and acclaim on all thy thousand thrones
Hewn out of multi-colored rocks and risen
Stained with the stored-up sunsets in all tones—
If in all tones and shades this shade I feel,
Come from the black cathedrals of Castille
Climbing these flat black stones of Catalonia,
To thy most merciful face of night I kneel.

THE RETURN OF EVE

When Man rose up out of the red mountains
    Of which Man was made
A giant ribbed out of the red mountains
    Reared and displayed.
Of him was not posterity nor parent
    Future or past
But the sun beheld him for a beauteous monster
    The first and last.

When God arose upon the red mountains
    Man had fallen prone
Flat and flung wide like a continent, capes and headlands,
    The vast limbs thrown.
And the Lord lamented over Man, saying "Never
    Shall there be but one
For no man born shall be mighty as he was mighty
    To amaze the sun.

"Not till I put upon me the red armour
    That was man's clay
And walk the world with the mask of man for a vizor
    Not till that day.
For on God alone shall the image of God be graven
    Which Adam wore
Seeing I alone can lift up this load of ruin
    To walk once more."

But the Lord looked down on the beauty of Woman shattered,
    A fallen sky,
Crying "O crown and wonder and world's desire
    Shall this too die?
Lo, it repenteth me that this too is taken;
    I will repay,
I will repair and repeat of the ancient pattern
    Even in this clay.

"And this alone out of all things fallen and formless
    I will form anew
And this red lily of all the uprooted garden
    Plant where it grew
That the dear dead thing that was all and only a woman
    Without stain or scar
Rise, fallen no more with Lucifer Son of Morning,
    The Morning Star."

The cloud came down upon the red mountains
    Long since untrod
Red quarries of incredible creation
    Red mines of God
And a dwarfed and dwindled race in the dark red deserts
    Stumbled and strayed
While one in the mortal shape that was once for immortals
    Made, was remade.

Till a face looked forth from a window in one white daybreak
    Small streets above
As the face of the first love of our first father,
    The world's first love.
And men looked up at the woman made for the morning
    When the stars were young,
For whom, more rude than a beggar's rhyme in the gutter,
    These songs are sung.

REGINA ANGELORUM

Our Lady went into a strange country,
    Our Lady, for she was ours
And had run on the little hills behind the houses
    And pulled small flowers;
But she rose up and went into a strange country
    With strange thrones and powers.

And there were giants in the land she walked in,
    Tall as their toppling towns,
With heads so high in heaven, the constellations
    Served them for crowns;
And their feet might have forded like a brook the abysses
    Where Babel drowns.

They were girt about with the wings of the morning and evening
    Furled and unfurled,
Round the speckled sky where our small spinning planet
    Like a top is twirled;
And the swords they waved were the unending comets
    That shall end the world.

And moving in innocence and in accident,
    She turned the face
That none had ever looked on without loving
    On the Lords of Space;
And one hailed her with her name in our own country
    That is full of grace.

Our Lady went into a strange country
    And they crowned her for a queen,
For she needed never to be stayed or questioned
    But only seen;
And they were broken down under unbearable beauty
    As we have been.

But ever she walked till away in the last high places
    One great light shone
From the pillared throne of the king of all that country
    Who sat thereon;
And she cried aloud as she cried under the gibbet
    For she saw her son.

Our Lady wears a crown in a strange country,
    The crown he gave,
But she has not forgotten to call to her old companions,
    To call and crave;

And to hear her calling a man might arise and thunder
On the doors of the grave.

CONAL O'RIORDAN

(1874–)

HYMN TO THE VIRGIN MARY

Queen of all Queens, oh! Wonder of the loveliness of women,
Heart which hath held in check for us the righteous wrath of
  God;
Strong Staff of Light, and Fosterer of the Bright Child of heaven,
Pray thou for us as we now pray that we may be forgiven.

She of the King of Stars beloved, stainless, undefiled,
Christ chose as His Mother-nurse, to Him, the stainless Child;
Within her breast, as in a nest, the Paraclete reposes,
Lily among fairest flowers, Rose amid red roses.

She, the bright unsheathèd sword to guard our souls in anguish,
She, the flawless limber-branch, to cover those that languish;
Where her healing mantle flows, may I find my hiding,
'Neath the fringes of her robe constantly abiding.

Hostile camps upon the plain, sharp swords clashed together,
Stricken fleets across the main stressed by wintry weather;
Weary sickness on my heart, sinful thoughts alluring,
All the fever of my soul clings to her for curing.

She the Maid the careful King of the wide wet world chooses,
In her speech forgiveness lies, no suppliant she refuses;
White Star of our troubled sea, on thy name I'm crying,
That Christ may draw in His spread net the living and the dying.

From the Gaelic by Eleanor Hull

RAINER MARIA RILKE

(1875–1926)

ON THE DEATH OF MARY

I

The same great angel who had once
brought her down the message of her bearing,
stood there, waiting for her to notice him,
and spoke: Now it is time that thou appear.
And she was startled as before and showed
herself the maid again, deeply confirming him.
But he shone, and infinitely nearing,
vanished as it were into her face—
and bade the evangelists gone forth afar
to come together in the house on the slope,
the house of the last supper. They came more heavily
and entered fearfully: There, along
the narrow bed, she lay, in her passing
and election mysteriously immersed,
quite inviolate, like one unused,
heeding angelic song.
Now that she saw them all waiting behind
their candles, she tore herself from the excess
of voices and with all her heart yet gave
away the two dresses she possessed,
and lifted her face to this one and to that . . . .
(o source of nameless brooks of tears).

But she lay back in her weakness
and drew the heavens so close to Jerusalem
that her soul, departing, needed but
to stretch itself a little:
already he, who knew everything about her,
was lifting her into her divine nature.

II

Who has considered that until her coming
the manifold heaven was incomplete?
The resurrected one had taken his place,
but next him, throughout four and twenty years,
the seat was empty. And already they began
to grow accustomed to the clean gap that was
as if healed over, for with his beautiful
outspreading shine the son filled it.

So even she, entering the heavens, went
not towards him, much as she longed to. There was
no room there, only He was there, resplendent
with a radiance that hurt her.
Yet as she now, that moving figure,
joined the newly blessed and took her place,
inconspicuous, light to light,
there broke out of her being a withheld store
of such glory, that the angel lighted up
by her cried out dazzled: Who is she?
Amazement reigned. Then they all saw how
above God the Father withheld our Lord
so that, with mild twilight playing round it,
the empty place showed like a bit of sorrow,
a trace of loneliness, like something
he was still enduring, a residue
of earthly time, a dried-up canker—.
They looked towards her: she was watching anxiously,
leaning far out, as though she felt: *I* am
his longest pain—: and suddenly plunged forward.
But the angels took her to themselves
and supported her and sang beatifically
and carried her the last stretch aloft.

III

But before the Apostle Thomas, who
came when it was too late, stepped the swift
angel, long since prepared for this,
and commanded at the burial-place:

Push the stone aside. Wouldst thou know
where she is who has moved thy heart:
See: like a cushion of lavender
she was laid in there a while,

that in future the earth smell of her
in its folds like a fine napkin.
Everything dead (thou feelest), everything sickly
is numbed with her good fragrance.

Behold the winding-sheet: where is a bleaching place
where it would grow dazzling and not shrink?
This light from this pure corpse
was more clarifying to it than sunshine.

Are you not astonished, how gently she went from it?
Almost as though it were still she, nothing is displaced.
Yet the heavens are shaken above:
Man, kneel down, look after me and sing.

From the German by M. D. Herter Norton

GERTRUDE VON LE FORT

(1875–   )

VIGIL OF THE ASSUMPTION

Your voice speaks:

The angel of the Lord came in unto Mary, and brought her the
home-call of infinite love.

Rise, soul of Mary, the heavenly messengers have come,

They are here to fetch the cradle that your Divine Child lay in.

Now take your rest on the heart under which His life slumbered,

Nestle deep in the garment that so tenderly enfolded Him.

Rise, soul of Mary, rise in the cradle of the All-high.

What is to befall you, snow-pure one? You shall be taken up
into Heaven.

From the German by Margaret Chanler

CHRISTMAS

Your voice speaks:

Little child out of Eternity, now will I sing to thy mother! The
song shall be fair as dawn-tinted snow.

Rejoice Mary Virgin, daughter of my earth, sister of my soul,
rejoice, O joy of my joy!

I am as one who wanders through the night, but you are a house
under stars.

I am a thirsty cup, but you are God's open sea.

Rejoice Mary Virgin, blessed are those who call you blessed,
never more shall child of man lose hope.

I am one love for all, I shall never cease from saying: one of you
has been exalted by the Lord.

Rejoice Mary Virgin, wings of my earth, crown of my soul, rejoice
joy of my joy!

Blessed are those who call you blessed.

From the German by Margaret Chanler

ANONYMOUS

THE KEENING OF MARY *

"O Peter, O Apostle, hast thou seen my bright love?"
M'óchón agus m'óchón, Ó! †
"I saw Him even now in the midst of His foemen,"
M'óchón agus m'óchón, Ó!

"Come hither, two Marys, till ye keen my bright love."
M'óchón agus m'óchón, Ó!
"What have we to keen if we keen not His bones?"
M'óchón agus m'óchón, Ó!

"Who is that stately man on the tree of the Passion?"
M'óchón agus m'óchón, Ó!
"Dost thou not know thy Son, O Mother?"
M'óchón agus m'óchón, Ó!

"And is that the little Son I carried nine months?"
M'óchón agus m'óchón, Ó!
"And is that the little Son that was born in a stable?"
M'óchón agus m'óchón, Ó!

"And is that the little Son that was nursed at Mary's breast?"
M'óchón agus m'óchón, Ó!
"Hush, O Mother, and be not sorrowful!"
M'óchón agus m'óchón, Ó!

"And is that the hammer that struck home nails through Thee?"
M'óchón agus m'óchón, Ó!
"And is that the spear that went through Thy white side?"
M'óchón agus m'óchón, Ó!

* Taken down from Mary Clancy of Moycullen, who keened it with great horror
in her voice, in a low sobbing recitative.
† "Alas, and alas, oh!"

"And is that the crown of thorns that crowned Thy beauteous
head?"
M'óchón agus m'óchón, Ó!
"Hush, O Mother, be not sorrowful."
M'óchón agus m'óchón, Ó!

"Hush, O Mother, and be not sorrowful,"
M'óchón agus m'óchón, Ó!
"The women of my keening are yet unborn, little Mother."
M'óchón agus m'óchón, Ó!

"O woman, who weepest by this My death,"
M'óchón agus m'óchón, Ó!
"There will be hundreds today in the Garden of Paradise!"
M'óchón agus m'óchón, Ó!

From the Gaelic by Padraic Pearse

PADRAIC COLUM

(1881–   )

FOURTH STATION

Jesus His Mother meets:
She looks on Him and sees
The Savior in Her Son:
The Angel's word comes back:
Within her heart she says,
"Unto me let this be done!"
Still is she full of grace.

By us, too be it one,
That grace that brings us revelation!

234

A CRADLE SONG

O men from the fields,
　Come gently within.
Tread softly, softly
　O men coming in!

Mavourneen is going
　From me and from you,
Where Mary will fold him
　With mantle of blue!

From reek of the smoke
　And cold of the floor
And the peering of things
　Across the half-door.

O men of the fields,
　Soft, softly come thro'
Mary puts round him
　Her mantle of blue.

SHANE LESLIE
(1885-　)

THE TWO MOTHERS

On the hill of weeping
Mother Mary spake unto Granuaile: *
"Little Mother, why so sad and pale?"
"Half my sons are sleeping,"
Unto Mother Mary said Granuaile,

* *Granuaile*—an Irish Sea-Queen whose name is symbolic for Ireland herself.

"And the rest are keeping
Weary watch beneath a windless sail."
"Mother, hush your weeping,"
Mary Mother said unto Granuaile:
"They are in my keeping
Where their hearts and hands can never fail,
And the rest are sleeping
But to rise again in freedom's gale,"
Mary Mother spake unto Granuaile.

RUPERT BROOKE

(1887–1915)

MARY AND GABRIEL

Young Mary, loitering once her garden way,
Felt a warm splendour grow in the April day,
As wine that blushes water through. And soon,
Out of the gold air of the afternoon,
One knelt before her: hair he had, or fire,
Bound back above his ears with golden wire,
Baring the eager marble of his face.
Not man's or woman's was the immortal grace
Rounding the limbs beneath that robe of white,
And lighting the proud eyes with changeless light,
Incurious. Calm as his wings, and fair,
That presence filled the garden.

                                        She stood there,
Saying, "What would you, Sir?"

                                        He told his word,
"Blessed art thou of women!" Half she heard,

Hands folded and face bowed, half long had known,
The message of that clear and holy tone,
That fluttered hot sweet sobs about her heart;
Such serene tidings moved such human smart.
Her breath came quick as little flakes of snow.
Her hands crept up her breast. She did but know
It was not hers. She felt a trembling stir
Within her body, a will too strong for her
That held and filled and mastered all. With eyes
Closed, and a thousand soft short broken sighs,
She gave submission; fearful, meek, and glad. . . .

She wished to speak. Under her breasts she had
Such multitudinous burnings, to and fro,
And throbs not understood; she did not know
If they were hurt or joy for her; but only
That she was grown strange to herself, half lonely,
All wonderful, filled full of pains to come
And thoughts she dare not think, swift thoughts
    and dumb,
Human, and quaint, her own, yet very far,
Divine, dear, terrible, familiar . . .
Her heart was faint for telling; to relate
Her limbs' sweet treachery, her strange high estate,
Over and over, whispering, half revealing,
Weeping; and so find kindness to her healing.
'Twixt tears and laughter, panic hurrying her,
She raised her eyes to that fair messenger.
He knelt unmoved, immortal; with his eyes
Gazing beyond her, calm to the calm skies;
Radiant, untroubled in his wisdom, kind.
His sheaf of lilies stirred not in the wind.
How should she, pitiful with mortality,
Try the wide peace of that felicity
With ripples of her perplexed shaken heart,
And hints of human ecstasy, human smart,
And whispers of the lonely weight she bore,
And how her womb within was hers no more

And at length hers?
            Being tired, she bowed her head;
And said, "So be it!"
            The great wings were spread
Showering glory on the fields, and fire.
The whole air, singing, bore him up, and higher,
Unswerving, unreluctant. Soon he shone
A gold speck in the gold skies; then was gone.

The air was colder, and grey. She stood alone.

SHEILA KAYE-SMITH

(1888–   )

LADY DAY IN HARVEST

(A Lullaby for the Falling Asleep of the Blessed Virgin Mary)

Mary sleeps—and as she sleeps the angels sing:

Sleep, sleep, sweetly sleep,
Sweetly sleep, sleep, sleep,
You who rocked the cradle—so—
In the stable long ago.
Golden Rose of David's stem,
Sleep, and dream of Bethlehem;
Dream of herald angels singing,
Dream of Christmas bells a-ringing
In the steeples of the town,
Telling of the Christ come down
To a stable long ago;
Dream in harvest of the snow;
Dream his head is on your breast,
Then, smiling, sleep and take your rest—

Gold Rose of David's stem,
Sleep and dream of Bethlehem.

Mary sleeps—and as she sleeps her Son sings:

Sleep, sleep, sweetly sleep,
Sweetly sleep, sleep, sleep:
You rocked the cradle once for me,
Mother of sweet liberty;
And now I sing your lullaby,
While angels watch us from the sky,
And the August stars are bright
In the dark, hop-scented night.
Rest, darling mother, rest
With your head upon my breast,
For all the hundred happy hours
That my head has lain on yours.
Mother whose hair is grey with love,
  With memories of Calvary's day. . . .
Darling, in the fields above
  The young angels wait to play,
And all the holy innocents,
  Who once laid down their lives for me,
Will climb into your lap and lie
  Where once I lay so lovingly.
Rest, darling mother, rest
With your head upon my breast.

Mary sleeps—and as she sleeps we all sing:

Sleep, sleep, mother, sleep,
Sweetly sleep, sleep, sleep;
On his bosom lay your head,
While the angels watch your bed,
And the August stars are red—
  Little mother of joy divine,
  Little mother of purity,
  Sweet mother of eternity—
  (You our mother and he our brother);

So shall heaven's windows shine
With lights of home, burning softly down,
　On your children on their way
　To your door—until the day
When we reach our native town:
And our hands shall knock, and yours unlatch,
And we shall come home to you under the thatch—
To you our mother, to him our brother,
So shall we love you and him and each other.
　Little mother of joy divine,
From your window in heaven look down,
And light the way to our native town.

HENRIETTE CHARASSON

(1890–　)

AVE MARIA

The third Sunday after Easter and the first dominical day of the
　white month of Mary,
And again I am before thee, who bearest the Child in thine arms,
　while my arms are empty and my heart is bare of hope.
I kneel before thee, who are full of grace, and look upon thy
　sweet and sad smile which the candles illumine.
Mother of the Human Race, I ask no more than is commonly
　allowed
　when I also would like to bring my small stone to the building!
Today the Gospel was read that I call the Gospel
　of Women in Travail:
"A woman when she is in labor hath sorrow, because her hour
　is come;
"But when she hath brought forth the child, she remembereth
　no more
　the anguish, for joy that a man is born into the world."

240

When these great words of Christ were read, my heart melted
    within me,
  because they spoke of a little child,
  and I suffered so . . .
Hail Mary, full of grace, the Lord is with thee, blessed art thou
    among women,
And blessed is the fruit of thy womb, Jesus.

From the French by Frederic Thompson

WILFRED ROWLAND CHILDE

(1890–   )

OUR LADY WITH TWO ANGELS

She sits in Sarras, delicate and strange
As Gryphons are, and from Her feet of crystal
Fall crystal rivers downward, healing streams
That wash away the slow stains of the world:
Her face is aureoled with an excessive beauty,
Calm as the radiant heart of irised Night,
And from her fingers weary petals keep dropping,
Which fall as answers to the tears and sighs
Of multitudes. Upon each side an Angel
Leans upon an immaculate theorbo,
Its strings his very heart's own, and from those
Plucked plangent strings such harmonies ensue
That Evening's hyacinthine cloud-castles
Blush into changeful rose-colour and bronze:
She is all ringed with lilies in Her castle,
Golden and white and sapphire, and Her grave
Child-brows are weighed down with such sweet innocence
They seem to need no crown, though Crown there is,
Clearer than peerless flashing diamond,

And liquid like the dreaming meres of Heaven,
 A lucid tiar for Eve's dewy rose,
A nimbus for the Sea-Star of bright Dawn—
God's Virgin sitting in her golden bower
Upon the walls of Syon . . . Such as She was
On earth beside the well in Nazareth,
So is She now in the serene Nazareth
Of Her Heavenly Coronation, in the Kingdom
Prepared by God All-Father for His Blessed,
Prepared by the Spouse-Emperor for His Bride.

LIAM P. CLANCY

(1897–)

A GAELIC CHRISTMAS

Their hearts are filled with Pity's mead,
And their souls are sorrow-laden,
When they hear of God's Handmaiden
Without *housheen* * in her need.

Did Mary walk the *bohreens* † green
From Shannon's shore to Galway's border,
The homes of Clare were set in order,
To shield her from the East winds keen.

My grief it is, and bitter woe,
That first to greet the Infant Treasure
Were men with love so mean of measure,
And not my kin by Shannon's flow,

* *How-sheen:* Little house.
† *Bo-reens:* Little roads.

Tho' Thomond heights be bleak and bare,
And Thomond folk but poor and lowly,
With a welcome warm and rapture holy
They'd share their store with the Strangers there.

If Mary went the winding road
From fair Aylroo to far Liscannor,
With matchless grace of mien and manner
Some *banathee* * would ease her load:

She'd lilt a haunting "Husheen-ho,"
Or croon an olden Gaelic number,
To lull the Babe to smiling slumber
Before the turf-fire's fitful glow.

O, would that Mary's feet but trod,
That Christmas Eve, some Thomond valley,—
With a joy untold my kin would rally
To dower with gifts the Lamb of God.

CHRISTMAS EVE

Let the door be open wide
And no blind be down at all,
For maybe she'd be walking
With the child within her shawl;
And how could we be bearing
The weight of shame and sin,
If she'd pass upon the roadway
With no light to guide her in?

* *Bann-ath-ee:* Woman of the house.

Let the chair be readied now,
And the fire kept burning bright;
For sorely she'll be needing
The rest and warmth this night.
The rushes too be spreading
Upon the earthen floor,
To make it sweet and wholesome
Her blessed feet before.

Full oft I've heard the story
How once this night were known
To rest within a shieling
Three strangers meek and lone;
But dawn did yield no tidings
Of man, or maid, or child:
'Twas Joseph's self was in it,
And Christ, and Mary mild.

So set the candles burning
Upon each window high,
And leave the door wide open
To guide their footsteps nigh:
Right warmly they'll be welcome
To share our hearth-fire bright—
For Mary's sake in heaven—
Who walk the wilds this night.

ARTHUR J. LITTLE

(1897–   )

INVOCATION

(From *Christ Unconquered,* Book IX)

Mother of God, mother of man reborn,
Majestic woman, who at the bitter tree
Besought the burden of the motherhood
Of men by immolation of your heart
To bear his pangs whom you had given to them,
And, by his gift of men, spoils of his pain,
To you, received your children to consort
With him, your only son, as you consort
Remember that award! For here I cry,
Here on the utmost kerf of the world's wall,
These iron bluffs that bar the western sea
Indomitable, and havoc of its storms
Hurl from the quiet lands, in this grey land,
The fierce and faithful, that another wall
Erects against the tempests of the mind
That ever would beguile us or torment
To banish you and him from your estate,
Ourselves, rich only in the servitude
That makes you ours. Here in this land were raised
Your altars first to show the wonder owed
To your untainted making; and its folk
Grew to the likeness of the thing they loved,
Yourself, even to elect the destiny
Of nearness to the cross and the disdain
That visits it, with loss of all delight,
All dignity, all liberty, all wealth,
The property of knowledge, outward grace,
For loyalty to the crucified, then know
Their weakness by the persecutors scorned
When at the conflict's close they rose in scars.
Now by the faithful valour of my race
Which to the highest never was untrue,

245

Though not all sinless, yet in that devout,
I call on you. How can my lips of clay
Fashion a song divine, unless through you
Made of its burden worthy? Through your prayers
Then, sorrowful, bring forth within my mind
The shape of Jesus crucified and scorned,
Which is the mind's act of becoming Christ
In impact of its knowledge, that transformed
Into your son divine I may declare
With faithful voice your passion which is his
Even to the authors of this alien tongue
Noble, and once the clarion of your fame,
Haply to mind them that your love endures.

RUTH SCHAUMANN
(1899–   )

MARY ON HER WAY TO THE TEMPLE

Scarce lay the blossoms of her golden hair
Warm as a leveret in her mother's hand
When on the wall her shadow gliding there
Haunted her young years with its stern demand.
She coveted no worldly vanity
As the tall steps she climbed with girlish grace,
Approaching unperturbed the galaxy
Of aged priests who kept the holy place.

She looked not back. There on the stone floor lay
The apple that her father gave as token
Of tenderness for all her tenderness.
She entered joyfully that blessed day
The templed walls, herself a shrine unbroken,
To wait till time shall reach its fruitfulness.

From the German by Edwin Buers, S.D.S.

246

FOURTH STATION

(The voice of a child:)

They say this is His mother,—
the people aged and tall.—
Who stands upon the roadway
rejected by them all;
her eyes are on the crosses.
Oh, why am I so small!

The heavy wood is pressing
the flesh that is her Son.
No word from her is wanted
whose cloak with dust is spun;
she may not cry in anguish.
Weep, mothers, gazing on!

His searching eyes have found you
and sent their love to you;
but now the hill up yonder
demands His life anew.
On tip-toe I was standing;
I saw your hand ascending
to bid a last adieu.

From the German by William J. Brell, P.S.M.

MARY KING

(1904–   )

MARY OF BETHLEHEM

When Mary came to Bethlehem,
To Bethlehem, to Bethlehem,
When Mary came to Bethlehem

And tarried near the Inn,
Every child in Bethlehem,
And every beast in Bethlehem
And every bird in Bethlehem,
Longed to be her kin.

When Mary rode from Bethlehem,
Everything was still—
All the birds of Bethlehem
Sang Aves from the hill;
Little children ceased their play,
Lowly oxen turned her way,
Because she had been one of them
And greatly loved in Bethlehem.

W. H. AUDEN
(1907–)

DIALOGUE BETWEEN MARY AND GABRIEL

(From *For the Time Being—A Christmas Oratorio*)

GABRIEL

Mary, in a dream of love
Playing as all children play,
For unsuspecting children may
Express in comic make-believe
The wish that later they will know
Is tragic and impossible;
Hear, child, what I am sent to tell:
Love wills your dream to happen, so
Love's will on earth may be, through you,
No longer a pretend but true.

MARY

What dancing joy would whirl
My ignorance away?
Light blazes out of the stone,
The taciturn water
Burst into music,
And warm wings throb within
The motionless rose:
What sudden rush of Power
Commands me to command?

GABRIEL

When Eve, in love with her own will,
Denied the will of Love and fell,
She turned the flesh Love knew so well
To knowledge of her love until
Both love and knowledge were of sin:
What her negation wounded, may
Your affirmation heal today;
Love's will requires your own, that in
The flesh whose love you do not know,
Love's knowledge into flesh may grow.

MARY

My flesh in terror and fire
Rejoices that the Word
Who utters the world out of nothing,
As a pledge of His word to love her
Against her will, and to turn
Her desperate longing to love,
Should ask to wear me,
From now to their wedding day,
For an engagement ring.

249

GABRIEL

Since Adam, being free to choose,
Chose to imagine he was free
To choose his own necessity,
Lost in his freedom, Man pursues
The shadow of his images:
Today the Unknown seeks the known;
What I am willed to ask, your own
Will has to answer; child, it lies
Within your power of choosing to
Conceive the Child who chooses you.

ROBERT FARREN
(1909–   )

MARY

Thou art God's sky,
in which the Sun arose:

Thou art His moon,
the window of His light.

Thou art God's earth,
God in thee taking root;
God's seed: He was thy tree;
God's tree . . . thy fruit.

Thou art God's spring
jetting out Life;
God's river-bed
through which His torrent rushed;

God's sea
in which He spawned His sacred fish;
God's oyster
secreting the pearl of Christ.
God's lake His cloud rose from
to rain on earth;
God's cloud:
by Him from thee was lightning struck;
God's lightning
blazing the encumbered Heaven;
God's Heaven,
for Heaven's where's God.

JOY'S PEAK

Was it at Nazareth
of the marvellous breath?
on the straw in the stable?
at the Cana wedding-table?
before at Jerusalem on the third day?
or at Jerusalem when
palms beat the wind and men
without the Magus' gold
extolled
kingship—was it then?

Was it in one of these
tremendous hours that you, Mary,
stood on the peak of Joy?
Or was the peak's name Calvary?
Or maybe yet—
Olivet?

MATER INCOGNITA

She came to me in hidden guise
  Before the sunrise of God's grace.
  I could not see her blessed face
Or know the marvel of her eyes.

Her mother-ear was quick to hark,
  As though to Heaven's keyhole laid,
  To listen to the child afraid
And crying in the frightening dark.

I did not know whose hands they were
  That came with solace in the night,
  Until at length she brought a light,
And I arose, beholding her.

With holy, healing waters first
  She laved me, and my fever fled;
  To me a-hungered brought she Bread,
And more than wine to stay my thirst.

Now folded close from every harm
  Within her very mantle's fold,
  I half forget the things of old
And all the grim night's dark alarm.

Mother, this thing I ask of you,
  That all my years be filled with praise,
  In reparation for the days
Of empty grief—before I knew.

LIAM BROPHY

ASSUMPTA EST MARIA

Angels

Lo, she cometh to us from afar,
Rising upward like the Morning Star
From that place where night and sorrow are:
　　Assumpta est Maria.

The People

Lo, she leaveth us in lonely dearth,
Leaveth now our long-remembering earth
Emptied of her and of all holy mirth:
　　Assumpta est Maria.

Angels

As she cometh, let us go to greet
Emmanuel's Mother, th' Father's Daughter sweet,
The Spouse Immaculate of the Paraclete:
　　Assumpta est Maria.

The People

Lo, she is gone from us, earth could not hold
So fair a Treasure; God hath halls of gold
To house her 'mong His mansions manifold:
　　Assumpta est Maria.

Angels

Her feet have touched at last our furthest coast,
Come, let the singing of the heavenly host
Surge round her, human nature's only boast:
　　Assumpta est Maria.

The People

See how our hymns still follow far behind,
She has a singing now of loftier kind,
Yet harken Heaven's hymns to our combin'd:
    Assumpta est Maria.

EILEEN DUGGAN

AFTER THE ANNUNCIATION

Mary, the maiden, walked out in the country,
Telling the wheat what the angel had told her;
The bees tumbled out of the flag-flowers to listen,
The birds stopped their fledglings and told them to heed her.

A woman in blue with wheat to her knees,
Mid the silence of birds and a stillness of bees,
Singing, "Golden, ah golden, with seedsprays unfurled,
Ripen within me, O wheat of the world!

Mary, bluewimpled, walked out in the country,
Telling the vine what none other must know yet;
The butterflies yearned to her hems as to harebells;
The flowers of the bushes fawned softly upon her.

A woman, gold-wet, with rainbow eyes,
And a border of living butterflies,
Singing, "Purple, ah purple, with tendrils close curled,
Ripen within me, O vine of the world!

EPIPHANY

Those who live in country places
Are not used to foreign faces.

Even of a pedlar selling
Some are frightened beyond telling;

Dust is dust in any village,
Even sooner than death's tillage,

And with rank there is a dryness,
Or an awkwardness, a shyness.

I, who am a paddocks-woman,
Think it would have been but human,

Though within her, poor, rough-fingered,
Some of David's blood still lingered,

And though shepherds, each a stranger,
Had knelt by that borrowed manger,

If the young and timid Mary
Of the three kings had been chary,

Hung her head and blushed and stammered
While with fear her pulses hammered

At their queer, grave sounds confiding
Some wild tale of a star riding.

To her, in the huge earth's pattern,
East from west was far as Saturn,

And what other village maiden,
Turning with her first-born laden,

255

Could confront with candid graces
Those proud-lidded Gentile faces?

Who has had within her doorway,
On one knee upon its floorway,

With his great wings slanted even
An archangel hot from heaven,

Telling her God's will upon her
Will make flesh His son within her,

Gives no ground to prince or pasha,
King of Europe, King of Asia!

THE NAME

We make that lovely sighing sound
A thing too far away,
A word and not the little name
His mother used to say.

Why do we never never think of her
As standing at the gate,
A dim, blue patience in the dusk?
"Jesus, come home; it's late."

Or in a dust of silver drops
When eaves are crying eyes,
"Jesus, the rain has made you grow,
You soon will touch the skies."

LITANY TO OUR LADY

Lady, giver of Bread,
Christ-bestowing,
give us the Bread of Life!

Fallow land for the sowing,
darkness over the seed,
secrecy for the growing:
give us the Living Bread.

Empty cup for the wine,
white linen, spread
without fold for the feast:
give us the Bread of Heaven,
yeast and leaven,
Christ-bestowing:
give us to eat.
Give us the Bread in the wheat,
Lady, giver of Bread.

Full grape in the vine,
give us the strong Wine
poured into the chalice
and lifted up.

Drained cup,
give us the broken Bread;
give us the crust of sorrow,
hard as rye,
Christ-bestowing.

Give us the emptiness
of the dark furrow,
while the great wind
of the Spirit is blowing
and sowing seed.

Lady, giver of Bread,
field sown by the wind,
snow white on the field,
darkness under the snow:
yield
the Bread of Life!
Wheat, leaven and yeast
and wine for the feast:
give us the Bread of Life,
Lady, giver of Bread,
Christ-bestowing.

THE REED

She is a reed,
straight and simple,
growing by a lake
in Nazareth:

a reed that is empty,
until the Breath of God
fills it with infinite music:

and the breath of the Spirit of Love
utters the Word of God
through an empty reed.

The Word of God
is infinite music
in a little reed:

it is the sound of a Virgin's heart,
beating in the solitude of adoration;
it is a girl's voice
speaking to an angel,
answering for the whole world;

it is the sound of the heart of Christ,
beating within the Virgin's heart;
it is the pulse of God,
timed by the breath of a Child.

The circle of a girl's arms
has changed the world—
the round sorrowful world—
to a cradle for God.

She has laid love in His cradle:
in every cot
Mary has laid her Child.

In each
comes Christ;
in each Christ comes
to birth;
comes Christ from the Mother's breast,
as the bird from the sun
returning—
returning again to the tree he knows,
and the nest,
to last year's rifled nest.

Into our hands
Mary has given her Child:
heir to the world's tears,
heir to the world's toil,
heir to the world's scars,
heir to the chill dawn
over the ruin of wars.
She has laid Love in His cradle,
answering, for us all,
"Be it done unto me":

The child in the wooden bed,
the light in the dark house,

the life in the failing soul,
the Host in the priest's hands,
the seed in the hard earth,
the man who is child again—
quiet in the burial bands,
waiting his birth.

Mary, Mother of God,
we are the poor soil
and the dry dust;
we are hard with a cold frost.

Be warmth to the world;
be the thaw,
warm on the cold frost;
be the thaw that melts,
that the tender shoot of Christ,
piercing the hard heart,
flower to a spring in us.

Be hands that are rocking the world
to a kind rhythm of love;
that the incoherence of war
and the chaos of our unrest
be soothed to a lullaby;
and the round and sorrowful world,
in your hands,
the cradle of God.

PART EIGHT

"LADY OF LETTERS"

Early and Contemporary American

HENRY WADSWORTH LONGFELLOW

(1807–1882)

THIS IS INDEED THE BLESSED MARY'S LAND

(From *The Golden Legend*)

This is indeed the Blessèd Mary's land,
Virgin and Mother of our dear Redeemer,
All hearts are touched and softened at her name;
Alike the bandit, with the bloody hand,
The priests, the prince, the scholar, and the peasant,
The man of deeds, the visionary dreamer,
Pay homage to her as one ever present.
And even as children, who have much offended
A too indulgent father, in great shame,
Penitent, and yet, not daring unattended
To go into his presence, at the gate
Speak with their sister, and confiding wait
Till she goes in before and intercedes;
So, men, repenting of their evil deeds,
And yet, not venturing rashly to draw near
With their requests an angry father's ear,
Offer to her their prayers and their confession,
And she for them in heaven makes intercession.
And, if our faith had given us nothing more
Than this Example of all Womanhood,
So mild, so merciful, so strong, so good,
So patient, peaceful, loyal, loving, pure—
This were enough to prove it higher and truer
Than all the creeds the world had known before.

Virgin, who lovest the poor and lonely,
If the loud cry of a mother's heart
Can ever ascend to where thou art,
Into thy blessèd hands and holy
Receive my prayer of praise and thanksgiving.
Let the hands that bore our Savior bear it
Into the awful presence of God;
For thy feet with holiness are shod,
And, if thou bearest it, he will hear it.

EDGAR ALLAN POE

(1809–1849)

HYMN

At morn, at noon, at twilight dim,
Maria, thou hast heard my hymn:
In joy and woe, in good and ill,
Mother of God, be with me still.
When the hours flew brightly by,
And not a cloud obscured the sky,
My soul, lest it should truant be,
Thy grace did guide to thine and thee.
Now, when storms of fate o'ercast
Darkly my present and my past,
Let my future radiant shine
With sweet hopes of thee and thine.

ABBY MARIA HEMENWAY

(1828–1899)

ANNUNCIATION NIGHT

(From *Mary of Nazareth*)

In through every lattice-bar
Where the trellis gapes ajar,
Flowing in, golden bright,
Beams of paradisal light,
With a wondrous lily-bloom
Flooding all the blessed room,
Silver most the snowy cover
Draping light the sleeper over.

Hush, a footfall on the floor;
Human step at chamber door.
Now with eyes of wonder mild,
Bending o'er her radiant child,
Gazing long doth Anna ponder
Till her loosed lips breathe the wonder.

"Never saw I moonbeams bright
As around this couch tonight
Gleaming o'er thy forehead fair,
Glistening in thy lustrous hair;
What a shining arrow dips
In the smile around thy lips!"
Bows her head to kiss the sleeper.
"O, Great Father, safely keep her!"
Saying, turning from the door,
" 'Tis a vision, nothing more.
'Tis a sweet and mystic dreaming—
Nights are never all in seeming."
Leaves her to her radiant rest
Guarded by an angel-guest.

HENRY ADAMS

(1838–1918)

PRAYER TO THE VIRGIN OF CHARTRES

Gracious Lady:—
Simple as when I asked your aid before;
   Humble as when I prayed for grace in vain
Seven hundred years ago; weak, weary, sore
   In heart and hope, I ask your help again.

You, who remember all, remember me;
   An English scholar of a Norman name,
I with a thousand who then crossed the sea
   To wrangle in the Paris schools for fame.

When your Byzantine portal was still young
   I prayed there with my master Abailard;
When Ave Maris Stella was first sung
   I helped to sing it here with Saint Bernard.

When Blanche set up your gorgeous Rose of France
   I stood among the servants of the Queen;
And when Saint Louis made his penitence
   I followed barefoot, where the King had been.

For centuries I brought you all my cares
   And vexed you with the murmurs of a child;
You heard the tedious burden of my prayers;
   You could not grant them, but at least you smiled.

If then I left you, it was not my crime,
   Or if a crime, it was not mine alone.
All children wander with the truant Time.
   Pardon me too; you pardoned once your Son!

For He said to you:—"Wist ye not that I
   Must be about my Father's business?" So,

Seeking His Father He pursued His way
  Straight to the Cross toward which we all must go.

So too I wandered off among the host
  That racked the earth to find the Father's clue.
I did not find the Father, but I lost
  What now I value more, the Mother, You!

I thought the fault was yours that foiled my search;
  I turned and broke your image on its throne,
Cast down my idol, and resumed my march
  To claim the Father's empire for my own.

Crossing the hostile sea, our greedy band
  Saw rising hills and forests in the blue;
Our Father's kingdom in the Promised Land!
  —We seized it and dethroned the Father too.

And now we are the Father, with our brood,
  Ruling the Infinite, not Three but One;
We made our world and saw that it was good;
  Ourselves we worship, and we have no Son.

Yet we have Gods, for even our strong nerve
  Falters before the Energy we own.
Which shall be master? Which of us shall serve?
  Which wears the fetters? Which shall bear the crown?

Brave though we be, we dread to face the Sphinx,
  Or answer the old riddle she still asks.
Strong as we are, our reckless courage shrinks
  To look beyond the piece-work of our tasks.

But when we must, we pray, as in the past
  Before the Cross on which your Son was nailed.
Listen, dear lady! You shall hear the last
  Of the strange prayers Humanity has wailed.

PRAYER TO THE DYNAMO

Mysterious Power! Gentle Friend!
Despotic Master! Tireless Force!
You and We are near the End.
Either You or We must bend
To bear the martyrs' Cross.

We know ourselves, what we can bear
As men; our strength and weakness too;
Down to the fraction of a hair;
And know that we, with all our care
And knowledge, know not you.

You come in silence, Primal Force,
We know not whence, or when, or why;
You stay a moment in your course
To play; and, lo! you leap across
To Alpha Centauri!

We know not whether you are kind,
Or cruel in your fiercer mood;
But be you Matter, be you Mind,
We think we know that you are blind,
And we alone are good.

We know that prayer is thrown away,
For you are only force and light;
A shifting current; night and day;
We know this well, and yet we pray,
For prayer is infinite,

Like you! Within the finite sphere
That bounds the impotence of thought,
We search an outlet everywhere
But only find that we are here
And that you are—are not!

What are we then? the lords of space?
  The master-mind whose tasks you do?
Jocky who rides you in the race?
Or are we atoms whirled apace,
  Shaped and controlled by you?

Still silence! Still no end in sight!
  No sound in answer to our cry!
Then, by the God we now hold tight,
Though we destroy soul, life and light,
  Answer you shall—or die!

We are no beggars! What care we
  For hopes or terrors, love or hate?
What for the universe? We see
Only our certain destiny
  And the last word of Fate.

Seize, then, the Atom! rack his joints!
  Tear out of him his secret spring!
Grind him to nothing!—though he points
To us, and his life-blood anoints
  Me—the dead Atom-King!

A curious prayer, dear lady! is it not?
  Strangely unlike the prayers I prayed to you!
Stranger because you find me at this spot,
  Here, at your feet, asking your help anew.

Strangest of all, that I have ceased to strive,
  Ceased even care what new coin fate shall strike.
In truth it does not matter. Fate will give
  Some answer; and all answers are alike.

So, while we slowly rack and torture death
  And wait for what the final void will show,
Waiting I feel the energy of faith
  Not in the future science, but in you!

The man who solves the Infinite, and needs
    The force of solar systems for his play,
Will not need me, nor greatly care what deeds
    Made me illustrious in the dawn of day.

He will send me, dethroned, to claim my rights,
    Fossil survival of an age of stone,
Among the cave-men and the troglodytes
    Who carved the mammoth on the mammoth's bone.

He will forget my thought, my acts, my fame,
    As we forget the shadows of the dusk,
Or catalogue the echo of a name
    As we the scratches on the mammoth's tusk.

But when, like me, he too has trod the track
    Which leads him up to power above control,
He too will have no choice but wander back
    And sink in helpless hopelessness of soul,

Before your majesty of grace and love,
    The purity, the beauty and the faith;
The depth of tenderness beneath; above,
    The glory of the life and of the death.

When your Byzantine portal still was young,
    I came here with my master Abailard;
When Ave Maris Stella was first sung,
    I joined to sing it here with Saint Bernard.

When Blanche set up your glorious Rose of France,
    In scholar's robes I waited on the Queen;
When good Saint Louis did his penitence,
    My prayer was deep like his: my faith as keen.

What loftier prize seven hundred years shall bring,
    What deadlier struggles for a larger air,
What immortality our strength shall wring
    From Time and Space, we may—or may not—care;

But years, or ages, or eternity,
   Will find me still in thought before your throne,
Pondering the mystery of Maternity,
   Soul within Soul,—Mother and Child in One!

Help me to see! not with my mimic sight—
   With yours! which carried radiance, like the sun,
Giving the rays you saw with—light in light—
   Tying all suns and stars and worlds in one.

Help me to know! not with my mocking art—
   With you, who knew yourself unbound by laws;
Gave God your strength, your life, your sight, your heart,
   And took from him the Thought that Is—the Cause.

Help me to feel! not with my insect sense,—
   With yours that felt all life alive in you;
Infinite heart beating at your expense;
   Infinite passion breathing the breath you drew!

Help me to bear! not my own baby load,
   But yours; who bore the failure of the light,
The strength, the knowledge and the thought of God,—
   The futile folly of the Infinite!

CHARLES WARREN STODDARD

(1843–1909)

AVE-MARIA BELLS

   At dawn, the joyful choir of bells,
     In consecrated citadels
   Flings on the sweet and drowsy air
   A brief, melodious call to prayer;

For Mary, Virgin meek and lowly,
Conceivèd of the Spirit Holy,
As the Lord's angel did declare.

At noon, above the fretful street,
Our souls are lifted to repeat
The prayer, with low and wistful voice:
'According to thy word and choice,
Though sorrowful and heavy laden,
So be it done to thy Handmaiden':
Then all the sacred bells rejoice.

At eve with roses in the west,
The daylight's withering bequest,
Ring, prayerful bells, while blossom bright
The stars, the lilies of the night:
Of all the songs the years have sung us,
'The Word made Flesh has dwelt among us,'
Is still our ever-new delight.

JOHN BANNISTER TABB

(1845–1909)

THE IMMACULATE CONCEPTION

A dewdrop of the darkness born,
Wherein no shadow lies;
The blossom of a barren thorn,
Whereof no petal dies;
A rainbow beauty passion-free,
Wherewith was veiled Divinity.

THE ANNUNCIATION

"Fiat!"—The flaming word
    Flashed, as the brooding bird
Uttered the doom far heard
    Of death and night.

"Fiat!"—A cloistered womb—
    A sealed, untainted tomb—
Wakes to the birth and bloom
    Of life and light.

THE ASSUMPTION

Behold! the mother bird
The Fledgling's voice hath heard!
He calls anew,
    "It was thy breast
    That warmed the nest
From whence I flew.
Upon a loftier tree
Of life I wait for thee;
Rise, mother-dove, and come;
Thy Fledgling calls thee home!"

MAURICE FRANCIS EGAN
(1852–1924)

MADONNA OF THE EMPTY ARMS

The Child was gone: the Mother stood alone
  Within her niche above the noisy street,
  Where varied sounds against the silence beat,
And children's footsteps echoed on the stone.
'What mean those empty arms; she makes no moan
  As if her Child were lost; her smile is sweet,
  And every child that passes she will greet
With loving eyes?' The answer seemed unknown.
And yet I found the key: from school each day
  The children trooped beneath our Lady's shrine,
    And as each passed, her empty arms were spread,
Like filling wings of angels when away
  They bear child-souls up to the Heart Divine.
    'I clasp you all; my own Child waits,' she said.

AGNES REPPLIER
(1858–   )

LE REPOS EN EGYPTE

All day I watch the stretch of burning sand;
  All night I brood beneath the golden stars;
Amid the silence of a desolate land,
  No touch of bitterness my reverie mars.

Built by the proudest of a kingly line,
  Over my head the centuries fly fast;
The secrets of the mighty dead are mine;
  I hold the key of a forgotten past.

Yet, ever hushed into a rapturous dream,
  I see again that night. A halo mild
Shone from the liquid moon. Beneath her beam
  Traveled a tired young Mother and the Child.

Within mine arms she slumbered, and alone
  Lay stretched o'er-wearied. On my breast of stone
Rested the Crucified.

LIZETTE WOODWORTH REESE
(1856–1935)

HIS MOTHER IN HER HOOD OF BLUE

When Jesus was a little thing,
  His mother, in her hood of blue,
Called to Him through the dusk of spring:
  "Jesus, my Jesus, where are you?"

Caught in a gust of whirling bloom
  She stood a moment at the door,
Then lit the candle in the room,
  In its pink earthen bowl of yore.

The little Jesus saw it all—
  The blur of yellow in the street;
The fair trees by the tumbling wall;
  The shadowy other lads whose feet

Struck a quick noise from out the grass;
  He saw, dim in the half-lit air,
As one sees folk within a glass,
  His mother with her candle there.
Jesus! Jesus!

When He a weary man became,
  I think, as He went to and fro,
He heard her calling just the same
  Across that dusk of long ago.
Jesus!

For men were tired that had been bold—
  And strange indeed this should befall—
One day so hot, one day so cold—
  But mothers never change at all.
Jesus!

BLISS CARMAN

(1861–1929)

A CHRISTMAS EVE CHORAL

Halleluja!
What sound is this across the dark
While all the earth is sleeping? Hark!
Halleluja! Halleluja! Halleluja!

Why are thy tender eyes so bright,
Mary, Mary?
On the prophetic deep of night
Joseph, Joseph,
I see the borders of the light,
And in the day that is to be
An aureoled man-child I see,
Great love's son, Joseph.

Halleluja!
He hears not, but she hears afar,
The Minstrel Angel of the star.
Halleluja! Halleluja! Halleluja!

Why is thy gentle smile so deep,
Mary, Mary?
It is the secret I must keep,
Joseph, Joseph,—
The joy that will not let me sleep,
The glory of the coming days,
When all the world shall turn to praise
God's goodness, Joseph.

Halleluja!
Clear as the bird that brings the morn
She hears the heavenly music borne.
Halleluja! Halleluja! Halleluja!

Why is thy radiant face so calm,
Mary, Mary?
His strength is like a royal palm,
Joseph, Joseph;
His beauty like the victor's psalm,
He moves like morning o'er the lands
And there is healing in his hands
For sorrow, Joseph.

Halleluja!
Tender as dew-fall on the earth
She hears the choral of love's birth.
Halleluja! Halleluja! Halleluja!

What is the message come to thee,
Mary, Mary?
I hear like wind within the tree,
Joseph, Joseph,
Or like a far-off melody
His deathless voice proclaiming peace,
And bidding ruthless wrong to cease,
For love's sake, Joseph.

277

Halleluja!
Moving as rain-wind in the spring
She hears the angel chorus ring.
Halleluja! Halleluja! Halleluja!

Why are thy patient hands so still,
Mary, Mary?
I see the shadow on the hill,
Joseph, Joseph,
And wonder if it is God's will
That courage, service, and glad youth
Shall perish in the cause of truth
Forever, Joseph.

Halleluja!
Her heart in that celestial chime
Has heard the harmony of time.
Halleluja! Halleluja! Halleluja!

Why is thy voice so strange and far,
Mary, Mary?
I see the glory of the star,
Joseph, Joseph,
And in its light all things that are
Made glad and wise beyond the sway
Of death and darkness and dismay,
In God's time, Joseph.

Halleluja!
To every heart in love 'tis given
To hear the ecstasy of heaven.
Halleluja! Halleluja! Halleluja!

LOUISE IMOGEN GUINEY

(1861–1920)

FIVE CAROLS FOR CHRISTMASTIDE

The Ox he openeth wide the Doore,
And from the Snowe he calls her inne,
And he hath seen her Smile therefor,
Our Ladye without Sinne.
Now soone from Sleep
A Starre shall leap,
And soone arrive both King and Hinde:
   Amen, Amen:
But O, the Place co'd I but finde!

The Ox hath hush'd his voyce and bent
Trewe eyes of Pitty ore the Mow,
And on his lovelie Neck, forspent,
The Blessed layes her Browe.
Around her feet
Full Warme and Sweete
His bowerie Breath doth meeklie dwell:
   Amen, Amen:
But sore am I with Vaine Travel!

The Ox is host in Judah stall
And Host of more than onelie one,
For close she gathereth withal
Our Lorde her littel Sonne.
Glad Hinde and King
Their Gyfte may bring,
But wo'd to-night my Teares were there,
   Amen, Amen:
Between her Bosom and His hayre!

II

Vines branching stilly
Shade the open door,
In the house of Zion's Lily,
Cleanly and poor.
Oh, brighter than wild laurel
The Babe bounds in her hand,
The King, who for apparel
Hath but a swaddling-band,
And sees her heavenlier smiling than stars in His command!

Soon, mystic changes
Part Him from her breast,
Yet there awhile He ranges
Gardens of rest:
Yea, she the first to ponder
Our ransom and recall,
Awhile may rock Him under
Her young curls' fall,
Against that only sinless love-loyal heart of all.

What shall inure Him
Unto the deadly dream,
When the Tetrarch shall abjure Him,
The thief blaspheme,
And scribe and soldier jostle
About the shameful tree,
And even an Apostle
Demand to touch and see?—
But she hath kissed her Flower where the
     Wounds are to be.

III

Three without slumber ride from afar,
Fain of the roads where palaces are;
All by a shed as they ride in a row,
"Here!" is the cry of their vanishing Star.

First doth a greybeard, glittering fine,
Look on Messiah in slant moonshine:
"This have I bought for Thee!" Vainly: for lo,
Shut like a fern is the young hand divine.

Next doth a magian, mantled and tall,
Bow to the Ruler that reigns from a stall:
"This have I sought for Thee!" Though it be rare,
Loathe little fingers are letting it fall.

Last doth a stripling, bare in his pride,
Kneel by the Lover as if to abide:
"This have I wrought for Thee!" Answer him there
Laugh of a Child, and His arms opened wide.

IV

Was a Soule from farre away
Stood wistful in the Hay,
And of the Babe a-sleeping hadde a sight:
Neither reck'd hee any more
Men behind him and before,
Nor a thousand busie Winges, flitting light:
But in middle of the night
This few-worded wight
    (Yule! Yule!)
Bespake Our Ladye bright:

"Fill mee, ere my corage faints,
With the lore of all the Saints:
Harte to harte against my Brother let mee be.
By the Fountaines that are His
I wo'd slumber where Hee is:
Prithee, Mother, give the other Brest to mee!"
The Soule that none co'd see
She hath taken on her knee:
    (Yule! Yule!)
Sing prayse to Our Ladye.

281

V

The Ox and the Ass,
Tell aloud of them:
Sing their pleasure as it was
In Bethlehem.

Still, as blowing rose, sudden as a sword,
Maidenly the Maiden bare Jesu Christ the Lord;
Yet for very lowlihood, such a Guest to greet,
Goeth in a little swoon while kissing of His feet.

Mary, drifted snow on the earthen floor,
Joseph, fallen wondrous weak now he would adore,—
(Oh, the surging might of love! Oh, the drowning bliss!)
Both are rapt to Heaven and lose their human Heaven that is.

From the Newly Born trails a lonely cry.
With a mind to heed, the Ox turns a glowing eye;
In the empty byre the Ass thinks her heart to blame:
Up for comforting of God the beasts of burden came,

Softly to inquire, thrusting as for cheer
There between the tender hands, furry faces dear.
Blessing on the honest coats! tawny coat and grey
Friended Our Delight so well when warmth had strayed away.

Crooks are on the sill; sceptres sail the wave;
All the hopes of all the years are thronging to the Cave.
Mother slept not long, nor long Father's sense was dim,
But another twain the while stood parent-wise to Him.

The Ox and the Ass,
Be you glad for them
Such a moment came to pass
In Bethlehem!

JAMES M. HAYES

(1875-   )

OUR LADY OF THE SKIES

And there appeared a great wonder in heaven;
A woman clothed with the sun, and the moon under her feet,
and upon her head a crown of twelve stars.

Revelation XII, i

Twelve stars upon the brow of her,
    No queen is crowned as she,
The foot stool for the feet of her,
    The moon stoops down to be.

The radiance that falls from her
    Has moon and stars outdone,
The glory of the robes of her
    Is woven of the sun.

She is the woman wonderful
    Who in the heaven appears;
God's splendor is the light of her
    That blinds the burning spheres.

St. John in sacred ecstasy
    Beholds, with raptured eyes,
Above the world, protecting it,
    Our Lady of the Skies.

THOMAS WALSH

(1875–1928)

LA PRECIOSA

On the marches of Pamplona—out to sun and wind and star—
Lift the airy spires and turrets of the kings of old Navarre;
Where the endless dirge is chanted o'er their alabaster tombs,
And the Canons drowse in scarlet mid the incense and the
    glooms.
Daily came the little goatherd Mariquita, lithe and brown,
Through the dusty gates to jangle with her flock across the town,
Lounging barefoot through the alleys and the squares at milking
    hour;
Calling shrilly round the doorway and the cloister by the tower.
There amid the ancient portal blazoned o'er with angels rare
Sculptured stands La Preciosa crowned upon her daïs fair.
Whilst upon her breast the Infant turns with smiling eyes to
    look
On the lesson she is reading in her graceful little book.
There the tousled country urchin used to come and shout in
    play—
"Mary, Mary, neighbor Mary,—watch the Child while I'm
    away"—
When—so read the Chapter annals—from the stone would come
    reply
With a gentle nod of greeting,—"Mariquita dear, good-by."
Till the Canon Don Arnaldo, passing when his mass was o'er,
Heard that banter so unseemly at La Preciosa's door,
Little knowing in his wisdom that the Virgin meek and mild
Answered through the stony image to the greeting of the child.
"When again you pray Our Lady, cease," he said, "your idle
    sport;
Kneel as though the queen or duchess passed you on her way to
    court;
Clasp your hands and bow your forehead as more humble words
    you say

Such as—'Heavenly Queen and Empress, House of Gold, to thee
    I pray.'"
Mindful of the solemn lesson Mariquita half-afraid
Ever, as the good old Canon taught her, clasped her hands and
    prayed;
Bowed in rustic salutation, ended with a long Amen—
But in stone the Virgin listened,—never smiled nor spoke again.

ADELAIDE CRAPSEY

(1878–1914)

CRADLE-SONG

Madonna, Madonna,
Sat by the grey road-side,
Saint Joseph her beside,
And Our Lord at her breast;
Oh, they were fain to rest,
Mary and Joseph and Jesus,
All by the grey road-side.

She said, Madonna Mary,
"I am hungry, Joseph, and weary,
All in the desert wide."
Then bent a tall palm-tree
Its branches low to her knee;
"Behold," the palm-tree said,
"My fruit that shall be your bread."
So were they satisfied,
Mary and Joseph and Jesus,
All by the grey road-side.

From Herod they were fled
Over the desert wide,

Mary and Joseph and Jesus,
In Egypt to abide:
Mary and Joseph and Jesus,
In Egypt to abide.

The blessèd Queen of Heaven
Her own dear Son hath given
For my son's sake; his sleep
Is safe and sweet and deep.

Lully . . . Lulley. . . .
So may you sleep alway,
My baby, my dear son:
Amen, Amen, Amen.

My baby, my dear son.

FRANCIS CARLIN

(1881–1945)

THE VIRGIN'S SLUMBER SONG

Shoon-a-shoon
I sing no psalm
    Little Man
Although I am
Out of David's
    House and Clann.
Shoon-a-shoon
I sing no psalm.

(Hush-a-hoo,
    Blowing of pine;
Hush-a-hoo,
    Lowing of kine:

286

Hush-a-hoo,
  Though even in sleep,
His ear can hear
  The shamrocks creep.)

Moons and moons
And suns galore,
  Match their gold
On Slumber's shore,
With Your glittering
  Eyes that hold,
Moons and moons
And suns galore.

(Hush-a-hoo,
  Oceans of earth;
Hush-a-hoo,
  Motions of mirth:
Hush-a-hoo,
  Though over all,
His ear can hear
  The planets fall.)

O'er and o'er
And under all,
  Every star
Is now a ball,
For Your little
  Hands that are
O'er and o'er
And under all.

(Hush-a-hoo,
  Whirring of wings;
Hush-a-hoo,
  Stirring of strings:
Hush-a-hoo,
  Though in slumber deep,
His ear can hear
  My Song of Sleep.)

(1881–   )

THE ROSARY

I

Et verbum caro factum est

A fragrant silence filled the purple air,
The midnight stars looked down in golden peace
Upon a world sleep-locked from haunting care;

But in high heaven, joy knew swift increase
As truth and mercy kissed, and Love supreme
Flashed from eternal heights to man's release.

One soul in shining Nazareth did not dream:
She prayed in rapture as the deep night sped,
And saw the splendid wings from heaven gleam

As Gabriel knelt and gave the message dread.
She paused; then spoke in roseate purity:
"Behold the handmaid of the Lord," she said.

In that one instant's fathomless mystery,
God was made flesh in spring-sweet Galilee.

II

Oriens ex alto

Beneath her heart, the maiden Mother's, dwelt
The Word made flesh, lived by her gentle life,
And each emotion of her being felt

As, through a world that had forgotten strife,
Over the hills on eager feet she passed
And down the vales with summer banners rife.

The Orient from on high His splendor cast
Upon the home that gave her welcome there;
For heaven had come to dwell on earth at last!

And all the gratitude of praise and prayer
And flaming love a human heart can hold,
The intimate communing deep and rare

Of those three months that flew on wings of gold,
In her Magnificat, the Virgin told.

XIV

Assumpta est Maria

Like son, like mother, so our Lady took
The shadowy road to cross life's farther bound
Into the clear resplendence of God's look.

No grisly specter lurking there she found
To vex her tranquil innocence with fear:
A velvet darkness wrapped her spirit round,

And left her body to its flowery bier
And the encircling sound of muted praise,
The sigh unguarded, and the silver tear.

Thomas came late from those far eastern ways
He walked for Christ, and broken-hearted, cried
Once only in the hallowed tomb to gaze;

But when they rolled the rocky portal wide,
Lo! her bright body lay no more inside.

XV

Mater coronata

Sweet ring the harps of heaven with such a joy
As earth can never dream. In mystic row
On row, the angels gloriously deploy,

But oh! in eager ranks far nearer go
The blessed souls. They throng the gates of pearl
As she, their queen and peer, like morning's glow

Passes the golden street, the crystal swirl,
On, till the Central Splendor crowns her brow,
And through the air new radiances whirl.

Still is she crowned in the eternal Now;
And still the earth keeps heaven's jubilee
And plucks what best prayer's garden will allow

Of mystic beauty, day by day, to be
Diadem for the Queen of the Rosary.

MARJORIE L. C. PICKTHALL
(1883–1922)

MARY SHEPHERDESS

When the heron's in the high wood and the last long furrow's
    sown,
With the herded cloud before her and her sea-sweet raiment
    blown,
Comes Mary, Mary Shepherdess, a-seeking for her own.

Saint James he calls the righteous folk, Saint John he calls the
    kind,
Saint Peter seeks the valiant men all to loose or bind,
But Mary seeks the little souls that are so hard to find.

All the little sighing souls born of dust's despair,
They who fed on bitter bread when the world was bare,
Frighted of the glory gates and the starry stair.

All about the windy down, housing in the ling,
Underneath the alder bough linnet-light they cling,
Frighted of the shining house where the martyrs sing.

Crying in the ivy-bloom, fingering at the pane,
Grieving in the hollow dark, lone along the rain,—
Mary, Mary Shepherdess gathers them again.

And O, the wandering women know, in workhouse and in shed,
They dream on Mary Shepherdess with doves about her head,
And pleasant posies in her hand, and sorrow comforted.

Saying: There's my little lass, faring fine and free,
There's the little lad I laid by the holly tree.
Dreaming: There's my nameless bairn laughing at her knee.

When the bracken-harvest's gathered and the frost is on the
   loam,
When the dream goes out in silence and the ebb runs out in foam,
Mary, Mary Shepherdess, she bids the lost lambs home.

If I had a little maid to turn my tears away,
If I had a little lad to lead me when I'm grey,
All to Mary Shepherdess they'd fold their hands and pray.

MARGUERITE WILKINSON

(1883–1928)

TO THE LIGHTED LADY WINDOW

I kiss my hand to you,
   Mary, Holy Mother!
I kiss my hand to you,
   Jesus, little brother!

Lady, I love your robe
 Like a wave in a deep sea;
Your aureole of stars
 Is very dear to me;

And the beauty of the soul
 That met the Holy Ghost,
And the wonder of the life
 Wherein the guest was Host.

But lady, even more,—
 And you would have it said,—
I love the little child
 That shines above your head.

I kiss my hand again,
 Mary, Holy Mother;
I kiss my hand again,
 Jesus, little brother.

CHARLES L. O'DONNELL

(1884–1934)

THE SHED

I.

Sweeter than honey and the honeycomb,
And fairer than the stars are after rain,
The young girl, in her anguish, far from home,
Knocks at their midnight doors, and knocks in vain.
I think she would put out her eyes with weeping—
Men die, they are not born, upon the street,—
Well, here a shed, with cattle dully sleeping,

Angels of God, have pity on her, sweet.
He was so helpless, the good man beside her;
But who would be accomplished in this hour?
There was not really anything denied her,
Heaven and earth were powerless in her power.
And who would ask for Him a cradle golden,
That in her arms and on her breast was folden?

II.

The legioned angels come at length, and sing,
Come wondering shepherds with their tardy sheep,
And, later, star-led, king shall ride with king
To lay their grandeur where He lies asleep.
She would be patient in that hour of splendor,
As she was silent in her lonely grief,—
The Mother is so wise, the Maid so tender,
And her good man believed beyond belief.
They two shall keep Him safe, the World's Desire,
And one, upon the breast that is the Lord's
Shall die—not she; the dread years shall conspire
Against her, and the edge of seven swords.
Ah, by the tears that blind my human eyes,
I shall not quit her feet in Paradise!

THE SPINNER

Mary the Mother of Jesus,
  A lady of high degree,
Sat by her cottage spinning
  In Nazareth of Galilee.

A light fell over her shoulder
  As she sat in the plane-tree's shade,

While a delicate lace of shadows
 The sun and the green leaves made.

Busy her foot on the treadle,
 And her wheel busily whirled
As a Child looked out from the doorway,
 A Child who had made the world.

Deftly she handled the distaff,
 And happily whirred her wheel
As the Child came down from the doorway
 And ran at her side to kneel.

"Mother," He said as He watched her
 There while she sat and spun,
"Some things are more fair than I dreamed them
 The day that I made the sun.

"And you are My heart of all beauty,
 My star of all seas, of all lands—"
"Hush, Child," whispered Mary His Mother,
 Her tears falling down on His hands.

JOYCE KILMER

(1886–1918)

A BLUE VALENTINE

Monsignore,
Right Reverend Bishop Valentinus,
Sometime of Interamna which is called Ferni,
Now of the delightful Court of Heaven,
I respectfully salute you,
I genuflect
And I kiss your episcopal ring.

It is not, Monsignore,
The fragrant memory of your holy life,
Nor that of your shining and joyous martyrdom,
Which causes me now to address you.
But since this is your august festival, Monsignore,
It seems appropriate to me to state
According to a venerable and agreeable custom,
That I love a beautiful lady.
Her eyes, Monsignore,
Are so blue that they put lovely little blue reflections
On everything that she looks at.
Such as a wall
Or the moon
Or my heart.
It is like the light coming through blue stained glass,
Yet not quite like it,
For the blueness is not transparent,
Only translucent.
Her soul's light shines through,
But her soul cannot be seen.
It is something elusive, whimsical, tender, wanton, infantile,
     wise
And noble.
She wears, Monsignore, a blue garment,
Made in the manner of the Japanese.
It is very blue—
I think that her eyes have made it more blue,
Sweetly staining it
As the pressure of her body has graciously given it form.
Loving her, Monsignore,
I love all her attributes;
But I believe
That even if I did not love her
I would love the blueness of her eyes,
And her blue garment, made in the manner of the Japanese.

Monsignore,
I have never before troubled you with a request.

The saints whose ears I chiefly worry with my pleas are the most
    exquisite and maternal Brigid,
Gallant Saint Stephen, who puts fire in my blood,
And your brother bishop, my patron,
The generous and jovial Saint Nicholas of Bari.
But of your courtesy, Monsignore,
Do me this favour:
When you this morning make your way
To the Ivory Throne that bursts into bloom with roses because
    of her who sits upon it.
When you come to pay your devoir to Our Lady,
I beg you, say to her:
"Madame, a poor poet, one of your singing servants yet on earth,
Has asked me to say that at this moment he is especially grateful
    to you
For wearing a blue gown."

DAVID MORTON

(1886–   )

PETITION FOR A MIRACLE

(From his *Boke of Two Ladies*)

I would make you,   (Mother Mary,
If I could,   Of your grace,
One small thing   Set intention
That's wholly good,   In the place
Wholly true   Of this faltering,
And wholly right;   Failing, blind
One small thing   Imperfect thing,
For your delight . . .   And let her find,
Small, it must be,   What was perfect
For the touch   In my thought,
Falters in   Shining through
Attempting much.   The thing I wrought.)

I—His Adoration

There was—and this was very long ago—
A Lady of such mien, so grave, so mild,
One would have said, without the need to know:
"Here, as God lives, is Mother for the Child."
The joy she had, by such election crowned,
Were theme beyond the mortal lords of rhyme—
And that most grievous grief wherein she drowned,
Must beggar utterance through all listening time.

Not I, alone, but every son of song,
Shapes here, shapes there, a syllable to fail
The accents reachless of that Joy, that Wrong—
And rhymes his own dear lady's boon or bale,
For sweetness' sake, as I have writ for you,
Aware of One most pleased at what I do.

SISTER M. MADELEVA
(1887-   )

A NUN SPEAKS TO MARY

I

In the Days of King Herod

You had no little maid, so I remember,
To help you sweep and tidy up the room,
To sit and watch with you that first December
Through shining twilights deep with golden gloom.

Through all those wistful days you had no mother
To know your wonder and to share your joy

Of fashioning—you could not let another!—
The darling swaddling garments for your Boy.

There was not any housewife to befriend you
The day word came to go to Bethlehem town;
No kinswoman bethought her to attend you
Of all the folk of David going down.

And when you held Him to your heart in wonder,
Emmanuel, God's Son, your Boy, the Word
Made flesh Who shook the skies with holy thunder,
In Bethlehem not any mother stirred.

II

Sequel

Now come again the sweet Isaian days,
Merciful, tender;
I know their loneliness; I dream their splendor.
Down their plain ways,
Mary, I come,
Confounded with this former shame, and dumb.
Take me in service, in complete surrender,
Waking and sleeping;
Take every daily task, take every duty,
Take little homely things as dusting, sweeping;
Change them into your heavenly housekeeping;
Touch them with Nazareth's most stricken beauty.
Think that my busy hands weave raiment fair
For Christ to wear;
Know that my hurrying feet
Run all your errands, Sweet;
And should they tarry
Hear how I promise them,
My Lady Mary,
That they at length may go with you to Bethlehem.

And at the last let be
On those three mute and piteous, fearful days
When none of all earth's womenfolk is near you,
That you will have to help you and to cheer you
In little foolish ways
Poor, simple me;
That when you stand outside the inn, the night wind
  blowing,
I will be there
Adoring, knowing;
That if the whole wide world should have no room,
I will be waiting through whatever gloom
To be your resting place.—But this is heaven I dare!

So, let my promise be my prayer.
And do not seek for any cave at all
With patient kine and manger crib and stall
Beyond the gates of little Bethlehem town
To lay your dear Son down.
Mother, all fair,
Lay Him within my hungry arms to sleep;
Lay Him within my hungry heart to keep,
Adorable, holy,
Little and lowly.
And let earth's shepherds, let heaven's seraphim
So find me with you Christmas night, adoring, loving
  Him.

OF WOUNDS

I have no word to match with its white wonder,
The garment of His body as He wore it
On that first dawning that He came to me
After His death.

Some things there were the soldiers played at dice for,
Kirtle and cloak, perhaps; each got a part
Of such dear raiment as He had about Him,
But not this single garment that He wore.

For that was mine, out of my body woven
Into the pattern of the Son of God,
Seamless from head to foot, and perfect,
Growing to fit His growth, strong with His strength,
Until the day He died.

That day the soldiers tore it, soiled it, spat upon it,
Flayed it to shreds, seared it with gaping rents.
Being His mother, I shall not forget it.

Only for joy I did forget on that first morning
That He returned to me, clad in its splendor
Cut from the loom of death.

Being His mother, I had wished His body flawless,
Fearing to think how beautiful might be
Five open wounds upon it.
I know now that they are beautiful as God.

MOTIF FOR MARY'S DOLORS

Seven notes of grief,
Seven points of pain,
Scale struck to start
What melodies and
What refrain
Within your song-swept heart!

T. S. ELIOT
(1888–   )

PART IV FROM "THE DRY SALVAGES" *

Lady, whose shrine stands on the promontory,
Pray for all those who are in ships, those
Whose business has to do with fish, and
Those concerned with every lawful traffic
And those who conduct them.

Repeat a prayer also on behalf of
Woman who have seen their sons or husbands
Setting forth, and not returning:
Figlia del tuo figlio,
Queen of Heaven.

Also pray for those who were in ships, and
Ended their voyage on the sand, in the sea's lips
Or in the dark throat which will not reject them
Or wherever cannot reach them the sound of the sea bell's
Perpetual angelus.

BENJAMIN   FRANCIS   MUSSER
(1889–   )

DER HEILIGE MANTEL VON AACHEN
(Aix-la-Chapelle, Rhine Province)

A good stout tankard at a Rhineland inn
Is the way to toast Our Lady when going to Aachen:
It's Catholic and honest, and it's masculine.

---

* The Dry Salvages—presumably *les trois sauvages*—is a small group of rocks, with
a beacon, off the northeast coast of Cape Ann, Massachusetts.

Charlemagne held court here; the German Parthenon
Flung its many chapels around his octagon,
Where forty kings were crowned in the Renaissance dawn.

A good stout tankard . . . men though we are, we need
Something strong to stay us, as into Aix we lead
Trembling hearts to holy treasures of our creed.

Not Barbarossa's lamp-ring, not windows that soar
A hundred feet, not pulpit from Henry the Emperor,
Not the shining armor that the dull kings wore.

These are worldly wonders. But in the treasury,
In the Magyar chapel, beyond earth's royalty
Are the four Great Relics; we kiss them manfully,—

Swaddling-clothes that knew His Mother's patient thread,
The loin-cloth He wore when on the Cross He bled;
The napkin that bore the Baptist's severed head;

And, for the last, Our Mother's humble cloak.
Up and down Palestine this her daily yoke,
Not a shining armor, nor lace for gentlefolk.

Then, while doughty pilgrim from his tankard slakes
Thirst, and sings her German songs, Our Lady takes
Her cloak and, questing souls, goes out from Aix.

THE HOLY LAND OF WALSINGHAM

(Norfolk, England)

Lay willows under Walsingham,
Strew laurels over Walsingham,
But mostly scatter prayers, tears and love in
Walsingham.

When England was Merrie England,
Because the Faith was England,
Of all Our Lady's English homes, this was her oriflamb.

Evesham, Glastonbury, Tewkes,
Worcester, Coventry—Saxon times
Held many a sanctuary and miracle of our Queen.
Walsingham and Ipswich
Stirred Norman love, that gave her
Walsingham's Austin priory and England as demesne.

Angels flew to Walsingham
And built her shrine at Walsingham,
And half the kings of all the earth paid homage at her
throne.
When Henry Tudor, dying,
Had most tormented conscience,
His wreck and theft of Walsingham caused his most
bitter groan.

But hold awhile your willow wreath,
For Mary's Dowry may again
Be flooding over Walsingham, her love may bring them
home.
The Palmer's Way has been restored,
And slowly, slowly comes alive
The beauty that was Walsingham, that patience
that is Rome.

LOUISE CRENSHAW RAY
(1890–   )

PHILIPPINE MADONNA

In every war, strange legends circulate,
As tenuous as fog, but some defy
Rejection, bringing comfort out of hate
And terror. . . . When our battle-darkened sky

Once more was brightened by Pacific dawn,
A boyish naval officer was found
Half dead across a charred ship timber on
A beachhead we had taken. All were drowned

When his torpedoed boat sank. "Let me tell
You how it was. I seized a plank, I know,"
He murmured from his cot, "but what befell
Me, Father, no one will believe, and so

"I sent for you. One thing is certain, that
I was not on the plank alone. For strange
Enough, at the far end, back to me, sat
A woman draped in white. She did not change

"From that position, so I could not see
Her face. Yet surely as one understands
A holy truth, I knew that it was she,
Our Lady, rowing the timber with her hands."

Another victim of hallucination,
Exposure to the sun and thirst! Small wonder,
Poor lad, I thought. Returning to my station,
I approached my chapel from the rear. From under

The door behind the altar a rivulet
Of water trickled. Rushing in, there stood
The lifelike statue of Our Lady, wet
And dripping. Then I ran for Chaplain Hood,

Afraid to trust my own bewildered sight.
Together, at the altar rail once more,
We saw Our Lady in the candle-light,
Her raiment dry, no water on the floor!

DANIEL SARGENT

(1890–   )

PREFERENCE

I should rather say one prayer to the Mother of God
Than have the whole of the planet pray to me,
I should rather kiss one place where her feet have trod
Than have the universe for my property.

I should rather see that shaking eglantine
At her shrine in Lourdes, than see old Rome made o'er,
Or Solomon's temple shine as it used to shine,
Or the Parthenon, its crown on its head once more.

I should rather die at the North Pole—which I dread—
Or starve in the darkest jail in the darkest city,
I should rather be buried alive when they think me dead,
Than step for an instant from Our Lady's pity.

I should rather have one place where I can stand
And gaze at her, than roam all roads in the land.

JAMES L. DUFF

(1891–   )

THE LOAN OF A STALL

At the inn there was no room—
    There was no room at all
For the carpenter's wife who was great with child,
    So she took the loan of a stall.

305

O, she was tired with journeying
  And a Baby in her womb.
The stable door stood welcome-wide.
  Her time was almost come.

The stable door stood welcome-wide,
  The straw was sweet and fresh,
And there, in a borrowed manger-crib,
  She bedded the Word made Flesh.

The scented breath of the oxen warmed
  The room for her little Son,
And a great star served for light when the brief
  December day was done.

There was no room in the inn for them—
  There was no room at all,
But the Mother of God was a humble maid,
  And she took the loan of a stall.

CRADLE SONG

Sleep enfold thee,
  Jesukin.
Close I hold Thee,
  Jesukin.
Never in palace or temple or shrine
Was there a comeliness like to Thine,
And Thou art mine, oh, Thou art mine,
  Jesukin.

Sweet sleep bless Thee,
  Jesukin.
Close I press Thee,
  Jesukin.

The brightest of the stars that shine
Is set above Thee for a sign,
But now—this moment—Thou art mine,
    Jesukin.

Sleep enfold Thee,
    Jesukin.
Soft I hold Thee,
    Jesukin.
King Thou art—of David's line—
But here, among the humble kine,
This little while, oh, Thou art mine,
    Jesukin.

CLIFFORD J. LAUBE
(1891–   )

AVE, VITA NOSTRA!

Attila's spirit rides again the red roads of the East;
    Caligula returns, a subtler tyrant, to the South;
King Herod's sword still seeks the Lord; with fury thrice
        increased
    It strikes at holy youth and maims the manna-nour-
        ished mouth.

    Mother of God, amid this strife,
    Amid this death, be thou our life!

Dark intellects, like Lucifer's, low-fallen in their pride,
    Have dimmed the philosophic lamp in Learning's
        ancient seats;
Despoiled of grace, a godless race thrusts purity aside,
    Slaying the lily in its bulb, the heart before it beats.

Mother of Christ's integrity,
Amid this blight, our sweetness be.

Yet while the Coliseums stand, the catacombs remain.
   The wolf-pack prowls, but Peter watches, faithful to
      his flock.
A martyred Pro in Mexico, the mangled priests of Spain,
   The hidden saints of Russia, show the texture of the
      Rock!

Mystical star above the slope,
Mother of men, be thou our hope!

Hail, holy Queen!
Mother of mercy,
Our life, our sweetness and our hope,
To thee do we cry, poor banished children of Eve!
To thee do we send up our sighs,
Mourning and weeping in this valley of tears.

M. WHITCOMB HESS
(1893–   )

THE VISION OF ST. BERNARD

(After the painting by Filippo Lippi)

Bernard reads late, alone; and twilight falls
Dimming the page. Soon must the keen eyes probe
Vainly for words. . . . But whence has spread
This glow illumining his cloister's walls
To stretch them to horizons past our globe?
What hand—divinely pure—is on his book?

(He knew her by the light about her head,
And by the cloak of heaven that she wore—
But more
He knew her by her grave regardful look.)

So stood she that swift shining moment through,
Her hand still touching where St. Bernard read
Of truth unchanged in changing time or place;
The while a corner of her mantle blue
Was folded round an earth child, and his face
Shone in the glory compassing her head.

DOROTHY PARKER

(1893–   )

THE GENTLEST LADY

They say He was a serious child,
   And quiet in His ways;
They say the gentlest lady smiled
   To hear the neighbors' praise.

The coffers of her heart would close
   Upon their smallest word.
Yet did they say, "How tall He grows!"
   They thought she had not heard.

They say upon His birthday eve
   She'd rock Him to His rest
As if she could not have Him leave
   The shelter of her breast.

The poor must go in bitter thrift,
   The poor must give in pain,

But ever did she set a gift
To greet His day again.

They say she'd kiss the boy awake,
And hail Him gay and clear,
But oh, her heart was like to break
To count another year.

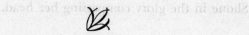

LEONARD FEENEY

(1897–   )

FAMILY PORTRAIT

Our Lady is my fear,
Not my peace,—
Whose Father guards His dear
From release.

Our Lady is my queen,
Not my mother;
I gave her at fourteen
To an Other.

I gave her as a spouse
To a Third
Who made her womb a house
For a Word.

Our Lady is a star,
Is a well,
Too deep for me, too far,
Too terrible.

But she dashes down the air
When I lock with Lucifer
And she hauls me by the hair
Out of Hell!

BECAUSE OF HER WHO FLOWERED SO FAIR

(From *Song For a Listener*)

29

Because of Her who flowered so fair
The poor old apple-wench will wear
A sprig of roses in her hair;

The strumpet strolling on the quay
Who puts in pawn her purity,
Will sue for sailors' chivalry;

The lily garbaged in a brawl
Out of her refuse-heap will crawl
Back to her trellis on the wall.

31

The crown and crest of creaturehood
Has not been seen so great, so good
As in our race, as in our brood.

The Cherubim and Seraphim
Have been o'er-vaulted and made dim
By something slender, something slim

311

Assembled on our satellite
To move as any maiden might
Familiar to our common sight.

32

Truth to attraction one must tether;
Reason and rapture rolled together
Will settle whether not or whether

The philosophic proof must pass
Inspection near the looking-glass
To learn the logic of a lass

And find if in mythology
What sense there is, if sense there be,
Was not a need for such as She.

33

A girl did God, I do believe,—
Created, courted by,—conceive;
And would that every word I weave

Her Sire, her Spouse, her Son might please
In this frail ditty darned in threes
With threads of triple harmonies.

One riddle, and my rhyme is through:
A bull will butt at red, but you,
Beelzebub, will butt at blue!

FRANCIS BURKE

(1898–   )

THE MEDIATRIX OF GRACE

Men in these our days, be it noted, do love Our Blessed Mother because
they sing to her, in the Latin tongue, *O Mediatrix Omnium Gratiarum!*
And our Holy Fathers, the Popes, having late reminded us that she is also
our *Co-Redemptrix;* and that likewise, because our Redemption is by sacrifice, and sacrifice a priestly work, she is somehow the *Priestly Virgin, Virgo
Sacerdos, la Vièrge-Prêtre:* it has seemed good to a certain word-craftsman
to make this tapisserie, out of the Holy Pontiffs, out of the Holy Council of
Chalcedon, out of Saint Bede who writes a lesson for her Office, and out of
Saint Chrysostomus and many a learned doctor of our own times. May it
be pleasing in her lovely and merciful eyes; and may all her daughters,
unraveling it, guess what mysteries, mayhap, may yet be shared in heaven—
through her and with her and in her through whom we have our All. Now
the piece should commence like this:

The Mother of Christ the Priest and of His
    royal and priestly people,
The consecrate Virgin, first Maid of immolation,
    the Spouse of the Spirit who is sacrificial Fire,
The sorrowful Mother ascending the steps of
    the altar of Golgotha, and standing between
    us and God, between earth and heaven,
The Madonna uplifting the Bread of Heaven in
    Bethlehem the house of bread;
The refuge of sinners, of Magdalen and Peter,
    of Teresa and Gabriel, with love for the strong
    or the feeblest,
Our mystical and golden temple, the ark of our
    covenant, the spiritual chalice and tabernacle
    of the Incarnate Word,
Being participant in her Son, the Priest, the King,
    the Prophet, surely no less than men who are
    her children,
Is Priestly Virgin truly, as she is His Prophetess
    and His Queen.

313

"Be it done unto me," she says, not as God
    said, *"Let there be light,"* but as a priest says,
    "This is My Body."
"They have no wine," she says as a priest would
    say, *"This is the cup of My Blood."*
And like the *Dominus vobiscum* her hands
    dispense the rains of His graces,
And like the *Agnus Dei* she is the sign of peace
    and longing,
And like the *Domine non sum dignus* she is the
    Magnificat of exultation,
Priestly Mother, O bless us with your tender Son!

She has put on the chasuble of the sun, and her
    stole of stars, and she takes the horns of the
    slender moon for her candelabrum,
And she walks in the way of the Light of the
    world, the sick lie in wait for her passing,
For she brings our daily bread and the oil that
    anoints all fevered foreheads,
The balm of all pierced hearts and the chrism for
    all our fears,
And she bears sweet charities like a seamless
    garment,
Full of lilies of the field and of five-for-a-farthing
    sparrows,
Down forbidden alleys and over flat hills by paths
    forgotten,
And the urn of living water by which death is
    immortality,
Closing eyes like the eyes of Joseph:
Jesus, Mary and Joseph, assist me in my last
    agony
May I breathe forth my soul in peace, with you.

In her is the Church Imperial, the Teacher and
    Sanctifier.
She is Shepherdess to the Pastor of the pastors
    of the sheep.

Out of the fold of her heart she leads us like
 guarded words,
Sentences of the Word Who is Jesus,
For she is the abode of wisdom and all echoes,
Hers is the speech of Jesus,
Thus paused at the Aleph and caressed the Lamed
When first they opened, the lips of the True.
And she is seated with prophets and doctors,
Armed like a Queen with a glittering army,
And none have spoken as she has been silent,
Theotokos, destroyer of heresies!
Homoousia to the Truth Incarnate!
Mother to the Word.

She is the morning star of all our nocturns.
She is Vesper kindled at each evening bell.
The virgin earth. The miraculous shower. The
 midnight and dawn and the field of wheat
 unblighted.
The vine of Engaddi. The threshing-floor and
 wine-press of Sion on the hill.
She is the Host immaculate. She is the water
 in the wine of our only offertory:
Virgin-victim with Jesus, daughter of her Son.
Like her children, the brothers of Jesus,
Like her sisters, the sisters of Jesus:
Priestly Virgin in Jesus,
At the right hand of Jesus at the right hand of
 the Father,
Whence she shall come, O tenderness of Jesus!
In the resurrection and judgment
And world without end. Amen.

JOHN GILLAND BRUNINI

(1899-   )

THE ASSUMPTION

O heart submissive in this martyrdom
Of love, this exile weary in the long long years
Beyond the Cross, is ended—death, like rain
On fleece, has gently brought release.
                              O, Mary, tears
Were oft, too oft, your drink, the swords of pain
Were cruel in your soul—at last, at last,
His Will has caught your breath.
                              O seraphs sing!
Among the blessèd she is highest blest,
She shelters men beneath the covert of her wing,
Exalt her like a cedar on the crest
Of Lebanon, a rose and cypress tree
By waters of the plain, for Mary is assumed
To Heaven.
                    Sweet above fine honey, she
Has taken mystic root in God and bloomed,
Her petals are perfumed in mercy, dewed in love,
Her leaves are burgeoned in compassion.
                              Sweet as myrrh
And cassia is her fragrance, holy is her well
Of purity, her brook has found the sea of grace,
The Mother of Fair Love has come to dwell
In God—O, angels, praise the glory of her face!

TO MARY AT CHRISTMAS

No stranger pilgrims wear the shepherd's way
Than those who seek the stabled Child alone;
In many inns where Mary's Son would lay
No stranger keepers Bethlehem had known
Than those who choose not none but One. Deny
The Virgin-Mother?—better both were barred
From hearth and threshold lest half-welcome cry
More insult than such doors that hold their guard
On any knock . . .
                    Where Jesus is there must
His Mother be!
              O Prince of Peace and Queen,
Whose love released our garden debt of dust,
Whose wills were manger laid for Cross foreseen,
Such severing would flout all ordered plan
And mock the heart which flamed with whiter fire
Of human love, divinely fanned, than man
Had known could ever burn and not expire.

Before day-star elect, O heart most pure,
Brought low and pierced, denials more unite
What they would cleave, for scourge and Cross abjure
The Lamb of God and her alike in plight.
"I thirst;" and so athirst in kind was she,
His earthly dearest, lone and last to cede,
That Mary too became Love's legacy,
As well the giver given with the deed
So broadly writ in pain. Deny? ah, claim
In awe-struck breath this wondrous grace
Of kinship, children got in Adam's shame
And born anew to hail our Mother's place
In power above all angels, saints and seers!

O Care, whose fulness is unceasing prayers
For us, our days are momented with tears,

Our years are tithed with waywardness and snares,
Our exile versed in questioned ills and plaints,
And prodigal in pride our courage faints . . .
Yet over all our sweetest tribute rings—
We fly to covert of our Mother's wings.

SISTER MARIS STELLA
(1899–   )

LINES FOR A FEAST OF OUR LADY

What shall be added to your praises?
The lip-worn, love-worn, heart-worn phrases
centuries out of choir and cell
and field and vineyard praise you well.
Like bells over the spinning earth
hour upon hour they tell your worth.
You are the Mother of Delight.
Over the sea you are the bright
star shining. You are the ivory tower,
the ark of gold, immortal flower
blossoming on a mortal root,
the good tree bringing forth good fruit.
You are the cloud raining the Just One.
Fair as the moon and bright as the sun,
out of the desert light of day
terrible as an army in array
you come—the Gate of Heaven to heaven's gate.
What can be added to your state?
The vast uncountable choir of voices
down aisles of centuries rejoices;
in endless litany proclaims
the fertile flowering of your names.

318

Hell will not thank you nor death raise
its voice. Only the living praise.
Then shed your grace upon the mind
That we here in these deeps may find
the words we seek, that like a vine
with strong roots in the soul may shine
the litany that climbs and grows
upon the lattice of the Rose.

CAUSE OF OUR JOY

O Mother of Fair Love, it was not alone
Christ whom you mothered on the first Christmas night,
not alone the Orient, the Splendor that outshone
daylight and suns and all created light.
It was not only this new dearness, kissed and held
in love and lullabies among the straw,
warmed by the breath of oxen that still smelled
of clover and sweet fields. But in deep awe
there crept in with the shepherd and his sheep
and bowed down with the oriental king
your other children who will always keep
the joy of your mysterious mothering,
cause of our joy, heaven's gate, at once our mother,
on that first Christmas night through Christ, our Brother.

PATRICK O'CONNOR

(1899-   )

THE MANTLE OF MARY

Fair is the hue of your mantle, Mary—
  (Take me to shelter, take me to hide!)
From the deep skies of Heaven it drank all its color,
  In the deep pools of Heaven my mantle was dyed.

Fine is the cloth of your mantle, Mary—
  (Take me to shelter, take me to hide!)
Ah, careful was the carding and careful the spinning,
  And piteous the shearing of my dear Lamb's side.

Warm is the web of your mantle, Mary—
  (Take me to shelter, take me to hide!)
It is woven of rare wool, woven of fair wool—
  The soft white fleece of my Lamb Who died.

Draped like a queen's is your mantle, Mary—
  (Take me to shelter, take me to hide!)
Yea, God hath exalted His handmaid, Who made me
  Mother of His Word and His Spirit's bride.

Full are the folds of your mantle, Mary—
  (Take me to shelter, take me to hide!)
That all generations be shielded and succored,
  The cloak of their Mother is a deep cloak and wide.

Ah, wrap me around with your mantle, Mary—
  (Take me to shelter, take me to hide!)
Child of my sword-pierced soul, I shall guard you,
  Little blood-brother of the Crucified.

RAYMOND E. F. LARSSON

(1901–   )

TO OUR LADY, THE ARK OF THE COVENANTS

—and if by such bright tokens,
such bright smiles, my Lady,
suddenly these streets
which had been glum dusts that led nowhere
to one stricken, isolate,
unarmed of ends and destinations,
befuddled of dust among this city's
bundles, very dustiness

and days

like a stubbled field, all, all harvested,
left thus with husks, husks only

were come unto

such quickness as the fields
come unto oh as fields come most brightly unto,
sprayed all with bells and with bell-sounding flowers
all bunched, all bouncing, all, all belled,

where then were

death, my Lady? where were not years like halls
illimitably marble, all arch and arcade?
where were the earth not gardened, and the wide
seas green and all fern-fronded, and the wide
brackened ambuscades of waves and the splashed waterfalls all
terraced there, all tumbled down to the gardened land
and the seas' wide windy grain?—
where walked An One there once as in a field.

Where were the earth
mean, unfruitful, where were the earth's
grain but the dust lain in mowed random bundles? Ah,
Lady!

where were death then?

where were the dead?

O Thou!
who hast undone with smiles
as though with thy dove-gentle hands
my heart from death where it was bitter,
not a brighter glitter in the dust;

               Thou who hast unchoked
my lips of sighs, and leafed the winter-bitten tree,
who hast most certainly leafed now my bitter heart
with season come unto a fruitfulness,

                   it is I
come now unto thee for the brightness
of my eyes—as sights
of afar and farther places and
the very place of brightness
thine eyes, my Lady,
as lanterns light.

          Lights! lights, my Lady!—
that the way of this clay be upward
above the dust.

CORNELIA OTIS SKINNER

(1901–)

TO THE SISTINE MADONNA

Mary, most serenely fair,
Hear an unbeliever's prayer.
Nurtured in an austere creed,
Sweetest Lady, she has need
Of the solace of thy grace;
See the tears that stain her face
As she kneels to beg your love,
You whom no one told her of.

SISTER M. THÉRÈSE

(1902–   )

I SEND OUR LADY

I may not venture to your door
And lift the latch, as I would do;
I send Our Lady in my stead
Tonight, to comfort you.

(For in the smiling of your eyes
I feel the dark where tears have lain,
Under the music of your voice,
The counterpoint of pain.)

Beneath the February moon,
A lithe, cool crescent in the sky,
She will be haloed regally
As she goes softly by.

In the white vigil of your prayer
Under the lintel she will tread
And know you by the curving light
You wear about your head.

She will shut out philosophy;
Lay your bright wisdom on the sill;
For there are caverns in the soul
That only love can fill—

Stark intervals of silence, when
Even the spirit poised in grace
Is chastened by the pity worn
Upon a woman's face.

Beyond the touch of any thought
Or little word that she may speak,
Will be the solace of her arms,
Her kiss upon your cheek.

And from my window at the dawn
My soul will fly like any bird
To nestle at her heart, and hear
The music she has heard.

NORBERT ENGELS

(1903–)

EX MARIA VIRGINE

*"And was incarnate by the Holy Ghost of the
Virgin Mary: and was made man."*

And Mary said, "Before the void was filled
With worlds He stirred within my womb;
I felt His blood surge like the seas of space
    Against His tomb.

"His pulse began the trembling of the winds,
The restless stars and rhythmic seed;
Started the trees and thorns, and in the waters
    The sponge and reed.

"Mine was not woman's pain, but pain of spear,
The scourging lash, and hempen bands;
Mine was the ragged pain of nails that pierced
    His unborn hands.

"And those He met along that dreadful road:
They were the voices that I heard
In the eternal night, before the dawn
    Brought forth the Word.

"Vast seas of stars kept tumbling in my breast,
Winds of a thousand heavens wept:
Men cried to me, 'Give us our Son!' and stirred
    Him where He slept.

"He reached His arms, and I could feel them moving,
No longer quiet there and curled;
I saw them opened on the Cross, as though
    To hold the world.

"I thought: Could I but keep Him in my heart,
This Seed of beauty and of pain,
Walled against death, a Flower that has no need
    Of sun and rain!

"And yet, if God had said: 'Choose love and pain
Together, to keep or share with them!'
I would have borne Him that age-destined day
    In Bethlehem."

JOHN W. LYNCH

(1904–   )

A WOMAN WRAPPED IN SILENCE

V

        A little girl
Had wandered in the night, and now within
The shadows of a broken stall, was waiting,
While the night winds and the breath of time
Were moving over her.

Of Joseph then?
O, did he rise and stealthily return
Before the cave's wide entrance, there to stare
Within the dark? And lift his eyes to search
The trembling stars? And did he feel the midnight's
Slow, sweet advent and the pulse of joy
That ached beneath the hours, as sharp as pain?
And did he mark again the barrenness
And with a craftsman's hand run sadly down
A length of broken beam? And suddenly
Did Joseph fall upon his knees and know
Our purest human helplessness, and hold
His heart the centre of a tide of sobs
That deepened, silently, least she might hear
Who did not need to hear? And were there prayers?
Uncertainties? What happened here until
A cry came that had not been heard before?
The beat of pulses and the hush of heart
Had made a silence more intent within
Surrounding silence. Deepening of night.
The last pure poise of prayer, more still and wordless
In an utter distillate of prayer.
Starlight moving imperceptibly.
The drift of time. And then a moment's fall,
The last that we should know of loneliness.
A sigh, unheard within the dark, and then . . .

She . . . wrapped him up in swaddling clothes, and laid him in a manger.

Only that. The brief, sweet offices
Of motherhood: the gentleness that cared
Thus for a Child's small need: the simple, calm,
Unhastened task, that in the very words
The telling takes, is strong with humanness,
And sure with peace, and must forever keep
Him ours, and say forever she is ours.

Only that. No word of great travail,
No word of pain, or fright, or ecstasy,
No strangeness. Only that. The quiet hands

Wrapped him up in swaddling clothes, and laid him in a manger.

Her first gift then to Him, and His first witness
To the ways of earth, the first of tribute,
And the gesture that began the long
Fulfillment was a simple care she brought
To Him, not as a creature comes to stoop,
But as a mother bends to love. We know
No more than this, and what exchange beyond
Lies gathered to the spaces of her heart
To turn forever there, inviolate.
O, did she fold the veil down with her hands,
And raise them over Him, like frail, white wings
Of prayer? And brush His brow in lightest touch?
And look beneath His eyes that opened then,
And for the first time *see,* and know that she
Was seen? O, this is why His birthplace holds
No more than emptiness, stripped bare and clean
Of all the proud pretension we might hang
For feeble fringes, fraudulent with stale
Dishonors. We can grant no purer gift
Than she, and we are helpless to provide
Him whiter tribute than is held in these
Pale hands that hovered over Him, and that
Which rose to meet Him from her eyes.

And then
She knelt and held Him close against her heart,
And in the midnight, adoration fused
With human love, and was not separate.

And very near, the man named Joseph came.
He was not tired now, nor worn, nor sad,
His step was gentle, and a lightness soared

Within him till the memory of angel
Voices heard in dreams was now a less
Remembrance for him than the sight of hands
That held a sleeping Child.

                                    He was the first
To find her thus, the first of all the world.
And when her faint smile called for him to take
Him for a breathless moment, he was first
To know there is no other blessedness.

The beat of pulses and the hush of heart
Had made again a silence more intent
Within surrounding silence . . . drift of time . . .
Starlight moving imperceptibly.

JESSICA POWERS

(1905–)

AND IN HER MORNING

The Virgin Mary cannot enter into
The soul for an indwelling; God alone
Has sealed this land as secretly His own
But being mother and implored, she comes
To stand along my eastern sky and be
A drift of sunrise over God and me.

God is a light and genitor of light
Yet for our weakness and our punishment
He hides Himself in midnights that prevent
All save the least awarenesses of Him.

328

We strain with dimmed eyes inward and perceive
No stir of what we clamored to believe.
Yet I say: God (if one may jest with God)
Thy hiding hath not reckoned with Our Lady
Who holds my east horizon and whose glow
Lights up my inner landscape, high and low.
All my soul's acres shine and shine with her!
Thou art discovered, God; awake, arise
Out of the dark of Thy Divine surprise!
Thine own reflection hath revealed Thy place,
For she is utter light by Thine own grace,
And in her light I find Thee hid within me,
And in her morning I can see Thy face.

THE CLOUD OF CARMEL

"The Lord promised that He would dwell in a cloud."
—2 Par. vi. 1.

Symbol of star or lily of the snows,
Rainbow or root or vine or fruit-filled tree:
These image the Immaculate to me
Less than a little cloud, a little light cloud rising
From Orient waters cleft by prophecy.
And as the Virgin in a most surprising
Maternity bore God and our doomed race,
I who bear God in mysteries of grace
Beseech her: Cloud, encompass God and me.

Nothing defiled can touch the cloud of Mary.
God as a child willed to be safe in her,
And the Divine Indweller sets His throne
Deep in a cloud in me, His sanctuary.

329

I pray, Oh, wrap me, Cloud, light Cloud of Carmel
Within whose purity my vows were sown
To lift their secrecies to God alone.
Say to my soul, the timorous and small
House of a Presence, that it cannot see
And frightened acre of a Deity,
Say in the fulness of thy clemency:
I have enclosed thee all.
Thou art in whiteness of a lighted lamb wool,
Thou art in softness of a summer wind lull.
O hut of God, hush thine anxiety.
Enfolded in this motherhood of mine
All that is beautiful and all divine
Is safe in thee.

JAMES EDWARD TOBIN

(1905–   )

MADONNA OF THE EXILES

I

We stumble down the pocked and cratered road,
Reft of eye-comfort of familiar scenes,
A thousand parchment faces in the gray
Dore of chiaroscuro char, and not
One birth-place tongue or hand among the lot;
Alone at dawn, stunned silence all the day,
Companionship of driven masses means
No comradeship at all; for nightmares cease,
But not this evil dream—world without peace—
Maniacal and modern Caesar's code.
Mother of loneliness, pray for us!

I fled to Egypt, treading alien sands,
A donkey's distance from a tyrant's sword;
No friends but puzzled Joseph—and the Word
Whose smile gave firmness to my trembling hands.

II

No man can paint without his tube and brush:
Where is the beauty of an endless path?
Our hands are empty—we have carried naught
From hate and horror but a memory
Better forgotten; there is left no fee
For charity, no cover for men caught
In night's dread net, no hearth-escape from wrath
Of rain:—nadir of nothingness we face
Without a hoe for earth or axe to brace
New walls to still the tempest to a hush.
Mother of comfort, pray for us!

I thought no handicraft was left when He
Emptied my life, staying for Temple talk,
And when He went with fishermen to walk:
But there is prayer in simple carpentry.

III

There in a bitter caricature of life,
The twitching fingers of our cottaged farms
Groped, in a skin-burned spasm, for the light,
To tremble back before the lash of fire;
The eyeless socket of the village spire,
Staring toward heaven, found it ever night;
The once proud wheat lay cowering, with its arms
Laid down; the limbless trees expired—and we,
Whose children rest in rubble dust, can see
No human gleam of solace in this strife.
Mother of courage, pray for us!

My heart was splintered when one awful day
I, too, seemed Sonless by that travesty
Of trees, raised in triune asymmetry.
He rose. There are things men can never slay.

ALFRED BARRETT

(1906–   )

CHANT OF DEPARTURE

(A Missionary's Prayer to Our Lady, Queen of Apostles)

Woman who walked home on the arm of John
Another way from that your Son had gone,
Woman who walked
And talked,
Unwavering, of what must yet be done—
Woman, behold your son!

Behold
Him who in boyhood haunts will not grow old;
Who goes predestined to an alien grave
In clay or sand or wave—
Yet sails enamored of one hope: to see,
As John from his dawn-lit boat on Galilee,
Christ in the haze-dim faces on the shore
Of Shantung or the coast of Travancore.

Woman who walked home on the arm of John,
When on
Some night of tears I hear the palm trees toss,
Stand by my side beneath the Southern Cross.

MARY'S ASSUMPTION

"Factum est silentium in coelo quasi media hora."
Apocalypse: viii, 1

There was silence in heaven, as if for half an hour—
 Isaian coals of wonder sealed the lips
Of Seraph, Principality and Power,
 Of all the nine angelic fellowships.

The archangels, those sheer intelligences,
 Were silent, with their eyes on heaven's door.
(So must our fancy dower them with senses,
 Make them incarnate in a metaphor.)

There was silence in heaven as Mary entered in,
 For even Gabriel had not foreseen
The glory of a soul immune from sin
 Throned in the body of the angels' Queen.

Blessed be God and Mary in whose womb
 Was woven God's incredible disguise.
She gave Our Lord His Body. In the tomb
 He gave her hers again and bade her rise.

Bright from death's slumber she arose, the flush
 Of a chaste joy illumining her cheeks;
Among the motherless in heaven there was a hush
 To hear the way a mother laughs and speaks.

Eye had not seen, nor ear of angel heard,
 Nor heart conceived—until Our Lady's death—
What God for those that love Him had prepared
 When heaven's synonym was Nazareth!

Her beauty opened slowly like a flower,
 Beauty to them eternally bequeathed.
There was silence in heaven; as if for half an hour
 No angel breathed.

JOHN LOUIS BONN
(1906–   )

MADONNA: 1936

The laborer to the lady: Yes, there are
Names like the day-spring and the morning star,
Gold arc and ivory tower, yet none of these
Meets my big need, O bitterness of the seas.

But Maiden, you have a name like a steely flower
Electrical and sharp—or is there power
Over wheel's crush and the grind of dynamos,
O lily of iron, of cleft in granite rose?

The lady to the laborer: I have heard
Voice under voice that speaks—the hiss that stirred
And steamed the sooty air—yet turn, turn wheel
Of braced and steady earth beneath my heel.

Coiled round my world, is he, and his coils are cold?
Yet though tooth be acid and the jaw be gold
Lo the worm! lo the serpent! lo the fanged with flame
And metal snake doth magnify my name.

JAMES J. DONOHUE
(1906–   )

LAST ANTIPHON: TO MARY

Dear Mother of the Savior, yet remaining
Star of the Sea and heaven's open door,
Come when we stumble, lifting and sustaining,
For in our hearts we long to rise once more.

You who, defying nature, still continue
Virgin before and after Gabriel's call,
You who, defying nature, wrought the sinew
Of Him Who made you, pity us who fall.

V. Eve's angel keeps a garden ringed with fire,
R. But Mary's angel answers Eve's desire.

Let us pray:

Pour, we beseech Thee, O Lord, the flood of Thy grace on our
    spirits,
That, as by an angel's voice we have known of Thy Son's
    Incarnation,
So by His Passion and Cross we may be led through to the glory
Of rising again from the dead: through the same Jesus Christ our
    Redeemer. *Amen.*

SISTER MARY IGNATIUS

(1907–   )

OUR LADY OF THE LIBRARIES

In Bodleian and Harleian
    Lurk ambushes of grace—
A secret siege Our Lady lays
    To many an ancient place. . . .

The Primer's gilded hieroglyphs
    Her lyric names conceal,
From manuscripts like winding-sheets
    Her risen praises steal!

SISTER MARY ST. VIRGINIA

(1907–   )

A NUN TO MARY, VIRGIN

I had gone fruitless and defenceless, Lady,
Had it not been for your strange blossoming:
Out of the sun and rain, in still and shady
And lonely moorlands, uncaressed by wing,
My having life had been a thing to mourn for,
Passing none on nor yielding up perfume—
Without you I had cringed beneath a scorn for
Skylarks that soar not, trees that do not bloom.
Without you I had had no answer to
The gibe against my love and my sweet mating—
Now, as I reach to take a Child from you,
These lips send far beyond my cloister grating
The canticle a million maids have cried,
Finding in you themselves: and justified.

SHRINE IN NAZARETH

Out of the garden in the gathering gloom
He turns, as twilight blurs the house where she
Will be a little shadow in the room—
Huddled over a parchment prophecy,
Heedless of shadows. Now that day is gone,
He must light and bring the candle from the door.
But, reaching out his hand, the man upon
The threshold stops—as any man would—, for
There at the latticed window fast asleep,
So beautiful that any pulse would stir,
The maid still kneels: still would she wish to keep

Watch for the little one asleep in her.
And any man would leave the light before her
And stumble away, trying not to adore her.

JOSEPH JOEL KEITH
(1908–   )

IMMACULATE PALM

Beautiful, Beautiful Mother, give
from your Immaculate Palm
a soothing, healing unseen balm
for boys who want to live.

Holiest, Holiest Mother, take
from the enveloping night
the sick boy's weeping for the light,
and whisper softly, "Wake."

Sorrowful, Sorrowful Mother, lift
salve that is borrowed above
for pierced ones. Let them feel His love,
and lead them out of tomb-like mind
where dwell believing blind,
You, who gave your Precious Gift.

THOUGH SHE SLUMBERS

Slumber, Small One.
Do not stir.
The Purest Bride's Your
comforter.

Though she sleeps this
holy hour,
as gentle as a
moonlight shower,

She will know Your
need, and keep
You warm, awake or
while You sleep.

Though she slumbers
till the day
she'll feel sweet Hands if
they touch hay.

Nothing's heard both
far and wide,
but heaven breathes softly
by her side.

SHE WALKS

She lies in silence
where the breath
of dumb things warm her
holiness.

338

She sees a halo
round His Head,
on earth, that heaven's
Love has made.

She walks gold streets of
God in praise
of dumb meek things and
golden hay.

FRANCIS X. CONNOLLY

(1909–   )

NO MORE DESTRUCTIVE FLAME

(*The Feast of the Immaculate Conception—1944*)

Once for our consolation it seemed, O Lord,
Was this Thy gift of perfect innocence
This isolation of the human seed
From all its sad and lying lusts
And all the subtler sophistries of greed.

Now not to console but to alarm
Comes this Thy mirror flashing heaven's face
Into the blood and dusty violence
Of our eyes, into the deep and ulcerous place
Where only cautery of her seven swords
Can cleanse the wounds inflicted in this strife
And wound us unto life.

Blind to her glory, we withered men
Swift only with our justifying words
(The malodorous conscience says we meant no harm)

339

Sweat in the desert of our fears
Evaporate in our desires.
Yet this last virtue, hope, whose fires
Though banked are warm
Shall still blaze bright
And the dry tinder, kindléd by Thy mirror, burn
No more destructive flame but light.

WILLIAM A. DONAGHY

(1909–   )

FOURTH STATION

He Meets His Mother

This afternoon in loud Jerusalem
They meet and part once more; no touch nor kiss
Can ease their anguish; while the mockers hiss:
"And he's the fool who thought his streaming hem
Could cure the woman. See the two of them,
The son and wife of Joseph come to this."
Two hearts cry out—abyss unto abyss,
And Jesse's flower is cut from Jesse's stem.

Perhaps she thinks of Nain—of all the land
Where wonders blossomed as He walked three years;
Of Jairus, Lazarus, the withered hand,
Of flowing mercies and of drying tears;
And still she knows her bitter place and part,
He will not heal her withered, widowed heart.

THIRTEENTH STATION

He Is Taken from the Cross

Now you may have Him, Mary, they are done,
The shepherd stricken lies; His little flock
Had fled before the crowing of the cock;
Now Caiphas is happy; he has won;
He does not heed the frightened crowds that run,
Jerusalem is shaken; shock on shock
Upheave the temple sanctum, rive the rock;
Now you may have the Thing that was your Son.

He cannot hear you, darling, He is dead—
Come, now, and we will hide Him from their sight;
He cannot feel your kisses on His head—
See—Nicodemus waits no more for night.
Look—he and John and Joseph stand in grief
And look to you for refuge and relief.

FRAY ANGELICO CHAVEZ

(1910–   )

LADY OF LIDICE

From God's lofty City
my Lady looks down,
the remembering lover
of every small town,
looks down less with pity
than wistfulness over
the town that is not;

341

for gone are its people,
each household and cot,
the quaint Slavic steeple
that tendered them cover,
a smoldering plot.

From God's lofty City
my Lady looks down,
forever the lover
of every small town.

LADY OF PEACE

Cathedral: Honolulu

I left a lei, Lady,
  To say goodby
Before we sailed away
  To where men die,
And vowed to bead on my return
  Fresh buds for dry.

Should I return not, Lady,
  When battles cease,
Grant my vow and promise
  Sweet release,
And lay your leis where I lie,
  And peace.

SEA-BIRDS

In days when Albion's seamen knew
Why they salute the quarterdeck
  (It held a shrine to Mary),
They named the hungry fowl that flew
About the galley at their beck,
  "Chickens *Matris Carae.*"

Dear Mother, with your apron blue
Shoo your chicks off reef and wreck
  (Gregory's angels, marry!)
Back to Peter's ship and crew—
And you upon the quarterdeck
  To feed them, Mother Carey.

MULIER AMICTA SOLE

Woman supremely blest
In woman's prime desire
To be most richly dressed:
Incomparable attire,
Blinding, iridescent
In robe of cloth-of-sun,
With Pleiad-plaited coronet,
And slippered with the crescent!
Gown sun-spun,
Crown star-set,
And the moon
For her shoon!
Woman supremely fit
To be so clothed, the one
Found truest, best, immaculate.

343

MARY

Miriam, Mary, Maria, Marie,
What voweled jewel might this be?

    Is it a sapphire love,
    Of purest water true?
    Or is it water of
    A sapphire hue?

Miriam, Marie, Maria, Mary,
So crystal-cut, yet limpid, airy!

    It flows in regal tones,
    Glitters like both of these:
    The sea-reflecting stones,
    The jeweled seas.

Mary, Marie, Maria, Miriam,
Ocean of beryl, sea-lit beryllium!

    Gem for the Father's ring,
    Stone of the Son's great crown,
    Glint on the Spirit's wing,
    Light pouring down.

Miriam, Mary, Marie, Maria,
Pendant for my lips, Maria!

344

JAMES J. GALVIN

(1911-   )

LADY OF O

By the seven stars of her halo
By her seven swords of woe
Oh Holy Spirit anneal my pen
To utter sweet words for the ears of men
In praise of Our Lady of O.

With seven O's we salute Thee
Each evening as Christmas comes;
We hail thee adazzle with sunset gold
Repeating prophecies new and old
Like salvoes of guns and drums.

O Woman, the word in Thy keeping
Thy secret from God most High,
Shall soon be whispered over the earth
And men shall listen and leap for mirth
Like stars in the Christmas sky.

O Lady, lone tent in the battle
Where our Leader awaits his time;
Though the day grow darker and Satan scorn
The tide of battle shall veer at morn
When He sallies forth to the cheer of horn
And trumpet and timbrel-chime.

O Stalk on the brink of blossom,
Shooting green through the frosty mire;
The peoples pray for thy Spring to come
And the mighty ones of the earth go dumb
For the Flower of the World's Desire.

O Tower of Grace untrespassed
Since Eden by God's decree;

345

At thine ivory spire and jasper gate
The pining kindred of Adam wait
For the turning of Christ the Key.

O Damsel more welcome than morning
To a world gone blind since the fall;
The stars go pale at Thy sandals' sound
And skylines glimmer, and men peer round
For a virgin in simplest homespun gowned
With the Sunrise under her shawl.

O milk-and-honey-run Mountain
Whence the crystal Cornerstone
Shall issue unsullied by tool or hand
The Stone that shall fasten each race and land
Together like flesh and bone.

O City ashine on the hill-tops
The nations uplift their eyes
From rainy island and sunken sea
And the ends of the earth they throng to Thee
To dwell in thy Christ-lit skies.

By the seven stars of Thy halo
By Thy seven swords of woe
Forgive us, O Lady, these phrases worn
In praise of Thy season with God unborn
O ineffable Lady of O.

OX-BONE MADONNA

(A Polish soldier in a Russian concentration camp, carved a statue of
Mary from a bone plucked out of the soup.)

Once they minted Our Lady in multiple golden medallions
Commingling her glories in smouldering roses of glass;
From gale-bellied mainsails she nodded on numberless galleons
Accorded a salvo at sunset on cannon of brass.

Time was when her icon was blazoned on jewel-spun banners
When lancers went plunging to battle huzzahing her Name
When guildsmen aspired to depict her ineffable manners
In spidery windows of moon-dappled amber and flame.

But now though the pitiless shock of artillery shake her
From lily-sprung pinnacles high on the spires of Cologne
Though matchless madonnas be splinters of quincewood and
  nacre
Her bell-plundered abbeys with clover and thorn overgrown
Neither flogging nor hunger nor death can make captives forsake
  her:
From a castaway ox-bone they carve her more splendid than
  stone.

MORNING STAR

"That *Lucifer* I mean: the Morning Star who never fell."
                                        (*Exultet*)

I loathe the very thought of Her
Who slewed my schemes awry
This *animal* of flesh and bone
Who makes the cherubim Her throne
Alongside the Most High.

I, Lucifer, the Sire of Light
Christened the *Morning Star*
Beheld this vision with the rest
But at His arrogant behest
I shrilled the first defiant jest
And girt myself for war!

To all His angel minions
He showed the Yet-to-be
And we saw in a world of kine and corn
A breed of beings yet unborn
Mortals with all but snout and horn
Lower by leagues than we.

And some of them sat counting stars
And some sat counting sheep
Then angels flickered by a bed
Of hay inside a cattle-shed
Where one of *them* inclined her head
Against a child asleep.

And then God startled angeldom
With words beyond belief,
Saying: "I am not One; but Three.
And this is Christ my Son you see
Cradled upon a human knee.
Take it for Grace or grief.

"And she who spun his frock of flesh
Softer than seraph-down
Shall be my Spirit's peerless Bride
And rule creation at Our side
And long as Heaven shall abide
Shall wear the stars for crown."

Because I would not hail her Queen
Because I dared rebel
(Unlike the spaniel Seraphim)

348

My blazing radiance grew dim;
And hurling blasphemy at Him
I hurtled into Hell.

But I will trick her kindred
With slyly candied lies
With apples sweetly dappled red
But sour at core with craven dread.
I'll snuff the stars about Her head
And wither Paradise.

ARTHUR MACGILLVRAY

(1912-)

MADONNA OF THE DONS

Before the stirring of the notes at the lecture
There is the time for learning,
Bread years and water and the single lamp,
Tracing the maze of a long thread through the hemmed mind.
We find this lonely going.

Not all are twelve year old instructors, Lady,
Giving graduate courses on the Father.

Has the desk a future and have the vacant chairs
Voices that we hear in the evening?
Are facts like flowers, pressed dead between the pages,
And can we run our business without the blossoming vase?
We want a blackboard answer.

The snakes beneath the flowered fact, Lady,
Need the finding and the crushing out.

The pencilling hands we talk to this young hour
Will hold other ammunition:
Fingering a throw-flame, grasp-knife, throttle-neck, drop-bomb.
The copyright of birds has elapsed. Air is man's road,
And that is where you come in:

Lady, breathe down the air you dress yourself with,
Cover the words we form with flesh.

ALBERT J. HEBERT, JR.

(1913–   )

HEART FOR ALL HER CHILDREN

I have seen Our Lady in Ireland, being carried in procession in
    May
A Loveliness on the shoulders of her faithful sodalists.
I have seen Our Lady sorrowing on her altar in a London church,
And by her feet a large white candle burning for the men in
    Normandy.
I have seen her in France, arriving before a cathedral
Amidst the shouts and tears of her children, a returned
Prisoner of War in an old, beautiful and venerated image.
I have seen her in Luxembourg, smiling down from niched
    corners
Of quaint streets, and even from an office building.
And, from her small shrines above the entrances of nearly every
    home,
In a small hamlet in Germany, on the Frankfort-Munich road,
I have seen her weeping over the guns and the refugees;
From the houses she looked down—and the town was not harmed.
I have seen Our Lady in so many lands; and in all those strange
And varied lands, men were her children, and men had her love.

JOHN DUFFY

(1914–   )

THE ANNUNCIATION

And was it true,
The stranger standing so,
And saying things that lifted her in two,
And put her back before the world's beginning?

Her eyes filled slowly with the morning glow.
Her drowsy ear drank in a first sweet dubious bird.
Her cheek against the pillow woke and stirred
To gales enriched by passage over dew,
And friendly fields and slopes of Galilee
Arose in tremulous intermixture with her dreams,
Till she remembered suddenly . . .

Although the morning beams
Came spilling in the gradual rubric known to every day,
And hills stood black and ruinous, as in eclipse,
Against the softly spreading ray,
Not touched by any strange apocalypse
Like that which yesterday had lifted her sublime,
And put her back before the first grey morn of Time—
Though nothing was disturbed from where she lay and saw,
Now she remembered with a quick and panting awe
That someone came, and took in hand her heart,
And broke it irresistibly apart,
With what he said, and how in tall suspense
He lingered, while the white celestial inference,
Pushing her fears apart, went softly home.
Then she had faltered her reply,
And felt the sudden burden of eternal years,
And shamed by the angelic stranger standing by
Had bowed her head to hide her human tears.

351

Never again would she awake
And find herself the buoyant Galilean lass,
But into her dissolving dreams would break
A hovering consciousness too terrible to pass—
A new awareness in her body when she stirred,
A sense of Light within her virgin gloom:
She was the Mother of the wandering Word,
Little and terrifying in her laboring womb.
And nothing would again be casual and small,
But everything with light invested, overspilled
With terror and divinity, the dawn, the first bird's call,
The silhouetted pitcher waiting to be filled.

OUR LADY'S LABOR

He is clothed with beauty.—Ps. xcii, 1.

Day after day
The muffled shuttling of Her blood
Wove His apparel's gradual array,
Silk stole and hushed unhurrying limb.
Day after day, night after night
Softly He buckled on, in the deep gloom,
The spotless labor of Her womb,
Softly the universe of dappled light,
The shine and shadow of our human years.

What beauty, with what weight of tears
The weaving of Her veins availed Her Child!
She, His elected, She, His undefiled,
Who cinctured Him in tangible delight,
Laying the universe against His soul—
The cap of Carmel for His searching sight,
The velvet of all roads to couch His feet,

To charge the chambers of His heart with mirth
The blue-green changes of Genesareth—
She, with these gifts of happy heaven and earth,
Gave (as He longed) the bite of bitter death.

O nights of secret tears that filled and felled
The tender lilies strewn before His feet!
O heavy, helpless flowers!
For all you smiled, and swept Him sweet on sweet,
And His huge heart with all your odors swelled,
One sweep there was you could not hold nor heal—
The last sharp gift of the invading steel.

And these shall never pass away,
Which sprang from her providing womb:
Remembered beauty and remembered pain,
Cherished in every wandering vein
She wove for him in darkness, day by day,
Out of the labor of a lovely loom.

OX-BONE MADONNA

We have minted her beauty in multiple golden medallions
Commingling her graces in smouldering roses of glass,
In banners have hued her that blazed over lancers and stallions
And pared her in plumwood to smile on the perilous pass.

Her splendor has dimpled the darkness of rafter and moulding
A luminous cheek in the cavernous dusk of Cologne,
From marvelous maple and marble her features unfolding
Her face has anointed the timber and sweetened the stone.

But haloed and holy and folded in fretted apparel
Incredibly crowned with the Child in her snowy embrace
Out of the silence of bone an ineffable carol
Out of the thigh of an ox her unspeakable face!

Ah, none but Our Lady could blazon a bone into glowing
Who stood without stain in the mire where the cattle had trod
And kept in the stench and the dark and the din and the lowing,
In the squalor of oxen the mien of the Mother of God.

THOMAS MERTON

(1915–   )

THE BLESSED VIRGIN MARY COMPARED
TO A WINDOW

Because my will is simple as a window
And knows no pride of original birth,
It is my life to die, like glass, by light:
Slain in the strong rays of the bridegroom sun.

Because my love is simple as a window
And knows no shame of original dust,
I longed all night, (when I was visible) for dawn my death:
When I would marry day, my Holy Spirit:
And die by transsubstantiation into light.

For light, my lover, steals my life in secret.
I vanish into day, and leave no shadow
But the geometry of my cross,
Whose frame and structure are the strength
By which I die, but only to the earth,
And am uplifted to the sky my life.

354

When I became the substance of my lover,
(Being obedient, sinless glass)
I love all things that need my lover's life,
And live to give my newborn Morning to your quiet rooms,

—Your rooms, that would be tombs,
Or vaults of night, and death, and terror,
Fill with the clarity of living Heaven,
Shine with the rays of God's Jerusalem:
O shine, bright Sions!

Because I die by brightness and the Holy Spirit,
The sun rejoices in your jail, my kneeling Christian,
(Where even now you weep and grin
To learn, from my simplicity, the strength of faith).

Therefore do not be troubled at the judgments of the thunder,
Stay still and pray, still stay, my other son,
And do not fear the armies and black ramparts
Of the advancing and retreating rains:
I'll let no lightning kill your room's white order.

Although it is the day's last hour,
Look with no fear:
For the torn storm lets in, at the world's rim,
Three streaming rays as straight as Jacob's ladder:

And you shall see the sun, my Son, my Substance,
Come to convince the world of the day's end, and of the night,
Smile to the lovers of the day in smiles of blood;
For through my love, He'll be their Brother,
My light—the Lamb of their Apocalypse.

THE EVENING OF THE VISITATION

Go, roads, to the four quarters of our quiet distance,
While you, full moon, wise queen,
Begin your evening journey to the hills of heaven,
And travel no less stately in the summer sky
Than Mary, going to the house of Zachary.

The woods are silent with the sleep of doves,
The valleys with the sleep of streams,
And all our barns are happy with peace of cattle gone to rest.
Still wakeful, in the fields, the shocks of wheat
Preach and say prayers:
You sheaves, make all your evensongs as sweet as ours,
Whose summer world, all ready for the granary and barn,
Seems to have seen, this day,
Into the secret of the Lord's Nativity.

Now at the fall of night, you shocks,
Still bend your heads like kind and humble kings
The way you did this golden morning when you saw God's
          Mother passing,
While all our windows fill and sweeten
With the mild vespers of the hay and barley.

You moon and rising stars, pour on our barns and houses
Your gentle benedictions.
Remind us how our Mother, with far subtler and more holy
          influence,
Blesses our rooves and eaves,
Our shutters, lattices and sills,
Our doors, and floors, and stairs, and rooms, and bedrooms,
Smiling by night upon her sleeping children:
O gentle Mary! Our lovely Mother in heaven!

SISTER MARY MAURA

(1916–)

TO THE QUEEN OF DOLORS

Seven times seven
the beads I toll,
chiming the music of your griefs
about my soul.

Long since my sires
and their sires before
chanted their charms against the storm,
against the hoar.

Charm for the foal,
a charm against rain,
potent potion for the newbud life
and woman in pain.

Poor were my sires
with never a bead
to fling at the Ivory Tower
and cry their need.

Seven times seven
the beads I press,
remember the seed of my sires, Queen,
in this distress.

OUR LADY OF THE REFUGEES

Mother, who knew
what hardship shakes
a woman bundling clothes
and putting by her wheaten cakes;

Mother who urged the donkey
 (making happy riot
on the straggling stones),
urged the beast to be more quiet;
Mother who heard the Child
whimper beneath the thin blue shawl,
our aching prayers cry out to thee,
Mother, pray for them all.

A thousand Bethlehems
mask dark tonight;
the eyes of little friendly homes
have lost their light;
pathetic heaps of poor dear things
are laid aside; a small bird sang
where a latched door swings.
Mother, whose sad Egyptian flight
preceded all of these,
guide them in faith beneath familiar stars—
Our Lady of the Refugees.

RAYMOND F. ROSELIEP

(1917–   )

LADY OF LETTERS

Lady of Letters,
Laureate of the Word,
by reason of your flamed *Magnificat,*
your nine-month interlude
of weaving life
into the urgent God-ripe Word
that spurred the night's blue range with singing,
and spurred the centuries, too;

Lady of Letters,
Laureate of the Word,
as the young dawn whence leapt
the Star of perfect song:

Bear up our prayer.

Our souls, our minds, our senses vault
with longing
to unleash their own magnificats;
to pierce the essence of the churning earth,
the essence of men's churning hearts
with the untroubled music of the Word.

Lady of Letters,
Laureate of the Word,
send down your Spirit spouse
as branding fire
on every troubadour thus consecrate,
for choruses
that would seize virgin height
and incarnate raptly, once again,
the Word.

WHERE DO I LOVE YOU, LOVELY MAID?

Where do I love you, lovely Maid?
I love you twice with urgency:
Poised in the light at Bethlehem,
Braced in the gloom at Calvary.

At Bethlehem where willing hands
Possess the Strong, yet very Small,
As I lift up white Love each dawn
Above my altar's Christmas stall.

At Calvary where steady palms
Caress the limbs' torn livery,
The way I hold red Love, secure,
Before my altar's dark rose tree.

TO MARY: AT THE THIRTEENTH STATION

You are the priest tonight:
The paten of your lap holds sacrifice.
You are the priest tonight,
Offering Peace and its price.
Star candles burn palely bright;
John is your faithful acolyte.
You are the priest tonight.

SYMPHONY IN BLUE

The gentian sleeps in waters
That are a maiden's eyes;
The maiden wears a mantle
Cut from the morning skies.

A wheel of stars is whirling
About her dawn-veiled hair;
The sparks flash blue and silver
Above the serpent's lair.

The maiden tends a fountain
Of Rain for grape and wheat,
Its torrent is immersing
The blue globe at her feet.

RICHARD WEBB SULLIVAN

(1917–

STAR OF THE SEA

Hail, Star of the Sea,
Hail, most blessèd lantern,
Star of love
Too deep for passion,
Queen of Heaven!
Hail, Queen of Heaven
And of All Sorrow!

Though the guns falter,
Lady and Queen,
And we have seen
Our stubborn foes given
In our power,
Lady, this
Is, beyond our knowledge,
A fearful hour,
And as much sorrow
As has been.

Not in this Now,
Grievous Queen,
Most bereav'd Lady,
Of the ancient tree
Where the Son
Of Heaven died
Think most poignantly,
But the newest cross
Where He for Sin
Is crucified
After the new
Gethsemeni.

Is this called Peace?
Our arms prevailed.
The guns are stilled.
We did not love
The men we killed,
And, thus, we failed.
We had no shame.
We cast the stone.
The Christ who came
With a great throng
Went on alone.

Whatever Pardon
May be sent
We shut out
With our intent.
Mother, pray for us.

Pray, untainted Virgin—
Pity what
You can not bless
And beseech
The kind Trinity
To prevent
Our wickedness,
Lest sweet mercy flee,
Oh, too far,
Beyond our reach.

Star of love,
Queen of Heaven,
Star of the Sea,
Most blessèd lantern,
Give us light.
Brightest of stars,
Lead us.

Holiest of stars,
Be mindful of us.
Mother of God,
Star of the Sea,
Pray for us.

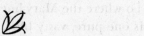

SISTER MARY CATHERINE

(1919–   )

NEW TESTAMENT: REVISED EDITION

This is a wrong that needs not my bespeaking
    To win your pity, Mary of Bethlehem,
That women with children go through our cities seeking
    (How hopelessly) a roof to shelter them.

This thing you know, of inns where any stranger
    Against his need can find some place to stay,
Where dogs have homes, and oxen still their manger,
    And only children may be turned away.

There are no new griefs; only for our weeping
    The old sorrows men have wept before.
And still Light comes; but we are blind or sleeping,
    And let a Child turn homeless from our door.

JOSEPH DEVER

(1919–   )

QUEEN OF HORIZONS

Oh Lord, give me a plane,
And waft me high again,
To where the Mary-hue
Is one pure, vasty blue.
Oh, I will romp the airy ocean,
Make sun-winks with my mothy motion.
Below, chameleon clouds obscure
My ethered glee, make sure
Men cannot see my suit
Of her, although the brute—
Blotch-steel may rend her gown,
And from her mantle claw me down
The blurring avenue of space.
Yet, richly have I known her face,
For sweet, abounding purity
Was bluely clad and smiled on me;
And every crimson blob of death
Becomes a lambent, crystal breath.
Howl-spatter-demons, have your riot,
You will be azured and be quiet.
Yankee, Jap and German, too,
Blue, my lady, fold in blue.
Fold them warmly in your arms,
Where the flung steel never harms,
Where the blinding wedge of dawning
Dazzles, yet is merely fawning
On the lady's world-embrace
Of azure. Do you know one place
In Heaven where there is no Mary?
You, with pinions, be not wary
Of the blood-fleck and the flame,
For blue can clean and blue can tame

The hotly spiked, infuriated sky
Blue-silently; and only death will die.
Therefore, Lord, give me a plane,
And waft me Mary-high again.

ROBERT MENTH

(1919–   )

CRY FROM THE BATTLEFIELD

(To Our Lady of Perpetual Help)

O Lady, together with the Child you take
In your frail arms to hush His frightened cries,
Cradle us against your heart and ache
To see the sorrow staring from our eyes.
O Lady strong beyond all ecstasy,
Young willow bent before the Breath of God,
Think still of us as little ones while we
Thrust puny chests at Heaven from this sod
And flail with futile fists against the Breast
Where beats the Beauty passion cannot taste.
O Lady, heal our wars, our dark unrest,
The lusts that lash our land a scarlet waste:
Mother of men, this bleeding face
Awaits the wonder of your love's embrace.

MARGARET DEVEREAUX CONWAY

(1921–   )

THE ANNUNCIATION

("Gramercy, my lady free," Gabriel to Mary in
the Ludus Coventriae.)

Not yesterday, nor yet a day
But at the core of time,
Gabriel came on wings of flame
To ask salvation's rhyme.

"Mary, thou lantern wrought of grace,
In thee would Light unmade
Hide its terror of radiance
Lest mankind be afraid."

And quiet eyes regarded him,
Holding their freedom high,
While Love and Light were hesitant
Before her soft reply.

"How shall this Light transmute itself,
Knowing my flesh not free?"
"Love shall invade where none may go,
And God shall dwell in thee."

So at the *trivium* of time
Heaven came within
The ark of thy unspotted flesh
That men might live again.

Envoi

We had not lived unless your will
Bowed to God's urgency.
By thy dear Son are we all saved—
Gramercy, lady free.

Lady and Mother—
if only she could weep!
But no, she is a queen,
and queens are brave
and full of strength,
Even a Mother-Queen.
Her Mother's heart
aches and swells
in an unbent breast
to lay that bloody head,
its crown of crimson thorns removed,
against its pillowed softness,
to soothe those burning eyes
with moist, light kisses;
to fold those hands in a long caress
against her cheeks
and pretend He is again
her little child
hurt in play
and comforted to sleep
in her arms.
But He is a Man,
a King
with a task to do
for truth
and all that men will claim
dear and just and beautiful
in the days to be
and through
eternity.

She must see Him through
His mission well done,
Ever Queen and Mother of God.

LUCY A. K. ADEE

OUR LADY OF GOOD VOYAGE

You hold a silver ship
Upon your arm,
As once you held
Your little Son asleep.
O blessed Mary,
Keep us from every harm
Our fishing ones
Far out upon the deep.

He chose the fishermen
To be His friends,
Peter the Rock,
Andrew his brother true—
They followed Him,
He met them on the shore—
You must have known them
And loved them, too.

Lady of Good Voyage
With silver ship held fast,
We light our candles—
Guard the souls
On boats with sail
And mast.

OUR LADY OF MERCY

Our Lady walks the parapets of heaven
(Her feet were sandaled once against the dust)
Our Lady's hands are beautiful with blessings
(The Nazareth beggars blessed them for a crust.)

She leans her head across the brilliant rampart—
(The latchless door at Nazareth stood wide)
Our Lady's hands are beautiful with blessings
(And angels watched the beggars there and sighed.)

She hears the mystic litany of angels,
A prayer no mortal knows and none could say,
But they who have no need can find no mercy—
"Most gracious advocate, turn thine eyes this way."

BIOGRAPHICAL NOTES

ADAM OF ST. VICTOR (1130–1180), was a Breton who, while young, entered one of the theological centers of his time, the Abbey of St. Victor near Paris, where he lived until his death. His is the most potent name in the revival of liturgical poetry in the twelfth century; he is looked upon by some as the foremost among the sacred Latin poets of the Middle Ages. Not only did he initiate but he also brought to perfection the Latin sequence. Some thirty-seven of his hymns and sequences were published in the *Elucidatorium Ecclestiasticum* of Clichtoveus, a theologian of the sixteenth century; the remaining seventy were preserved at the Abbey of St. Victor until the Revolution, when they were transferred to the Bibliothèque Nationale; here they were discovered by Léon Gautier who edited the first complete edition in Paris in 1858.

ADAMS, HENRY (1838–1918), was born in Boston, Mass., and educated at Harvard and the University of Berlin. John Quincy Adams, sixth president of the United States was his grandfather; John Adams, second president, his great-grandfather. In 1861 he went with his father, recently appointed United States minister to England, where he met the leaders in social and literary circles. In 1868 he returned to America and spent two years in Washington contributing political articles and correspondence to *The North American Review, The Nation* and *The New York Evening Post.* In 1870 he was appointed assistant professor of history at Harvard, and became editor of *The North American Review.* Two years later he married Marian Hooper of Boston, and in 1877, having retired from Harvard and the editorship of the *Review,* he settled in Washington and devoted himself to historical research. In 1879 he published *The Life of Albert Gallatin;* in 1880, *Democracy,* an anonymous novel. His nine-volume

History of the United States of America During the Administrations of Thomas Jefferson and James Adams, a masterpiece of research, was published (two volumes in 1889, four in 1890, and the final three in 1891), and *Mont Saint Michel and Chartres* (1904, but revised and privately printed again in 1912). About this time he wrote his "Prayer to the Virgin of Chartres," which did not appear until after his death. *The Education of Henry Adams* was privately printed in folio in 1906, and posthumously published in 1918. In 1930 his letters were edited by Worthington Chauncy Ford, and his nine-volume history reprinted in four volumes.

ADEE, LUCY A. K. (contemporary), lives in Washington, D. C., and has contributed "Our Lady of Good Voyage" together with a number of other poems to the Summer, 1945, issue of *Poet Lore.*

AKATHISTOS HYMN, THE, is an office in honor of Our Lady, sung in churches of the Byzantine rite. When it is sung in its entirety as on the fifth Saturday of Lent, accordingly called "Akathistos Saturday," it is divided into four *staseis* ("standing parts") interpolated by psalms and hymns during which the faithful are permitted to sit down. Hence its name, *"Non-sitting Hymn";* or, perhaps, because the clergy and people spent the entire night before the fifth Sunday of Lent standing in church singing the praise of Our Lady. Its origin, as given in the historical lesson in the Byzantine office for the day, assigns it to the year 626 when Heraclius being emperor, and Sergius, Patriarch, Constantinople was attacked by the Persians and Avars, and saved by the Patriarch leading his people around the city walls, while carrying the great relics, and calling to Our Lord and His Mother for protection. After a mighty wind scattered the enemy fleet, casting up its vessels on the shore near the Church of the Mother of God at Blachernae, the faithful spent the entire night in thanksgiving, standing and singing hymns of praise and gratitude. Some consider only the first *kontákion* as the only original part relating to the victory of 626, which was added to an ensemble of hymns and psalms already known. The authorship of "The Akathistos Hymn" is uncertain; many attribute it to Sergius I, Patriarch; others to George Pisides, a deacon and contemporary, archivist and sacristan of the Great Church of St. Sophia at Constantinople. The hymn has been translated into all liturgical languages: Byzantine (Staroslav, Rumenian, Arabic, etc.), Latin (many times), Italian, German, Russian, French and Ukrainian.

One of the best English translations is that by Father McNabb; other translations have been done by G. W. Woodward, Anita Bartle and Dr. John Christopher. The hymn has an indulgence of fifty days, both in the Eastern and Latin rites, bestowed by Benedict XIV (*Ex auditu sancti Pontificis,* May 4, 1756), for each recitation, and a plenary indulgence for its recitation on the Feast of the Annunciation, March 25.

ALIGHIERI, DANTE (1265–1321), author of the *Divina Commedia,* and one of the greatest writers of all time, was born in Florence of an old Guelph family of former nobility. His education was entrusted to the philosopher, Brunetto Latini. Pursuing his studies at Bologna, Padua and Naples, he excelled in languages, theology, painting and music. According to Boccaccio, it was at the age of nine that he first met Beatrice Portinari, a little girl in dress "of subdued and goodly crimson," as he later wrote, who made him the greatest poet of all Christendom. Their love was always to be one "in the spirit" since she was already betrothed. Dante's *Vita Nuova,* completed in 1294, recounts their love. Her death in 1290 occasioned the poet to transmute her memory into a symbol of all truth, all grace, all love and all wisdom. As he wrote of their first meeting on the bridge "that wonderful vision came to me, and I determined to say nothing further of that most blessed one until I should be able to put into words what hath not before been written of any woman." He wrote a matchless poem which all the world has consented to call *"divine."* Dante married Gemma di Manetto Donati and had four children. For the greater part of his life he was involved in the political rivalries of the Whites and Blacks of the Guelph party. He was banished from his beloved Florence because of his anti-papal activities and spent his last years in Ravenna with his friend, Guido Novello da Polenta, at whose house he died suddenly of a fever. His tomb is at Ravenna. Dante's writings include *Vita Nuova, Divina Commedia, Convito, De Monarchia, De Vulgari Eloquio* and a collection of sonnets and short poems known as the *Canzoniere.*

ALMA REDEMPTORIS MATER, "Gracious Mother of the Redeemer," is the first of the four antiphons of Our Lady in the *Roman Breviary.* It is said or sung after the Divine Office from the Vespers of the Saturday before the first Sunday of Advent to the Feast of the Purification inclusive. The hymn is ascribed to Hermann Contractus (1013–1054).

ASGRÍMSSON, EYSTEINN (d. 1361), was a Canon Regular who, in 1343 resided in the monastery of Thykkvabaer; a decade later, he acted in the capacity of an official at Helgafell and was intimate with Gyrd, the Norwegian Bishop of Skalholt. From 1355 to 1357 he lived in Norway where he was made a canon of the cloister of Helgisetr, near Trondhjem. In 1357 he returned to Iceland as Visitator of his order. He died in 1361 at the monastery of Helgisetr. It is not certain when and where he wrote his one great poem, *Lilja* ("The Lily"), consisting of one hundred stanzas in honor of the Mother of God and composed in a rather free adaptation of eight-stressed court-meter. The poem has been translated into a number of languages.

AUDEN, WYSTAN HUGH (1907–   ), was born in York and educated at Gresham's School, Holt, and Christ's Church, Oxford. In 1929 he went to Berlin, then taught for five years in Scotland and Malvern. In 1935 he married Erika Mann, daughter of Thomas Mann, the novelist, and in the summer of 1936 both he and Louis MacNeice went to Iceland, whence they wrote their *Letters from Iceland* (1937). For some months of 1938 he traveled in China with Christopher Isherwood, and gathered material for *Journey to a War* (1939). In 1939 he came to the United States and lectured for two years at the New School for Social Research, N. Y. During 1941–42 he held an appointment at the University of Michigan, was awarded the Guggenheim fellowship for 1942, but relinquished it because of the war, and accepted an appointment at Swarthmore College. At the time of Auden's coming to America, Richard Eberhardt publicly remarked that it was as significant a literary event as Eliot's going to Europe was in the ex-patriotic days. First regarded as one of the daring "modernes," his attitude reflected by his verse has grown increasingly Christian. His publications include: *Poems* (1930), *The Orators* (1932), *The Dance of Death* (1933), with Christopher Isherwood, *The Dog Beneath the Skin* (1935), with John Garrett, *The Poet's Tongue* (1935), with C. Isherwood, edited *The Oxford Book of Light Verse* (1939), with C. Isherwood, *Selected Poems* (1940), *Another Time* (1940), *New York Letter* (1941) and *For the Time Being—A Christmas Oratorio* (1944).

AVE MARIS STELLA, "Hail, Star of the Sea," is a liturgical hymn of unknown authorship. It is at least as old as the ninth century, and occurs in the *Roman Breviary* in Vespers of the Common Office of the Blessed Virgin Mary, in the Office for Saturdays, in the Little Office of the Blessed Virgin Mary, as well as on all feasts of Our Lady. Discovered in a St. Gall manuscript of the ninth century, its frequent use in the Divine Office made it a most popular hymn of the Middle Ages. Many other hymns have been founded upon it. It has been wrongly attributed both to Venantius Fortunatus and to St. Bernard of Clairvaux.

AVE REGINA COELORUM, "Hail, Queen of Heaven," is a liturgical hymn in use since the twelfth century; its author and date of composition have not been determined. In the sixteenth century it was introduced into the *Roman Breviary* as one of the four antiphons of the Virgin Mary, but it had been used by the Franciscans as early as the thirteenth. The antiphon is assigned from Compline on the Feast of the Purification (February 2), even when the feast is transferred, to Holy Thursday exclusively. It is found in the *St. Alban's Book* of the twelfth century; in a Munich manuscript of about the thirteenth century; in a Sarum breviary of the fourteenth, and in York and Roman breviaries of the fifteenth. Certain theological scholars have traced in it "noble accents . . . aspirations of many Doctors, such as St. Anthanasius, St. Ephrem, St. Ildephonsus." It is thought by Th. Bernard (*Le Bréviaire*, Paris, 1887) to have been introduced into the Divine Office by Clement VI in the fourteenth century, earlier than the other antiphons.

BARCLAY, ALEXANDER (1475–1552), was a monk of Ely and Canterbury, priest in the College of Ottery St. Mary, vicar of Much Badew in Essex and rector of All Hallows, Lombard Street, London. He translated into English an allegorical French poem called "The Castle of Labor," also Sallust's "Jugurthine War," and wrote the lives of several saints. His "Ballade to Our Lady" is the conclusion and dedication of *The Ship of Fools*, a famous satire on the follies of people of all ranks. The poem is of special historical interest because of the fact that it was the first English book in which any specific mention is made of the New World. It has been translated into Latin, and into the principal European languages. The complete title of the ballade is "A conclusyon of this Boke with a Balade of the translatour in honoure of the blessyd Virgyn Mary, Moder of God." Even at this early day Mary was invoked under the title of "Mother Immaculate," as this poem gives evidence.

BARRETT, ALFRED J., S.J. (1906–   ), was born in Flushing, New York (August 26). He attended St. Francis Xavier College, New

York City, graduating in 1924, when he entered the Jesuit novitiate of St. Andrew-on-Hudson, at Poughkeepsie, New York. He received his B.A. degree at Woodstock, Md., in 1930, his M.A., in 1931, and was ordained to the priesthood in June, 1937. He has been professor of poetry at Canisius College, Buffalo, New York, 1931–34; director of thirty-five schools in the Sodality movement; associate director of the Apostleship of Prayer, and is now a chaplain in the United States Army. He is the author of a book of poems, *Mint by Night* (1938).

BEAUMONT, JOSEPH (1616–1699), attended Peterhouse, Cambridge, in 1634; held a Fellowship there in 1636, and was dismissed as a Royalist in 1644. His epic poem "Psyche," was published in 1648. He held the following positions: canon of Ely, 1646; domestic chaplain to Whren, Bishop of Ely, 1650; Doctor of Divinity, and chaplain to the King, 1660; Master of Jesus' College, 1662, and of Peterhouse, 1663; and regius professor of divinity, 1624.

BELLOC, HILAIRE (1870–   ), historian, essayist, biographer, poet and novelist, was born of English-French parentage in Edgbaston, France, and studied at the Oratory School under Newman. After two years in the French Army, he went to Oxford, thence to London as editor. In 1896 he married an American, and has four children. Probably the most variously endowed of contemporary writers, his numerous works include historical, critical and literary subjects. Well known as a lecturer and controversialist, he is also acclaimed an excellent poet. Sheed and Ward has published a recent collection of his poems entitled *Sonnets and Verse,* which contains all of his verses that Belloc wishes to preserve (except his humorous verse) ; of which Hugh Walpole wrote: "Here are the collected poems of the greatest living English poet. Yeats is an Irishman. Who otherwise is Belloc's rival? Masefield, De la Mare, T. S. Eliot? The younger men might talk of Auden and Spender. But none of these has Belloc's variety, audacity, and especially his fiery, sarcastic humor . . . Mr. Belloc is a very great man. Only after his death will it be seen how truly great he is." Among his multitudinous writings are: *Marie Antoinette* (1924), *Milton* (1933), *Wolsey* (1933), *Richelieu* (1934) ; essays: *Survivals and New Arrivals* (1929), *Towns of Destiny* (1931) ; and *Sonnets and Verse* (1924).

BENVENUTA, SISTER MARY, O.P. (Dorothy I. Little), is an English Dominican contemplative of All Souls Priory, Headington, Oxford. Among her works are the following: *The Months and Other*

Poems, By-Paths of the Presence of God, Mane Mecum, Domine (1928), and *Eucharistic Meditations of St. John Vianney* (a translation). Her poems have appeared in several anthologies.

BERTRAND, SISTER MARY, R.S.M. (contemporary), is a member of the Sisters of Mercy of the Albany, New York, diocese; has written for *The Catholic World, Spirit* and other magazines. A member of the Catholic Poetry Society of America, she is literary agent and executor of the late poet, Francis Carlin. She is at present touring England and Ireland visiting convents of her Order, in preparation for a biography of Catherine McAuley, foundress of the Sisters of Mercy.

BOCCACCIO, GIOVANNI (1313–1375), was born in Paris of a Florentine family. While very young he was brought to Florence where he attended school until he was ten, then entered business with his father. In 1327 he went to Naples to study law, but devoted the greater portion of his time to literature, coming into contact with the most prominent members of the court of Anjou. In 1334 he is thought to have first met Maria d'Aquino, daughter of King Robert, who inspired his early works as his literary heroine, Fiammetta. He returned to Florence in 1340, where he held public office, and engaged in diplomatic missions to Padua, the Romagna, Avignon and elsewhere. His long friendship with Petrarch dates from 1350. In 1373, he began his lectures on the poems of Dante, and died two years later in Certaldo. *The Decameron,* finished in 1353, is his principal work. Like so much of the literature of his time, it is lamentably blotted by indecencies. However, it is said that in his later years he repented of his too free manner of writing in his youth. As a man he was upright, loyal and of good will.

BONAVENTURE, SAINT GIOVANNI DI FIDENZA (1221–1274), Doctor of the Church, Cardinal-Bishop of Albano and Minister General of the Friars Minor, was born in Bagnorea near Viterbo. Some have attributed the change from his baptismal name of John to that of Bonaventure to the exclamation of St. Francis, "*O buona ventura,*" when, as an infant, John was brought to him to be cured of a dangerous illness. He entered the Order of Friars Minor about 1238, was sent to Paris to complete his studies under Alexander of Hales, and received the "licentiate" which authorized him to teach at the University as *Magister regens;* here he remained until 1255, when he was forced to discontinue because of the opposition to Mendicant Orders. When these

379

Orders were reëstablished in their privileges, both he and St. Thomas Aquinas received the degree of Doctor on October 23, 1257. A few months previous, though only thirty-six years old, he had been elected Minister General of the Friars Minor, which office was rendered particularly difficult because of the two factions among the friars—the *Spirituales,* who insisted on literal observance of the original rule, and the *Relaxti,* who desired adaptations and mitigations. At the chapter of 1263 he fixed the limits of the Order's provinces, and designated that a bell be rung at nightfall in honor of the Annunciation, the practice of which, many believe, was the origin of the Angelus. In 1265 Clement IV nominated Bonaventure to the vacant Archbishopric of York, but the saint declined the honor. On June 23, 1273, much against his will, he was created Cardinal-Bishop of Albano, by Gregory X. It is said that the pope's envoys, who brought him the cardinal's hat, found him washing dishes outside a convent near Florence, and he requested them to hang the hat on a nearby bush until he had finished his task. At the Council of Lyons in 1274 he was in charge of the deliberations. While the Council was still in session Bonaventure died. He wrote on almost every subject discussed by the Schoolmen, but mainly on philosophy and theology. His chief works are the *Breviloquium, Centiloquium* and *Biblia Pauperum.*

BONN, JOHN LOUIS, S.J. (1906–   ), was born in Waterbury, Conn., studied at Crosby High School, later at Shadowbrook, Lenox, Mass., Weston and Boston Colleges, and the Gregorian University in Rome. He was ordained in the Jesuit Order June 21, 1935, and has since held professorships in literature and poetry at various Jesuit colleges. From 1935–36 he was chaplain in the CCC camps. His works include *Canticle,* a book of poems (1936), *So Falls the Elm Tree* (1940) and *Down the Days* (1942).

BRELL, WILLIAM J., P.S.M. (1911–   ), whose birthplace is Witten, Germany (September 8), took his high school, college and philosophical training in Germany. He came to America in September of 1935, and pursued his theological courses at the Catholic University of America, Washington, D. C. A member of the Society of the Pallottine Fathers, he was ordained to the priesthood in June of 1937 at Baltimore, Md. He received his M.A. degree from Marquette University, Milwaukee, Wis., in 1945. At the present time he is teaching at Pallottine College, Milwaukee. Besides writing poetry, he has done a translation of a German play, *The Peasant and the Princess.*

BRIDGES, ROBERT (1844–1930), was born at Walmer, on the Isle of Thanet, and educated at Eton, and at Corpus Christi College, Oxford. He later studied medicine at St. Bartholomew's Hospital, London. After years of success in the medical profession, he was made a Fellow of the Royal College of Physicians and a member of the staff of two London hospitals. In his thirty-eighth year he retired, and devoted his entire time to writing. He was appointed Poet Laureate in 1913. Among his best known works are: *Prometheus the Firegiver* (1884) ; *Eros and Psyche* (1885); *Shorter Poems* (1890–94) ; *October and Other Poems* (1920) ; *New Verse* (1925) ; *The Spirit of Man* (an anthology in English and French) (1916); and *The Testament of Beauty* (1930). He was an intimate friend of Canon Dixon, Digby Dolben, and the Jesuit poet, Gerard Manley Hopkins. It is to Robert Bridges that we owe the preservation and publication of the latter's poems.

BROOKE, RUPERT (1887–1915), was born at Rugby, and educated at King's College, Cambridge. In 1911 he traveled on the continent and in May of 1913 came to New York and traveled through the United States and Canada, sending periodical travel letters to the *Westminster Gazette.* He then sailed to the South Sea Islands, spending three months on Tahiti where he wrote much poetry. He returned to England in 1914, and when war broke out enlisted in the Royal Naval Division. He was commissioned sub-lieutenant, and in February 1915, sailed with the British Mediterranean Fleet for the Dardanelles. When the transport anchored off the coast of Greece he went ashore and was taken suddenly ill of blood-poisoning. Removed to a French hospital, he died April 23, 1915, at Lemnos. His works are: *Poems* (1911) and *Letters from America* (1916). His *Collected Poems,* with a preface by Edward Marsh, were published in 1918.

BROPHY, LIAM (contemporary), lives at "Garnavilla," Ballygall Road, Finglas, Dublin, Eire, and writes for the *Ave Maria, Holy Name Journal, Catholic Digest, The Catholic World* and *The Magnificat* here, and for the *Irish Ecclesiastical Record,* and the *Irish World* in his native Ireland.

BROWNING, ELIZABETH BARRETT (1806–1861), was born in Coxhoe Hall, Durham. Soon after her birth the family moved to the estate of Hope End, near Ledbury, Herefordshire, among the Malvern Hills, where Elizabeth passed her childhood reading

Greek and Latin classics. As a child she wrote an epic, *The Battle of Marathon,* in the style of Pope's *Iliad* which was privately printed by her father. After her mother's death the family moved to Sidmouth, and two years later to a residence in Gloucester Place, London. In 1833 she published *Prometheus and Other Poems;* in 1838, *The Seraphim and Other Poems.* Despite delicate health and confinement to her room, she continued her literary activity, and in 1844 published another volume of poems which included "The Cry of the Children" and "The Lady Geraldine's Courtship." After her meeting with the poet Robert Browning, who literally took her from "her couch to the altar," she went with him to Florence where she spent fifteen happy, busy years until her death. She is especially remembered for the poetic novel, *Aurora Leigh* (1857) and *Sonnets from the Portuguese* (1847, 1850).

BRUNINI, JOHN GILLAND (1899–   ), was born in Vicksburg, Miss., and educated at St. Aloysius College, Vicksburg, and at Georgetown University. He has been the secretary of the Catholic Poetry Society of America since its founding and the editor of *Spirit,* a magazine of verse and the official organ of the society. He has also worked as a reporter for the New York journals and has been on the editorial staff of *The Commonweal.* During the World's Fair in 1939 he was director of Religious Participation. He is the indefatigable organizer of the Catholic Poetry Congresses, held at Fordham University in 1941, on the occasion of the tenth anniversary of the society's founding, and at Hunter College in 1946, the fifteenth anniversary year. His book of poems is entitled *The Mysteries of the Rosary* (1932); *Whereon to Stand* (1946) is a modern synthesis for laymen, of the Church and the Faith.

BUERS, EDWIN, S.D.S. (1901–   ), was born in Essen, Rhineland (September 24), and was educated abroad and at the Catholic University of America, where he pursued special studies in philosophy, taking his Master's degree in philosophy in 1934. A member of the Society of the Divine Savior, he was ordained to the priesthood in the Shrine of the Immaculate Conception, Washington, D. C., June 13, 1933. He was Superior and Rector of the Salvatorian Seminary, St. Nazianz, Wis. (1936–39), of the Salvatorian Monastery, Milwaukee, Wis. (1939–46) and is at present assigned to the Salvatorian Novitiate House, Menominee, Mich. An exceptional scholar, Father Edwin Buers is widely known as a lecturer, missionary and retreat-master.

BURKE, FRANCIS, S.J. (1898–   ), was born in New Jersey and educated at Woodstock, Md., and at Louvain. He was a former lecturer in philosophy at Georgetown University, and has contributed to *Thought*, *The Ecclesiastical Review*, *America*, and *The Commonweal*. He is the author of *Pius XI, Pope of Missions* (1929).

BYROM, JOHN (1692–1763), was born at Broughton, near Manchester, England, of an old country family. His father was a prosperous linen-draper, and young John matriculated in Merchant Taylors' School and at Trinity College, Cambridge. He was an excellent student. In France, where he went for his health after finishing Cambridge, he became an admirer of Malebranche and Bourignon. He later married and became a stenographer. In 1742 he obtained from Parliament the privilege for twenty-one years of teaching his own system of shorthand, a system first published in 1767. He wrote a quantity of religious verse.

BYRON, GEORGE GORDON, LORD (1788–1824), was born in London and attended Harrow and Trinity College, Cambridge. His publication of the first two cantos of *Childe Harold's Pilgrimage* in 1812 established him as one of the great poets of England. In 1815 he married Anne Isabella Milbanke, and their separation the following year with its attendant scandal caused a reversal in public feeling toward Byron, and embittered, he left for Switzerland where he formed a close friendship with Shelley, settled in Italy. A passionate lover of freedom he threw himself into the cause of Greece, then struggling for her independence from Turkey, and died of fever at Missolonghi, April 19, 1824. His works include: *Hours of Idleness* (1807); *English Bards and Scotch Reviewers* (1809); *Childe Harold's Pilgrimage* (1812–16); *The Prisoner of Chillon* (1816); *Beppo* (1817); *Manfred* (1817); *Don Juan* (1819–24); and *The Vision of Judgment* (1822), and many others.

CARLIN, FRANCIS (1881–1945), was born at Bay Shore, Long Island, N. Y., and was educated in St. Mary's School at Norwalk, Conn. He has been a show-maker, a salesman and a floor-walker. His first book, *My Ireland*, was published in 1917, and was followed by *The Cairn of Stars* in 1920. His real name is James Francis Carlin MacDonald.

CARMAN, WILLIAM BLISS (1861–1929), was born at Fredericton, New Brunswick. He was graduated from the University of New Brunswick and later studied at the Universities of Edinburgh and Harvard, after which he read law for two years. He was successively editor, teacher and engineer; but is best known as a poet and lecturer. His first book of poetry was *Low Tide on Grand Pré* (1893) and his last, *Wild Garden* (1929). In 1921 he was crowned Canada's major poet by the Canadian Authors' Association, and in 1928 he was awarded the Lorne Pierce Medal of the Royal Society of Canada, highest literary distinction.

CHANLER, MARGARET (1862–   ), was born in Rome, the daughter of a portrait artist, Luther Terry of Connecticut. Privately tutored, the only formal examination she ever took was for her certificate in piano at the St. Cecilia Conservatory in Rome. She married Winthrop Chanler in 1886, and has six living children. In 1933 she entered the Roman Catholic Church. The novelist, Marion Crawford, became her half-brother when her own mother died and her father married the widow of Thomas Crawford. She was awarded a degree of Doctor of Letters by Nazareth College, Rochester, N. Y.. Her home is at Dudley Farms, Bedford, Mass. She has published *Roman Spring* (1934), *Autumn in the Valley* (1936) and *Hymns to the Church* (1937) a translation of Gertrud von Le Fort's poems. At present she is preparing a book of musical memoirs.

CHARASSON, HENRIETTE (Mme. René Johannet) (1890–   ), is a French poet and critic, who states that her main purpose in writing is "to show foreigners that all French women are not hoydens, Thérèse Desqueyroux's or Albertines dear to Proust." She has published four volumes of verse: *Attente* (1919), *Les Heures Du Foyer* (1926), *Deux Petits Hommes et Leur Mère* (1928) and *Mon Seigneur et Mon Dieu* (1934). It is said of her poetry that "she relates the happenings of daily life, tells her experiences as a mother and prays to God for the things for which all women pray, but she clothes these commonplace acts with poetic sentiments and sings them in lyric notes."

CHAUCER, GEOFFREY (c. 1340–1400), was the son of John Chaucer, vintner, of London. He held various positions in court and in the king's service, and was sent on a mission to Genoa and Florence in 1372–73, when he probably met Boccaccio and Petrarch. His career was varied and colorful, and included secret service to Flanders, embassies to France and Lombardy, controlling of customs in the port of London, knight duties of the shire for Kent, and clerk activities in behalf of the king at many places, including Westminster Abbey. (He made a pilgrimage to Canterbury in the April of 1388. His writing falls into three periods. (1) The period of the French influence, in which he uses the octosyllabic couplet, comprises *The Boke of the Duchesse* (1369) and the *Romaunt of the Rose,* so far as written by Chaucer. (2) The period of Italian influence, which marks the frequent use of the "heroic" stanza of seven lines and the beginning of the employment of the heroic couplet, has the following works: *The House of Fame, The Assembly of Foules, Troylus and Cryseyde, The Legende of Good Women* and the first drafts of some of his tales. (3) The period of his maturity, in which he worked the heroic couplet, witnessed the birth of the *Canterbury Tales,* designed about 1387. His prose works include a translation of Boethius, and a *Treatise on the Astrolabe.* Chaucer stands out as one of the three greatest figures in English literature. Nature had endowed him with broad and ardent interests and with keen and sympathetic understanding. As a writer he developed such imagination and skill that he has preserved for future generations, very much as he saw them, the entire wide diversity of medieval English types, from high to low, in their dress and manners. He died October 25, 1400, and was buried in the south transept of Westminster Abbey, which later became known as Poets' Corner.

CHAVEZ, FRAY ANGELICO (1910–   ), was born in Wagon Mound, N. M., and received his education in the public school at Mora, N. M.; St. Francis Seminary, Cincinnati; Dun Scotus College, Detroit, and the Franciscan Seminary in Oldenburg. He made his solemn profession in the Order of Friars Minor, Detroit, August 18, 1933. Since then, his apostolate has been spent in parochial duties, missionary activities among the Indians and retreat work both in Spanish and in English. As an author he is known for his *Clothed with the Sun* (1939), *New Mexico Triptych* (1940) and numerous magazine articles. His *Eleven Lady-Lyrics* was published in 1946. Fray Angelico is also an artist, specializing in church murals and book illustrations. He has spent the last years as a chaplain in the United States Army.

CHESTERTON, GILBERT KEITH (1874–1936), the son of Edward Chesterton, a retired realtor, whose wife had Scottish and French-Swiss blood in her veins, was born at Camden Hill, Kensington, London. He attended Colet Court and St. Paul's School, and spent a short time at a School of Art in St. John's Wood, whence he passed to Slade School (1892–95). Save for lectures on English at University College, this completed his formal education. In 1901 he married Francis Blogg and in 1922 became a Roman Catholic. His career as a writer was initiated by reviews in the *Bookman* and writings in the *Daily News,* where he not only gained a journalistic and literary reputation, but met many prominent Liberals. His great friendship was that with Hilaire Belloc and the two were often facetiously spoken of as "The Chesterbelloc." He likewise wrote for the *Speaker,* the *Illustrated London News* and a multitude of journals. He founded and edited *G. K.'s Weekly,* and together with Belloc and his own brother Cecil established the *New Witness.* After living in London for a short time he moved to Beaconsfield in the Chiltern Hills, where he died at the age of 62. Chesterton was a high-spirited, combative, opinionated man, leaving on everything he wrote the impress of a strong, whimsical and at times humorous personality. A Galahad of Letters, he devoted his best energies to the defense of the most treasured things of Western culture. The critics insist that he is primarily a poet. His poetry rings with the voice of battle, and treats invariably of themes of crises. Some of his finest poems are those which celebrate the Virgin Mary; Maisie Ward has called him "Our Lady's tumbler." None but the simple, sincere Marian troubadour could exclaim of a torch-light procession at Lourdes, "This is the only real League of Nations." Of his writings in diversified fields are the following: Essay: *All Things Considered* (1908), *Tremendous Trifles* (1909); Fiction: *The Napoleon of Notting Hill* (1903–11), *The Man Who was Thursday* (1930), *The Father Brown Stories* (1933); Polemical views on religious, political and social subjects: *Orthodoxy* (1908–21); History, Literary Criticism, and Art; volumes on Dickens, Stevenson, Blake, Cobbett, Chaucer; Poetry: *Poems* (1922), *Ballad of St. Barbara* (1923), *New Poems* (1929), *Ballad of the White Horse* (1931) and *Queen of Seven Swords* (1933). In 1935 a volume of *Collected Poems* was published, containing the poems of seven previously published books.

CHILDE, WILFRID ROWLAND (1890–   ), was born at Wakefield, Yorkshire, England, and educated at Harrow and Magdalen College, Oxford. He became a Catholic in 1914, and is lecturer in English Literature at the University of Leeds. Of twelve books of poems his best known is *The Gothic Rose* (1923).

CLANCY, LIAM P. (1897–   ), was born in County Clare, Ireland, and for some years was a Civil Servant in both England and Ireland, resigning his post as Customs and Excise Officer in Galway in 1926 to take up a commercial career in London. He returned to Ireland in 1943. He has contributed to many Irish, English and American periodicals, securing several times *The Bookman* award for "the best lyric of the month." One of these lyrics brought a request from faraway South Africa for permission to set the words to music, but the rights had already been acquired by an English publisher. One of the *Catholic World* lyrics has been set to music by an American composer. Besides contributions to *The Bookman* and *The Catholic World,* his lyrics have also appeared in the *Spectator, Pall Mall, Magazine, Poetry and the Play* (London); *Irish Fun, Irish Independent, Sunday Independent* (Dublin); *Columbia,* (United States). Since 1928 he has published some thirty poems in *The Catholic World.*

CLAUDEL, PAUL (1868–   ), was born at Ville-Neuve-sur-Fère, in Tardenois, France. In 1882 his family moved to Paris in order that his sister might study sculpture with Rodin. He attended the Lycée of Louis le Grand, having as companions, Léon Daudet, Fortunat Strowski and Joseph Bédier. It was Renan himself who crowned him at the distribution of prizes at the close of his college career in 1883. Though baptized in the Catholic Church he early came under the influence of scientific materialism and became hostile to religion until his eighteenth year. On Christmas day, while attending High Mass at Notre Dame in Paris with his companions, not out of reverence, but for inspiration, he was struck by grace, and, after some four years of struggle, returned wholeheartedly to the faith of his baptism. Since 1890 both he and his writings have been militantly Catholic. This "unusual ambassador" has served in the French consular service in the United States, Pekin, Prague, Frankfurt, and Hamburg, and as Minister to Brazil, Denmark, Japan, and the United States (1927–33). His dramatic works were gathered together in 1901 and published under the title of *L'Arbre.* Best known among his later dramas are *L'Annonce Faite a Marie,* which in translation was performed by the New York Theatre Guild in 1923–24, and his remarkable *Le Soulier de Satin,* whose message is that "all things minister to a Divine Purpose and so to one another, be it events or personalities. Even the falterings of circumstance and the patternings of personality, sin and falsehood, are made to serve truth and justice, and above all, salvation in the long run." (English translation by Rev. John O'Connor, page ii.) Perhaps the best known of his prose works is his correspondence with Jacques Rivière, the French poet—in its translation known as *Letters to a Doubter*—a vital commentary upon religious thought of the present century. His poetry comprises: *Cinq Grandes Odes* (1910), *Corona Benignitatis Anni Dei* (1914), *Cette Heure qui est entre le Printemps et L'Été* (1913), *La Messe Là-Bas* (1919) and *Feuilles de Saints* (1925).

COLERIDGE, SAMUEL TAYLOR (1772–1834), son of the vicar of Ottery St. Mary, Devon, received his education at Christ's Hospital and at Jesus College, Cambridge, which he left to go to London and enlist in the 15th Dragoons. After a few months he was discharged and returned to Cambridge, where he met Robert Southey, and together they devoted their energies to a pantisocratic dream to be realized on the banks of the Susquehanna. The dream however, collapsed. In 1795 he married Sarah Fricker, whose sister Edith later became the wife of Southey. In 1796 he published a volume of poems and started a periodical, which he had to discontinue at the tenth issue for lack of funds. His friendship with Wordsworth dates from 1797. *The Lyrical Ballads* (1798), written in collaboration with Wordsworth, contain some of his finest work. His *Biographia Literaria* was published in 1817, *Aids to Reflection* in 1825, *Confessions of an Enquiring Spirit* in 1844, *Table Talk* in 1884 and *Anima Poetae* in 1895. His poetic works are: *Poems* (1796), *The Ancient Mariner* (in Lyrical Ballads, 1798), translations of Schiller's *Wallenstein* (1800), *Remorse* (1813), *Christabel, Kubla Khan* (1816), and *Sibylline Leaves* (1817). After a period of ineffectual struggle to throw off the opium habit, Coleridge entered the home of Dr. James Gillman, at Highgate, where he spent the remaining eighteen years of his life.

COLUM, PADRAIC (1881–   ), was born in Longford, Ireland. "My childhood," he writes, "was spent in the Ireland of the countryside and the small market town, of the street-singers and an odd storyteller; the first verses I knew were from ballads I heard sung." He attended school in a town called Kingston, at Dublin, and first gained literary prominence as the editor of the *Irish Review* and a writer of delicate lyrics. In 1914 he came to the

United States where his work was instrumental in acquainting Americans with the current trends in Irish literature. He was one of the founders of the National Theatre Society, which later developed into the Abbey Theatre. Both he and his wife are attached to the Philosophy Department at Columbia University. Among his distinguished writings are: *Wild Earth and Other Poems* (1916–22), *Dramatic Legends and Other Poems* (1922), *Collected Poems* (1932) and *Legend of St. Columba* (1936).

CONNOLLY, FRANCIS X. (1909–   ), was born in New York City (June 24). He received his M. A. degree from Fordham Unisity in 1933, and his Ph.D. degree in 1937. A poet and discerning critic, he has contributed to *America, The Commonweal* and *Spirit*. From 1938 to 1940 he was the editor of *Spain,* and has served several years as lieutenant in the United States Navy. At the present time he is on the English faculty at Fordham University, and is chairman of the board of directors for the Catholic Poetry Society of America.

CONSTABLE, HENRY (1562–1613), was born at Newark, England, and attended Cambridge. After entering the Catholic Church he settled in Paris. On his return to England in 1603 he was imprisoned in the Tower of London. His sonnet-sequence, *Diana,* was published in 1592.

CONSTANTINE OF RHODES (6th or 7th century), translated poems from the Greek. He is the author of three epigrams in the *Greek Anthology*. Reiske supposed him to be the same person as Constantinus Cephalas who compiled the *Palatine Anthology*.

CONTRACTUS, HERMANUS (1013–1054), was born at Altshausen, in Suabia. He was a cripple from birth, hence his surname Contractus. He entered the school of St. Gall at the age of seven and became adept in Greek, Latin, Arabic, history, music, mathematics, philosophy and theology. At the age of thirty he entered the Benedictine monastery of Reichenau, where he became abbot, and spent the remainder of his days. He was one of the most learned men of his time. The hymns "Alma Redemptoris, Mater" and "Salve Regina," are attributed to him. The latter forms a part of the prayers which Pope Leo XIII ordered to be recited after every Low Mass.

CONWAY, MARGARET DEVEREAUX (1921–   ), was born at Wilkes-Barre, Pa. (January 29), and was educated at St. Ann's Academy, Wilkes-Barre (1937), and Marywood College, Scranton (1944). She is now employed in the Youth Department of the National

Catholic Welfare Conference, and is working toward an LL.B. degree at the Catholic University, Washington. Her poems have appeared in leading Catholic literary magazines.

COSMAS, SAINT (d. 760), surnamed the "Melodist," also called Hagiopolites, and Cosmas of Jerusalem, was a hymn-writer of the Greek Church and foster-brother of St. John Damascene. Both Cosmas and his brother went from Damascus to Jerusalem where they became monks in the monastery of St. Sabas near that city. In 743, he was appointed Bishop of Maiuma, the port of ancient Gaza, on the southern coast of Phoenicia. As a prose-writer he contributed commentaries on the poems of Gregory of Nazianzen; as a poet he is highly regarded by the Greek Church. His hymns, though originally intended for the services at Jerusalem, ultimately became universal in the Greek Orthodox Church. His liturgical chant, the "Golden Canon," is considered "the grandest piece in Greek sacred poetry."

CRAPSEY, ADELAIDE (1878–1914), was born in Rochester, N. Y., the daughter of Algernon Sidney and Adelaide Trowbridge Crapsey, the former an Episcopalian clergyman. She enrolled at Kemper Hall, Kenosha, Wisconsin, where she graduated in 1897, and entered Vassar, graduating in 1901. Two years later she began her work as teacher of history and literature in Kemper Hall. In 1905 she went abroad as student in the School of Archaeology in Rome, and the following year taught in Miss Lowe's Preparatory School in Stamford, Conn. In 1908 her health compelled her to abandon teaching, and she spent the following two years in Italy and England working on her *Analysis of English Metrics*. In 1911 she became instructor in Poetics at Smith College, but in 1913 the serious condition of her health forced her to give up her work. The remaining year of her life, spent in exile at Saranac Lake, was one of courage and brave lyric utterance. She herself arranged the collection of her poems, entitled *Verse* posthumously published (1915, 1919).

CRASHAW, RICHARD (1613–1649), was born in London, and was educated at the Charterhouse and at Cambridge, where he obtained a fellowship in 1637. He entered the Catholic Church at Paris. About 1648, through the influence of Cowley, he was introduced to Queen Henrietta Maria, through whom he came in contact with Church dignitaries in Italy, and was named a member of the household of Cardinal Palotta. However, his criticism of the private lives of his Italian companions induced His Eminence to obtain for him a benefice sub-canon at the shrine of Our Lady at Loretto, where he died a few months later. Crashaw is considered one of the greatest religious poets of the Church. His works are the *Epigrammatum Sacrorum Liber* (1634), *Carmen Deo Nostro* (1652) and *The Delights of the Muses* (1648).

CYNEWULF (c. 750–c. 825), probably a Northumbrian poet, was the author of four poems in Old English contained in the *Exeter* and *Vercelli* Books. The epilogues of these poems contain runic characters corresponding to the letters which compose the name Cynewulf. The poems treat of the Ascension, the legend of St. Juliana, the *Elene*, or story of the discovery of the True Cross by the Empress Helena, and the *Fates of the Apostles*. The first of these is found in the manuscript between a poem on the Incarnation and one on the Last Judgment, which have also been doubtfully ascribed to Cynewulf, the three together oftentimes alluded to as the *Christ*. Of the four poems named, the finest is the *Elene*, which consists of fifteen cantos, carrying descriptive passages of great beauty. Certain likenesses between this poem and the *Dream of the Rood* make it possible that Cynewulf was also the author of the latter. "The richness of Cynewulf's work, and its high technical excellence," Margaret Williams notes, "mark his poetry as 'classic.'"

DAVID, KING (born 1085 B.C.), is the name of the second king of Israel, great-grandson of Boaz and Ruth, who was born at Bethlehem and reigned from 1055–1015 B.C. His singing to the accompaniment of his own harp so pleased the restless Saul that he made the youth his armor-bearer for a short time. After his victory over Goliath, the youth won the tender friendship of Jonathan, Saul's son. Jealous of the harpist's popularity at court, Saul made life difficult for him, stipulating that he kill 1000 Philistines before he could marry Michol, Saul's daughter. Even after his success and marriage, he was hated by Saul. His succession to the throne of Saul resulted in the independence of Israel and the building of his famous palace, in addition to other civic improvements. War and famine visited his people and his last days were disturbed by Adonais. In the *Books of Kings* his life is told without palliation of his faults. He actually founded the Jewish dynasty, was tried in the school of suffering. To his son Solomon he bequeathed the completion of organization of the religious worship, very likely planning much of the temple's rebuilding before his death. The important part which music and song played in the ceremonies emphasizes his artistic abilities and appreciation for these arts. Beyond being king and musician, he was a prophet of the Messias with Whom he had in common a birthplace, the role of shepherd, five stones to match the five wounds, and betrayal by a trusted follower. (See also *Psalms, The Book Of.*)

DAVID, SISTER MARY, S.S.N.D., Elizabeth Cameron (1906–   ), was born in Yonkers, N. Y. (November 27), and was educated in the public schools of New York and Maryland, and at the Preparatory School and College of Notre Dame of Maryland in Baltimore, where she was graduated in 1927 with a B.A. degree, and High School teacher's certificate. In August of that year she entered the Congregation of the School Sisters of Notre Dame, and three years later was professed. After some years of teaching in the high schools of her order at Westminster and Cumberland, Md., she returned to her Alma Mater in 1931 as instructor in Latin and History. She has since taught English, French, Greek, and Liturgy, and in 1939 was made assistant librarian. She received her M.A. from Catholic University (1938), and a B.S. in Library Science (1943). She has contributed poems and essays to *America, The Catholic Library World, Contemporary Poetry, Modern Language Notes,* and *Thought.* Her translations include Paul Claudel's *Coronal* (1943), *Brother Lawrence of the Resurrection, The Practice of the Presence of God* (1945).

DEVER, JOSEPH (1919–   ), was born in Boston and is a graduate of Boston College. He is author of "Fifty Missions," which won first prize in the *Yank* short story contest, and has been reprinted several times in anthologies. He is a contributor to *The Sign, America, The Commonweal, Extension* and other religious and literary periodicals.

DE VERE, AUBREY (1814–1902), was born at Curragh Chase, Limerick, Ireland. He studied at Trinity College, Oxford, and at Rome, and in 1857 was received into the Catholic Church. He wrote both drama and poetry, his sonnets being greatly admired by Wordsworth. His chief works are: *The Search After Proserpine* (1843), *May Carols* (1857), *The Legend of St. Patrick* (1872), *Recollections* (1897), and *Medieval Records and Sonnets* (1898).

DONAGHY, WILLIAM A., S.J. (1909–   ), was educated at Holy Cross College, entered the Society of Jesus in 1929, and after studies at Weston College was ordained in 1941. He took graduate work in English at St. Louis University, taught poetry for a year at Holy Cross College and was Rector of a retreat house in N. Andover, Mass. At present he is on the editorial staff of *America*. His poems and critical articles have appeared in many Catholic periodicals. He is remembered for his sonnet sequence, "The Stations of the Cross," which appeared in *Spirit*.

DONNE, JOHN (1573–1631), was born in London, and was reared a Roman Catholic. He received his education at Hart Hall, Oxford, and Cambridge. Later he abjured his Faith, and in 1596 served under Essex in the expedition to Cadiz. On his return he was appointed secretary to Sir Thomas Egerton, Keeper of the Great Seal. During the next years he wrote much poetry. Because of a secret marriage he was dismissed from his office and committed to the Fleet from which he soon obtained his release. He continued to write, his first publication being *The Pseudo-Martyr* (1610), an argument against the attitude of Catholics toward the oath of allegiance, which he composed for the King. He then looked toward the Church for a career, and in 1615 was ordained in London. After living at Keyston in Huntingdonshire, and Sevenoaks in Kent, he was appointed divinity reader at Lincoln's Inn, and in 1621, dean of St. Paul's, where he attained eminence as a preacher. His writings consist of satire, elegies, religious poems, epistles and epigrams. He is one of the first of the so-called Metaphysical Poets of the seventeenth Century, and set a fashion which has been followed in much writing of the late decades. A collection of his poems was published in 1633 and eighty sermons in 1640, to which was prefixed a *Life* by Izaak Walton.

DONOHUE, JAMES J. (1906–   ), was born in Cedar Rapids, Iowa (June 28). He received his B.A. degree from Loras College, Dubuque, Iowa, in 1928, and attended the American College at the University of Louvain, Louvain, Belgium, where he was ordained to the priesthood in 1932. He took his M.A. degree at the Catholic University of America (1935), and his Ph.D. degree at the State University of Iowa (1941). Having served as assistant pastor in Denver, Col., during 1933, he was that year appointed to the faculty of Loras College as professor of English. His publications include: *Hid Battlements,* a pageant (1937), *The Torch-bearers* (1937), *The Theory of Literary Kinds* (1943) and *Exile in the Stars* (1945), a book of poetry based on the Divine Office for the First Sunday of Advent. Three of his dramas have been produced at Loras College: *Hid Battlements* (1938), *The Wranglers* (1944) and *Queen Esther* (1946).

DUFF, JAMES L. (1891–   ), was born in Menlo Park, Cal. (October 24). He is an alumnus of Stanford University and is now a coffee-broker in Los Angeles. A member of the Catholic Poetry Society of America, and poetry editor of *The Tidings*, it was through his efforts that the best poems from *The Tidings*, have been collected in anthologies. His poetry has appeared in Joyce Kilmer's *Anthology of Catholic Poets* and *Drink from the Rock*, as well as in such periodicals as *Poetry, Spirit, America, The New Yorker,* and *Saturday Evening Post.*

DUFFY, JOHN, C.SS.R. (1914–   ), was born in Roxbury, Mass. (May 28), and was educated at the Grammar School of Our Lady of Perpetual Help in Roxbury, St. Mary's College, North East, Pa., Mt. St. Alphonsus, Esopus, N. Y., and the Catholic University of America, Washington, D. C., where he received his doctor's degree in 1944. He made his religious profession as a Redemptorist on August 2, 1935, and was ordained priest on June 23, 1940. His present duties as professor of English are at the Redemptorist Preparatory College, North East, Pa. His poetry has appeared in discriminating Catholic literary magazines, and his book of poems, *Thou and I,* was published in 1947.

DUGGAN, EILEEN (contemporary), was born of Irish parentage at Wellington, New Zealand. She is considered one of the most authentic lyric poets of our time. "Her spirit is Gaelic, her outlook, Catholic," Theodore Maynard says of her. She published *New Zealand Poems* in 1940, and *Poems* in 1937.

DUNBAR, WILLIAM (c. 1460–c. 1520), called "the Chaucer of Scotland," was born probably in East Lothian, and was educated at St. Andrew's University, graduating in 1479. Though little is known of his life, from his poem "Visitation of St. Francis," it appears that he joined the Franciscans and as a begging friar traveled from Berwick to Canterbury. By 1500 he was in the service of James IV of Scotland; in 1501 he visited England with the ambassadors sent to conclude negotiations for the King's marriage to Margaret Tudor. In 1503, he composed an allegorical poem, "The Thistle and the Rose," honoring the Queen's arrival. He was ordained to the priesthood and celebrated his first Mass in 1504, and appears to have lived at court, writing poems and waiting for a benefice. After the defeat of Flodden, the King's death and the regency, his name disappears. He died probably

394

between 1520 and 1530. His writings include: *The Golden Targe, The Two Married Women and the Widow* and *The Dance of the Seven Deadly Sins.*

EGAN, MAURICE FRANCIS (1852–1924), was born in Philadelphia of Irish parentage and studied at La Salle College, Philadelphia, and Georgetown University. He became assistant to James Mc-Master, editor of the *Freeman's Journal,* at whose death he began lectures in English literature at Notre Dame University, and St. Mary's College, South Bend, Ind. Later he was elected professor of English at the Catholic University of America, whence he was sent as American minister to Copenhagen, remaining in Denmark until 1918. President Theodore Roosevelt termed him "unofficial diplomatic adviser" of three presidents. He thus stated his literary creed: "God, Who is center of life, is the center of the written expression of life, which is literature." His works include: *Songs and Sonnets* (1885), *Lectures in English Literature* (1889), *St. Martin's Summer* (1905), *Amélie in France* (1912), *Everybody's St. Francis* (1912), *The Ivy Hedge* (1914) and *Ten Years on the German Frontier* (1919).

ELIOT, THOMAS STEARNS (1888–   ), was born in St. Louis (September 26), and was educated at Harvard, the Sorbonne, and Oxford. His father, a prominent St. Louis businessman, was the son of the Reverend William Greenleaf Eliot, who had established the first Unitarian Church in St. Louis. In the spring of 1915 he married an Englishwoman, Vivienne Haigh, and since that time has resided in London. His first poems were published that same year (1915) in *Poetry: A Magazine of Verse,* of which Ezra Pound was foreign editor. In 1922 *The Waste Land* appeared, for which he received the *Dial* award of two thousand dollars. Among his critical works are *The Sacred Wood* (1920), *For Lancelot Andrewes* (1928), *John Dryden* (1932), *Selected Essays* (1932). In 1926 Eliot was Clark Lecturer in Trinity College, Cambridge; in 1932 he returned to the United States as Charles Eliot Norton, Professor of Poetry at Harvard (1932–33), and in 1933 gave the Page-Barbour lectures at the University of Virginia. He holds the honorary degree of Litt.D. from the universities of Columbia, Cambridge, Bristol, Leeds, Edinburgh, and is an honorary Fellow of Magdalen College, Oxford. His most recent volume of poetry, *Four Quartets* (1943) has been much admired. As a literary critic, Dr. Eliot has exerted a great influence on contemporary literature.

ENGELS, NORBERT (1903–   ), a native of Green Bay, Wis., attended the parish schools and the public high schools of that city, and later the University of Notre Dame, where he took a degree in music in 1926. He married Eleanore Perry of Hillsdale, Mich., in 1929. He has toured Europe, taught music in Green Bay and is now instructor in English at the University of Notre Dame. His poems appear in current literary periodicals.

ENNODIUS, MAGNUS FELIX (474–521), was bishop of Ticinum (Pavia), having been appointed to that see by Pope Hormisdas in 514. He was sent on two occasions as ambassador to Constantinople, but was unsuccessful in his attempt to heal the schism between the Eastern and Western Church. He is distinguished by his championing the papacy. His "Hymnus Sanctae Marie" is the first long poem entirely devoted to the praise of Our Lady.

EPHREM, SAINT, THE SYRIAN (c. 310–373), was born in Nisibis, Mesopotamia, and in his young manhood, was instructed and baptized by St. James, bishop of his birthplace. His controversy with the heretic Bardesanes and his followers is one among the many in which he fearlessly engaged. Beyond his deep influence on the Syrian Christians of Edessa, his career is obscure. As one of the founders and most distinguished teachers of the Christian Persian School at Nisibis, he wrote many scriptural commentaries, among them one on the apocryphal Third Epistle to the Corinthians; he also made a text of the Acts of the Apostles. The rest of his works are homilies and hymns, many of the latter being versified sermons. For use in nuns' choirs, he divides some of the hymns into strophes, the last verses of each strophe serving as the repeated refrain. Not the inventor but the supreme artist in Syriac poetry, he must be judged in his own time and setting, without Greek prejudice. Called "the Harp of the Holy Ghost," he has the distinction of being the first Christian writer of hymns. He was proclaimed Doctor of the Church by Pope Benedict XV in 1920.

EPIGRAMS, THE CHRISTIAN, are to be found among the some 4000 verses in *The Greek Anthology*. Book I of the anthology presents the later Christian epigrams, which are for the most part inscriptions from Byzantine Churches, at the time when the language of the Church was Greek. In *The Greek Anthology*, translated and edited by Shane Leslie (Ernest Benn, London, 1929) are found the epigrams to the crucifix and to the ikon of Our Lady, by Constantine of Rhodes, the latter of which is included in this anthology.

ERASMUS, DESIDERIUS (1467–1536), the great Dutch humanist, was born at Rotterdam. One of the most conspicuous figures of the Renaissance, at the age of nine he was the pupil of Hegius at Deventer and then squandered two years at the monastery school of Hertogenbosch. Urged by material necessity only and with no belief in his vocation, he was ordained to the priesthood. His tremendous learning, spontaneous wit and careful style set him up as a model for his contemporaries. At Paris in 1496 he fostered a sturdy contempt for scholasticism. Two years later at Oxford he came under the influence of Colet and Thomas More and began a study of Scripture. He undertook the first scholarly modern edition of the New Testament, *Novum Instrumentum,* with a commentary, which was published in 1516. Other works of his are: *Encomium Moriae* ("The Praise of Folly"), 1512, a satire suggested by More, chiefly aimed at theologians and Church dignitaries; *Enchiridion Militis Christiani,* 1503, a manual of piety; *Institutio Christiani Principis* ("Education of a Christian Prince"), giving autobiographical data and commentary on contemporary life; and *Adagia,* 1500, an assemblage of Latin and Greek proverbs. He freely expressed his antagonism towards Lutheranism, harshly criticized the medieval philosophers and theologians, and wrote with bitterness against ecclesiastical abuses. He condemned the religious life, and although he neither repudiated the Catholic Faith nor denied the authority of the Holy See, he did a great deal to propagate the spirit of mockery and irreverence.

EUGENIUS III, BLESSED BERNARDO PIGNATELLI (d. 1153), born at Pisa, was somewhat forcibly elected to the papacy, in 1145, as the successor to Eugenius II. Famous for initiating the dual system of government for church and state and for the unsuccessful Second Crusade, in the great Synod of Rheims of 1148 he did much to enact canons regarding dress and conduct of the clergy, particularly in France whence he had fled in 1146. An observant Cistercian throughout his religious life, his charity and mildness impressed all who had occasion to meet him. He was admired by his confrère, St. Bernard, who wrote for him the estimable papal handbook, *De Consideratione.*

FABER, FREDERICK WILLIAM (1814–1863), was born in Yorkshire, England, received his education at Shrewsbury, Harrow and Balliol

College. Puzzled by Calvinism and the philosophy of Newman, the Tractarian Movement drew him ultimately to conversion in 1845. Already an ordained Anglican, he received Holy Orders in 1847, and became a novice under Newman in the then incipient Oratory of St. Philip Neri of Maryvale. He soon founded a new Oratory in London where, in poverty of circumstance and fervor of religious dedication, he began to write sermons and the hymns for his own services. With the works published by him in that period his reputation was established: *All for Jesus* (1853), *Growth in Holiness* (1854), *The Blessed Sacrament* (1855), *The Creator and the Creature* (1858), *The Foot of the Cross* (1858), *Spiritual Conferences* (1859), *The Precious Blood* (1860) and *Bethlehem* (1860). The *Lives of Modern Saints* begun by him in 1847, are not so much biographies as studies of the operations of grace and the attainment of perfection. He also wrote two volumes of *Notes on Doctrinal Subjects* (1866). He claimed friendship with both Newman and Coleridge.

FABYAN, ROBERT (d. 1513), an English chronicler, and sheriff of London in 1493, vainly attempted to combine his London history with that of the country. His *Concordance of Histories* (first printed in 1516), a compilation commemorating this effort, extends from the arrival of Brutus in England to the death of Henry VII.

FARREN, ROBERT (Roibéard O Faracháin) (1909–   ), was born in Dublin, and studied at St. Patrick's Training College and the National University of Ireland. He was a teacher at the latter place from 1929 to 1930. A supervisor of radio work, and a director at the Abbey Theatre since 1940, he is also the author of *Thronging Feet* (1936), *Time's Wall Asunder* (1939) and *This Man Was Ireland* (1943). The latter book, an epic on the life of St. Colmcille, has elicited high praise from critics everywhere.

FEENEY, LEONARD, S.J. (1897–   ), was born in Lynn, Mass. (February 15), and was educated at St. Andrew-on-the-Hudson, novitiate of the Jesuits of the Eastern Province, Poughkeepsie, N. Y., Woodstock College, Woodstock, Md., and Weston College, Weston, Mass. After his ordination to the priesthood, he spent two years in Europe, studying at Oxford and the Sorbonne. He was instructor in English at Boston College (1931–36), literary editor of *America* (1936–40), and is now advising Catholic students at Harvard. He is a past president of the Catholic Poetry Society of America. Among his essays are: *Fish on Friday* (1934) and *You'd Better Come Quietly* (1939). He has written *An American Woman* (1936), a biography of Mother Seton, and several volumes of verse: *In Towns and Little Towns* (1927), *Riddle and Reverie* (1933), *Song for a Listener* (1936), and recently the verses in *Your Second Childhood* (1945).

FORTUNATUS, VENANTIUS (530–c. 609), was born near Treviso, Italy, and received his education at Ravenna. A troubadour wandering through Germany and France, absorbing classical knowledge and a rare command of the ancient meters, he settled at Poitiers where St. Radegunde had founded an imposing monastery. Under her beneficent influence he was ordained priest in 567, became chaplain of the monastery of Saint Croix, and in 597 was raised to the see of Poitiers. The simplicity of the man veils the keenness of the scholar more often than not. Voluminous and versatile as his writings are, he has often been underrated. He wrote the favorite hymn of the crusaders, "Vexilla Regis" (569) for the procession which honored the relic of the true Cross, received in Poitiers by the Emperor Justin. Thought by Raby to be superior to the "Vexilla Regis" is the "Pange Lingua," composed for the same occasion. The "Quem Terra, Pontus, Sidera," in honor of the Virgin Mother, is ascribed to him by ancient manuscripts.

GALVIN, JAMES J., C.SS.R. (1911–   ), was born at Newton Centre, Mass. (April 22), and made his studies at Our Lady of Perpetual Help Grammar School, Roxbury, Mass., St. Mary's College, North East, Pa., and Mt. St. Alphonsus, N. Y. He made his religious profession as a Redemptorist in 1932, and was ordained to the priesthood in 1937. After an assignment to the foreign missions of Puerto Rico (1939–42), he returned to the United States and has become editor of the Redemptorist magazine, *Our Lady of Perpetual Help*. He is a member of the Catholic Poetry Society of America. Some of his finest poetry has been printed in *Spirit*, among which is "The Song of the Khaki Christ."

GOETHE, JOHANN WOLFGANG VON (1748–1832), born at Frankfort-on-the-Main, the son of an Imperial Councillor, ranks with Voltaire and Rousseau in European literature, although he was more reverent than either of his predecessors. Schiller's friendship was happily influential in his life. He attended the University of Leipzig, and that of Strassburg, and wrote drama in both places. His most comprehensive work, the great dramatic poem, *Faust*, was in the process of completion throughout half of his life. A novel, *The Sorrows of Werther*, published in 1774, made him famous. In his writings Goethe covers a wide range, from translations and other prose works to classic poetry and drama. He is buried beside his friend, Schiller, in the ducal vault at Weimar.

GREEN, JULIAN (1900–   ), was born of American parents in Paris, where at the age of fifteen he became a Catholic. In joint authorship with Jacques Maritain he published *Oeuvres Nouvelles*. His novels are for the most part introspective tales of psychic gloom. Until *Memories of Happy Days* appeared in 1942, his writings were all in French. His recent translations of French authors are highly commendable, particularly his rendering of the poetry of Charles Péguy. He is likewise an alert critic, thorough and discerning.

GROSSETESTE, ROBERT (1175–1253), native of Suffolk, and trained at Oxford and at Paris, was a learned philosopher and scholar, and at one time head of Oxford. He later became Bishop of Lincoln. His interest lay predominantly in moral questions. *The Eudemian Ethics* and *The Nichomachean* are his most valuable Aristotelian translations. So trustworthy are his translations of the letters of St. Ignatius, that they have been used by the Cambridge Modern History to set the date of the Christian Renaissance. Despite controversy relative to the visitation of religious houses and his relations with the papacy, after his death he was commended for heroic virtue.

GUINEY, LOUISE IMOGEN (1861–1920), was born at Roxbury, Mass., of mingled Irish, Scotch and French ancestry, and was educated in private schools in Providence. After the death of her father, a general in the Union Army, she was for several years postmistress of Auburndale, and then cataloguer in the Boston Public Library. From 1901 she lived in England, and is buried at Oxford. With her duties of literary editor, essayist and poet, she kept up a voluminous correspondence. Her verse is spontaneous and full of courage. Notable among her books are *The White Sail and Other Poems* (1887), *A Roadside Harp* (1893), which she believed was her "best book," and *Patrins* (1897), a group of essays. She devoted years of preparation for a book on Henry Vaughan, the Silurist, which her death left unfinished. Her likewise incomplete *Recusant Poets,* which she and the Reverend Geoffrey Bliss, S.J., had compiled with so much labor, was published in 1939.

HAWKER, ROBERT STEPHEN (1803–1875), was born at Plymouth. As student at the Cheltenham Grammar School he published *Tendrils* in 1821. Two years later he married, and in 1827, during undergraduate studies at Oxford won the Newdigate Prize for a poem on Pompei. He took his degree in 1828 and orders in the Anglican Church in 1831. He became vicar of Morwenstow where he restored the church, established a school and cared for the shipwrecked. In 1832 he published *Records of a Western Shore*. His best poems are "The Quest of the San Graal" and the "Ballad of Trelawney." On his deathbed he was received into the Roman Catholic Church.

HAYES, JAMES M. (1875–   ), was born at Wexford, Ireland, of American parents visiting in Ireland. He was educated at All Saints School and St. Ignatius College, Chicago, and at St. Mary's Seminary, Baltimore. Ordained to the priesthood by Cardinal Gibbons in 1898, he became Rector of Sacred Heart Cathedral, Dallas, Texas, the following year, and in 1904 chancellor of the diocese of Dallas. He served as instructor in English at the Catholic University and at Catholic Sisters' College, Washington, D. C. (1921–24). From 1915 to 1924 he edited *The Sisters' College Messenger* at the Catholic University of America. His works are: *The Grave of Dreams* (1917), *Arrows of Desire* (1928), *History of the Bon Secours Sisters in the U. S.* (1931) and *In Praise of Nuns,* an anthology of verse (1942).

HEBERT, ALBERT J., JR. (1913–   ), was born in New Orleans (October 4), and educated in parochial schools. He spent three years in the European Theatre of Operations with the Eighth and Ninth Air Forces and Air Disarmament Command. As D/Sgt., he saw service in Ireland, England, France, Luxembourg and Germany. Of these years he treasures especially a "pilgrimage" to the ancient shrine of Our Lady of Walsingham in England, and visits to Our Lady of Buckfast, Devon, Notre Dame de Paris, Notre Dame de Reims, Notre Dame de la Garde at Marseilles, and Our Lady of Luxembourg. He is a charter member of the New Orleans Catholic Evidence Guild, and a licensed general chairman. At present he is pursuing higher studies. He has contributed fiction and non-fiction to such magazines as *Extension, St. Anthony's Messenger* and *The Savior's Call;* poetry to *Spirit, America, The Magnificat, Extension,* and other periodicals. He is a member of the Catholic Poetry Society of America.

HEMENWAY, ABBY MARIA (1828–1899), who wrote under the pseudonym "Marie Josephine," lived at Ludlow, Vt., and was an editor and historian of the counties and towns in her own state. She is the author of a trilogy of poems dealing with Our Lady and St. Joseph, *Mary of Nazareth*, in seven books (1867), *Rosa Immaculata or the Tower of Ivory* (1867), and *The Saint of Nazareth*, a life of St. Joseph (1873). In her foreword to the first book she wrote: "The Holy Family belong to the world; we took as our motto, and have appropriated every coveted relic or tradition handed down by historians, Christian or pagan, from the archives of Latin Church, Hebrew, or Greek, coming within scope of our original plan, only careful to note wherever a tradition has been thus introduced." The book grew, she says, "in the quiet of Sabbaths, in the calms before the ringing of bells, in the hush of holy eves," and touchingly adds, "Never felt we incompleteness as in this. . . . Go forth, and tell in the garden of Mary every breeze sighs of Him whom to know is life and love." In 1860 she edited *Poets and Poetry of Vermont*, and in 1863, *Songs of the War*.

HESS, M. WHITCOMB (1893–   ), studied philosophy and took degrees at Ohio University. Now residing at Athens, Ohio, she is the author of *The Name Is Living*, and a contributor to the philosophic reviews. Her poem in this anthology was written some years before her conversion to the Catholic Church, "which came," she states, "as I know completely, by Our Lady's prayers." She was baptized on the eve of the Assumption, and received her first Holy Communion on the Feast of the Assumption, 1942.

HINKSON, KATHERINE TYNAN (1861–1931), was born at Clondalkin, Dublin, Ireland, and educated at the Dominican convent, Drogheda. She was one of the leaders in the Celtic branch of the Catholic Literary Revival. A close friend of the Meynells, she was oftentimes a visitor at Palace Court where Alice held her literary salon, and was often accompanied thither by William Butler Yeats. She was the youngest contributor to the volume *Poems and Ballads of Your Ireland* published in 1888. In 1885 she had published *Louise de la Vallière and Other Poems*, and *Shamrocks* in 1887. Her best work is perhaps *Ballads and Lyrics* (1891). In 1922 she published *The Wandering Years*. Her *Collected Poems* appeared in 1930.

HOPKINS, GERARD MANLEY, S.J. (1844–1889), was born in the town of Stratford, Essex. He attended Highgate School and Balliol

College, Oxford, where he became the pupil of Jowett and Pater. Among his friends were Robert Bridges and Digby M. Dolben, and later in life, Coventry Patmore. Before his conversion to the Catholic Church in 1866 he had been a disciple of Pusey and Liddon; afterwards he allied himself with Cardinal Newman. In 1868 he entered the Jesuit novitiate, and was active in parish work until 1884 when he was appointed to the chair of Greek at Dublin University. A poet of remarkable originality, his "sprung rhythm," "inscape" and "instress" are among his cardinal legacies to the world of letters. John Pick, outstanding Hopkins scholar, has well summarized the life and writing of this priest and poet with the statement: "(he is) at the same time a priest true to heaven and a poet true to earth . . . all that (he) ever wrote (is his) *Laudate Dominum* in which he calls on all creation to praise their Creator." His last years were weighted with soul anguish. Though, as Dr. Pick remarks, "for Hopkins spiritual aridity was poetic aridity," he yet wrote the seven sonnets "which bear the marks of having issued from his soul in a catharsis of his burdened spirit." Yet there was a supreme triumph in the very last moments of his life: as he lay dying, he repeated three times the words, "I am so happy." His works are: *Poems of Gerard Manley Hopkins*, edited by Robert Bridges (1918), and *Letters*, edited by Claude Colleer Abbott (1935). *Gerard Manley Hopkins, Priest and Poet* (1943) by John Pick, is a discerning critical study of the spiritual wellsprings of his poetry.

THE HOROLOGIUM is the Latin title of the Hours of the *Menaea*. See *Menaea*.

HOUSELANDER, CARYLL (contemporary), who works in a London office doing advertising layouts, is also an artist with words. Her book *This War Is the Passion* (1940) surprised the world with its beauty, its freshness, its sound penetration of spiritual truth and its intangible impression of sympathy for all souls. *The Reed of God* (1943) another unique volume, deals with the joys and sorrows of the Virgin Mary. The author's plan of "rhythms" is demonstrated in the book, *The Flowering Tree* (1945). "The idea that I have," she states in a letter to Maisie Ward, "is that we are part, as it were, of a vast rhythm, and that when we become more recollected we become more and more conscious of it." She sees this Rhythm as part of God's arrangement for human living manifested by the cycles of the seasons, by the

Church's liturgy through the year, even by dawn, day and night's darkness. She believes that the writing of rhythms, or even the reading of them, becomes by practice a definite help to recollection.

HOUSMAN, LAURENCE (1865–   ), brother of the poet, A. E., is an English dramatist, novelist, poet and illustrator. At eighteen he went with his sister to London for an education in art. Some five or six years later he began to write, beginning with fairy tales, legends and poems, which he himself illustrated. Between 1912 and 1918 he published three novels. He considers his play on the life of St. Francis his best work. In America his *Victoria Regina,* with Helen Hayes in the title role, was a great success. Agnes Repplier called him "so brilliantly versatile that there is hardly a field of letters which he has left untried and unadorned." His plays are numerous. His poems include: *Spikenard* (1898), *Rue* (1899), *Selected Poems* (1909), *The Heart of Peace* (1919), *The Love Concealed* (1928) and *Collected Poems* (1937).

HOW, LOUIS (contemporary), was born in St. Louis, Mo., and educated at Harvard. He served in the Spanish American War. He is best known as a translator for his translation of *Montaigne's Essay on Friendship and Twenty-nine Sonnets by Étienne de la Boétie,* published by Houghton Mifflin and now a collector's item. Professor Northrup considers his translation from the Spanish of *Lazarillo de Tormes* the finest in existence. His translation of Baroja's *Caesar or Nothing,* and his poems, *Nursery Rhymes of New York City,* were published by Knopf. A second and illustrated edition of this latter volume, *Narcissus, The Other Don Juan, The Years Relent, Regional Rhymes of New York City, An Evening with Ninon,* and *The Divine Comedy of Dante* were published by the Harbor Press. His American version of Dante was undertaken "to convey some adumbration of the interest and charm of the 'Divine Comedy'; to make a readable version of a great classic that is eminently readable."

IGNATIUS, SISTER MARY, C.S.J., Anna Meany (1907–   ), who was born and raised in Brooklyn, attended St. Jerome's School and St. James Academy there, received her B.A. degree from St. Joseph's College for Women and her M.A. from the Catholic University of America, Washington, D.C. At present she is teaching English at St. Angela Hall Academy, Brooklyn, and is writing her dissertation in partial fulfillment of the Ph.D. requirements at St. John's University, Brooklyn. Her poems have appeared in *America, The Sign, Spirit, Sentinel of the Blessed Sacrament* and *The Magnificat*.

ISAIAS (died c.690 B.C.), whose name signifies "Yahweh is salvation," is foremost among the Latter Prophets. Details of his life are obscure. Said to be the son of Amos (not the Prophet), he is believed to have been about twenty years old when he began his ministry, from the closing year of Ozias, King of Juda, possibly up to that of Manasses. His book in the Bible is a collection of prophecies, uttered during many years and on many different occasions. They are all in Hebrew verse with the exception of the thirty-sixth and thirty-ninth chapters, which are historical and in prose. The Book of Isaias contains a number of Messianic prophecies which make it a gospel before the Gospel. In 1908 The Biblical Commission issued a declaration defending the unity and the truly prophetic character of the book. Isaias is traditionally believed to have died a martyr under the wicked king Manasses and is named in the Roman Martyrology on July 6.

JACAPONE DA TODI (1228–1306), was properly known as Jacopo Benedicti or Benedetti. After witnessing the tragic death of his young wife, he forsook the world, donned the garb of a Franciscan tertiary, did severe penance and for ten years roamed the Italian highways, scandalizing his conservative family and friends by his religious enthusiasms. As a lay brother of the Order of Friars Minor, he sided vehemently with the Spirituales whom Boniface VIII had deprived of certain privileges. From his prison fortress he wrote some of his most touching and aggressive lines. After five years' incarceration he was released by Benedict XI, and finally retired to a convent of St. Clare near Todi. His friend, Blessed LaVerna, administered to him the Last Sacraments just before death. Most of his poems are in the Umbrian dialect. The sequence "Stabat Mater Dolorosa" is attributed to him.

JOHN OF THE CROSS, SAINT (1542–1591), co-founder with St. Teresa, of the Carmelite Reform, was born in Fontiveros in Old Castile, the youngest child of Gonzalo de Yepes and Catherine Alvarez. His father, disinherited for marrying beneath him, earned his living as a silk-weaver, and, at his death left his wife and three children almost destitute. Young John attended the poor-school at Medina del Campo and, while continuing his studies at the Jesuit college acted as servant in the hospital. When he was twenty-one he received the Carmelite habit and the name of John of St. Mathias; in 1567 he was ordained to the priesthood. At a moment when, through a desire for greater austerity and retirement, he was considering a transference to the Carthusians, St. Teresa came to Medina and, hearing of John's virtues, asked to see him. In their conversation she told him pointedly that God wished him to become a member of the Reform (Discalced Carmelites) which she was establishing. Accordingly, he joined their first monastery in Duruelo and took the name of John of the Cross. It was here that he entered deeply into a life of contemplation. In 1571 he became spiritual director of the convent of the Incarnation at Avila, and his counsel was sought by religious and seculars alike. Teresa wrote of him to Philip II, "The people take him for a saint." However, in the difficulties between the Mitigated and Discalced branches of the order, St. John became innocently involved, and was carried off to prison at Toledo, placed in a small cell, and treated with much severity. It was here in seclusion and suffering that many of his great poems were written. After nine months he was freed and made superior of the little convent at Calvary; in 1579 he founded that of Baeza, and in 1581 became prior of Granada. In the negotiations which surrounded the establishment of the Discalced Carmelites as a distinct province, St. John took little part, but devoted his time to the great writings for which he has been acclaimed a Doctor of Mystical Theology. They are: *The Ascent of Mount Carmel, The Dark Night, The Living Flame of Love* and *The Spiritual Canticle,* all stamped with the seal of Catholic traditional teaching. In 1582, after St. Teresa's death, opposition was again stirred up against him, and in the status of a simple friar he was sent to the house at Peñuela. Taken ill, he was ordered out of Peñuela, with choice of Baeza, where a friend of his was prior, or Ubeda, where one who was not his friend presided. He chose the latter, and after some three months of even brutal treatment, died December 14, 1591, still under the cloud which certain members of his own order had raised against him. After his death his sanctity was at once acknowledged. He was beatified in 1675, canonized in 1726 and, for his mystical writings proclaimed a Doctor of the Church, in 1926. A biography, *St. John of the Cross,* by the Carmelite, Fr. Bruno, with introduction by Jacques Maritain, published in 1936, is the most excellent and authoritative work on St. John. *The Complete Works of*

St. John of the Cross, edited by E. Allison Peers, has been reprinted by the Newman Book Shop, Westminster, Md. (1945).

JOHN THE EVANGELIST, SAINT (died c.100), was the son of Zebedee and the brother of James who shared with him Christ's epithet, "Sons of Thunder." He was called "the disciple whom Jesus loved," and his presence at the raising to life of Jairus' daughter, the Transfiguration, the Agony in Gethsemane and beneath the cross on Calvary, only verified the esteem in which Christ held him. One of the Twelve Apostles, he is also known as "the Theologian" or "the Divine." After the first Pentecost he aided Peter in guiding the early Church and shared with him imprisonment. For about twelve years he labored in Palestine, fleeing during the persecution of Herod Agrippa I, returning in 51 for the Apostolic Council and apparently leaving again about 52 or 55. Tradition holds that he died at an advanced age in Ephesus, having returned from a long exile on the island of Patmos. The Church in the West keeps his feast on December 27. He is the only one of the Apostles who did not die a martyr. He is author of the Gospel which bears his name, three canonical epistles, and the *Apocalypse.*

JOHNSON, LIONEL (1867–1902), a native of Broadstairs, Kent, attended Durham Down, Clifton, Winchester College and New College, Oxford. From his early boyhood he wrote verse. On leaving Oxford in 1890 he went to London where he began a literary career by writing scholarly reviews for the *Academy, Anti-Jacobin, National Observer, Daily Chronicle, Pall Mall Gazette* and other journals. Some of his early poems appeared in the *Century Guild Hobby-Horse* and in the first and second *Book of the Rhymers' Club* (1892–94). In 1891 he became a Roman Catholic. Asceticism, reverence for Catholic tradition, sympathy with orthodox mysticism and a love of the niceties of ritual became thereafter the prevailing subject-matter of his poems. He wrote well in Latin, and even his English verse carries a strong Latin flavor. His critical writings are supreme. "Poet and critic" he called himself. Considered by many as the most definite literary personality of the '90's, he numbered among his friends William Butler Yeats, Katherine Tynan Hinkson, Walter Pater, the Meynells, Louise Imogen Guiney and a score of others; the quaint italicized dedications under his individual poems are a record of both his friends and his heroes. His death was the result of an accident. Among his best works are: *The Art of*

Thomas Hardy (1894), *Poems* (1895), *Ireland, with Other Poems* (1897), and *Post Liminium: Essays and Critical Papers* (1911). John Pick is at present preparing a critical-biographical study of Lionel Johnson.

JONSON, BEN (1573–1637), English dramatist whose birthplace was Westminster, served in the English constituent in the Low Countries. He and Shakespeare were friends, and when in 1598 *Every Man in His Humor* was produced, Shakespeare played a part in it. *Eastward Ho!, Sejanus* (1604), and *Volpone* (1605) followed, and were produced successfully. The most elaborate of his writings is *The Alchemist* (1610). "Drink to Me Only with Thine Eyes" remains the best known of his songs. He likewise wrote numerous elegies, epistles, epigrams, lyrics and epitaphs. In 1638 a memorial volume of his poems, entitled *Jonsonus Virbius,* was published.

KAYE-SMITH, SHEILA (1888–   ), was born at St. Leonards-on-Sea, near Hastings, England, and educated privately. In 1924 she married T. Penrose Fry, an Anglican minister, and in 1929 both she and her husband entered the Church of Rome. Her art has for the most part been developed away from Catholicism. Among her novels are: *Sussex Gorse* (1916), *Tamarisk Town* (1919), *Joanna Godden* (1922), *The End of the House of Alard* (1923), *Shepherds in Sackcloth* (1930), *Superstition Corner* (1934) and *Gallybird* (1934).

KEITH, JOSEPH JOEL (1908–   ), a native of Pittsburgh, now claims Los Angeles as his home. He is a member of the Catholic Poetry Society of America, Secretary-Treasurer of the Los Angeles Center of the P.E.N. Club, a world association of professional writers, director of publicity for the Book and Author Club and host to guest speakers at the Ambassador Hotel (Los Angeles) meetings. He has written texts for music published by C. C. Birchard of Boston, and is the author of the poetry volumes, *The Proud People* (1943), *The Long Nights* (1944), and *The Hearth Lit* (1946). His poems have been published in the following magazines: *America, The Saturday Review of Literature, Spirit, The Saturday Evening Post, Poetry, Ladies' Home Journal, The New York Times Book Review, Argosy* (London) and *Comment* (Australia). He has also had poems included in these anthologies: Moult's *Jonathan Cape;* Harcourt Brace's *Best Poems of 1941; Best Poems of 1942* and *Best Poems of 1943; The Tidings Poets,* vols. 1, 2 and 3; *This Is My America* (best poems chosen by Kenton Kilmer from *The Washington Post*); *Prairie Schooner Caravan,* and *Drink From the Rock.*

KILMER, JOYCE (1886–1918), was born in New Brunswick, N. J., and was graduated from Rutgers (1904) and Columbia (1906). After graduation from Columbia he taught for a year at a New Jersey preparatory school. In 1916 both he and his wife Aline, herself a distinguished poet, entered the Catholic Church. Of that event he remarked, "If what I write nowadays is considered poetry, then I became a poet in November, 1913" (date of his reception into the Church). When America entered the war he enlisted at once. He was killed while leading an attack on a machine-gun nest in the summer offensive of 1918. No one poet did more for the Catholic Revival as an American literary movement than did he. His works include: *Circus and Other Essays* (1916), *Dreams and Images* (1917), *Main Street and Other Poems* (1917), *Trees* (1914–24). In 1940 a collection, *Joyce Kilmer* (poems, essays, letters) was published with a memoir by Robert Cortes Holliday. His *Anthology of Catholic Poets* (1917–37) is well known.

KING, MARY (WHITE) (1904–   ), adopted daughter of Sir Frederick Truby, late Director of Child Welfare in New Zealand, was born in Dunedin, N. Z., and educated in a private school. Since 1928 she has resided in Adelaide, Australia, and is married to Anthony H. White (late Flg. Lieut. R.A.A.F.) and has one child. She was received into the Catholic Church in Sidney in 1931. Her works include: *Mothercraft,* a simple handbook for mothers and nurses on the Truby King system of child-rearing (now in its 17th edition), and *Mary of Bethlehem and Other Poems* (1944), poems of keen spiritual vision, many of which have first appeared in *The Southern Cross, Australian Woman's Mirror,* and other periodicals. Her biography of Frederick Truby King will shortly be published by Messrs. George Allen and Unwin, London.

KIPLING, RUDYARD (1865–1936), was born in Bombay, India, and was educated there and in England. He began to write at an early age, his first volume of verse, *Departmental Ditties,* appearing when he was but twenty-one, and his first volume of stories, *Plain Tales from the Hills,* a year later. When he arrived in London in 1890, he found himself famous. From 1892, when he married the daughter of H. Wolcott Balestier of New York and settled in Vermont, he remained in the United States until 1896. To this second period of his life belong the *Barrack Room Ballads* (1892), *The Seven Seas,* poems (1896), and much fiction. His two poems, "The Recessional" (1897), written on the occasion of Queen Victoria's Diamond Jubilee, and "The White Man's Burden," became especially popular. In 1907 he was awarded the Nobel Prize for Literature. He was rector of the University of St. Andrew's (1922–25), Doctor of Philosophy at Athens (1924) and received the gold medal of the Royal Society of Literature (1926). During World War I, in which his only son was killed, he wrote much on subjects connected with the British army and nation.

LAMB, CHARLES (1775–1834), and MARY ANN (1764–1847), collaborated in *Tales from Shakespeare* (1807), *Mrs. Leicester's School* (1807) and *Poetry for Children* (1809). Charles' individuality had already been apparent in *Old Familiar Faces,* published in 1798, in which year he likewise published a little prose romance, *The Tale of Rosamund Gray.* In 1820 his first essay appeared in the pages of the *London Magazine:* "Recollections of the Old South Sea House," to which he attached the famous pseudonym Elia, which clung to him ever after. The *Last Essays of Elia* were collected in a second volume in 1833.

LAMENT OF WALSINGHAM, THE, is of debatable authorship. In the January 1896 issue of *The Month,* Father Thurston has suggested Blessed Robert Southwell as its possible author. The poem has also been attributed without any proof to Blessed Philip Howard, Earl of Arundel. It was printed by Hale and Furnivall and Edmund Waterton. Waterton gives a lengthy account of the chapel at Walsingham, the most famous English shrine of Our Lady, and of the visit of Erasmus to the shrine in 1511 (cf. *Pietas Mariana Britannica*). In 1538 the image of the Virgin was sent by cart to Chelsea by Cromwell's orders and there publicly burned. At the same time the shrine was stripped and the fabric allowed to decay.

LARSSON, RAYMOND E. (1901–   ), born in Green Bay, Wis. (March 26), was educated at East High School, in that city. He worked in an editorial and reportorial capacity on papers in Green Bay, Appleton, Marquette, Milwaukee, Boston and New York. He is a convert to the Catholic Church, an art critic as well as a poet. His books of poetry are: *O City, Cities!* (1929), *A Sheaf* (1931), *Wherefore Is Peace* (1932), *Weep and Prepare* (1940) and *Perfect Vessel* (1941). Acting as joint editor with August Derleth, he published the volume *Poetry Out of Wisconsin* (1937), and has recently compiled *Saints at Prayer* (1942).

LAUBE, CLIFFORD JAMES (1891–   ), was born in Telluride, San Miguel County, Col. He received his education at Mount St. Vincent's Home, Denver, Col., Public School, Rico, Col., and the High School in Durango, Col. His career as an editor is long and distinguished. He joined the staff of the *New York Times* in 1929, acting as suburban editor. He is an authentic poet and published *Crags* in 1938. His poetry has appeared in such publications as the *New York Times, The Commonweal, The Sign, The New York Sun, Spirit, Literary Digest, Catholic Anthology* and others. He was one of the founders of *Spirit,* official magazine of the Catholic Poetry Society of America since 1934, and an associate editor, and one of the charter members of that society. In 1937 he founded the Monastine Press, which has published among other volumes Jessica Powers' *The Lantern Burns.*

LAUDES BEATAE MARIAE VIRGINIS, a collection of Latin quatrains based on the Psalms and honoring the Blessed Virgin, were "written by an English scribe, most likely in one of the Midland counties, early in the thirteenth century." The following note appears in the edition printed by William Morris at the Kelmscott Press, Upper Mall, Hammersmith, in the county of Middlesex (1896): "The Reverend E. S. Dewick has pointed out that these poems were printed in 1579, in a 16mo. volume, with the title *Psalterium Divae Virginis Mariae, rhythmice conscriptum a Reverendissimo domino Stephano, olim Archiepiscopo Cantuariensi, ex Bibliotheca Tegrinseensi depromptum, Cantandum sub melodia, Patris sapientia. Cum gratia & privilegio Caesareo. Excusum Tegernsee. Anno MDLXXIX.* This Tegernsee edition contains a *Conclusio* of four verses in the same metre as the Aves, but the text is otherwise inferior to that printed by William Morris. The ascription of the authorship to Stephen Langton is doubly interesting, as the manuscript transcribed for the Kelmscott Press was probably written before his death in 1228." Besides the quatrains on the individual Psalms there are introductory and conclusory verses. There is remarkable beauty in these salutations to the Virgin, many of which employ images that are unique and arresting. There is, however, a great unevenness in the work, some of the stanzas deviating too much to the subject of Christ, while others use more than one image, often unrelated, or do not carry out to a satisfactory conclusion the original image chosen. Father Roseliep's selection will give an idea of the spirit and tenor prevailing in the Laudes; his is an interpretative rendering rather than a literal or even a free translation. The edition used is that found in the rare book section at the Newberry Library, Chicago.

LE COMPTE, CALVIN (1922–   ), poet and musician, was born in Washington, D.C. (August 30). He attended high school in Washington, and is now working for his M.A. degree at the Catholic University of America, as well as teaching in the public schools. In 1942 he entered the Catholic Church. Twice he was awarded the O'Hagan Prize for English Poetry. He has produced a number of musical scores for Catholic University productions.

LE FORT, GERTRUD VON (1875–   ), was born of a French Protestant titled family who for religious reasons had fled to Germany. She was educated at the Universities of Heidelberg and Berlin, and worked under the Protestant philosopher Ernst Troeltsh, whose works she edited in 1925, the year that she entered the Catholic Church. The author of three historical novels: *The Song at the Scaffold* (1933), *The Pope from the Ghetto* (1934), and *The Veil of Veronica* (1936)—she has further distinguished herself as an authentic poet in her *Hymns to the Church* (1937), of which Sheed and Ward published an excellent English translation by Margaret Chanler (1944).

LEO XIII, POPE (1810–1903), was born at Carpineto. Gioacchino Vincenzo Raffaele Luigi was the sixth of seven sons of Count Ludovico Pecci and Anna Prosperi-Buzi. In the six years from 1818 to 1824 at the Jesuit school in Viterbo he acquired his later much envied facility with the Latin and Italian languages. While deciding his future, after a course in rhetoric and three years' study of philosophy with Jesuit teachers, he took up theology under Perrone and Patrizi. He was ordained in 1837 by the Vicar of Rome, and took over the difficult assignment of Benevento. Thence he was sent to Perugia, hotbed of the anti-papal revolutionary party where his energy and efficiency were outstanding. As nuncio to Brussels, he greatly improved the Catholic school situation, and in 1844 effected the nucleus of a Belgian college in Rome. For thirty-two years he was bishop of Perugia where his spiritual ambition had full play. He brought out a new diocesan catechism and wrote a guide for his clergy. In 1872 he established his Accademia di S. Tommaso, planned as far back as 1858, and introduced government standards for studies of the secondary schools and colleges. In 1878 he was elected Pope. He asked Catholics to coöperate with the French Republic, ameliorated the German situation, was mediator between Germany and Spain, established a rapprochement with Russia, and appointed the Apostolic Delegation to the United States in 1892. His writings in the twenty-five years of his pontificate dealt specifically with freemasonry, the invalidity of Anglican Orders, Christian marriage, liberty, capital, and labor. His Latin poems were published in English version by Msgr. H. T. Henry.

LESLIE, SHANE (1885–   ), is a native of County Monaghan, Ireland. He studied at Eton, the University of Paris and King's College, Cambridge, and in 1908 became a convert to the Catholic Faith. He is a former editor of *The Dublin Review,* and as an associate of the Irish Academy, holds an honorary degree from the University of Notre Dame. Among his diversified works are the following: *Songs of Oriel* (1922), *The End of a Chapter* (1918), *Verses in Peace and War* (1918), *Henry Edward Manning* (1920), *An Anthology of Catholic Poets* (1926), *The Skull of Swift* (1928), *Poems* (1933) and *The Epic of Jutland* (1930). His translation of *The Greek Anthology* was published in 1929.

LIGOURI, ALPHONSUS DE, SAINT (1696–1787), was born near Naples (September 27). A precocious child, his early boyhood was filled with the arts and sports common to a young heir of his day. At the age of sixteen he became a doctor of laws, and successfully practiced the profession for eight years. One serious failure, an oversight in the defense of a famous case, broke his devotion to the world and confidence in its promises. Returning in his humiliation to prayer which had once been a habit (fostered by yearly retreats made with his father), he laid his sword before Our Lady of the Redemption of Captives, braved difficulties of parental opposition and at the age of thirty was ordained to the priesthood. In 1731, under circumstances in which the providence of God was plainly evident, he became the supporter of a new religious order. In 1732 the future Congregation of the Most Holy Redeemer (Redemptorists) was founded in a little hospice belonging to the nuns of Scala, and in 1743 he was elected Superior General. In 1762 he was forced to accept the bishopric of St. Agatha, near Capua, an assignment which, amid great difficulties, he held for thirteen years. In 1769 a long attack of rheumatic fever left him paralyzed until his death. By a strange design of Providence, in 1781, he was dismissed from his own Order by the same Pope who was later to declare him Venerable, and under this shadow he died peacefully in his ninetieth year.

He was beatified in 1816, and canonized in 1839. Except for a few poems written in 1733 he wrote little until 1744 or 1745, when his *Visits to the Blessed Sacrament* appeared. In 1748 he completed the first sketch of his *Moral Theology*. He was a poet, musician, and charming letter-writer. Among his works are: *The Glories of Mary, The True Spouse of Christ, The History of the Council of Trent* and *Sermons for All the Sundays in the Year.*

LITANY FROM THE GAELIC, dates from the middle of the eighth century and is to be found in the *Leabhar Breac* or Speckled Book. Its titles of Our Lady are almost oriental in their rich imagery, and resemble those in the familiar Litany of Loretto. When the *Leabhar Breac* was brought to the notice of Pope Pius IX, the Litany was accorded an indulgence of one hundred days to those who devoutly recite it.

LITTLE, ARTHUR, S.J., (1897–   ), was born in Ireland (March 31), and entered the Irish Province of the Society of Jesus, September 15, 1914, taking his final vows on February 2, 1934. He taught Theodicy, and History of Philosophy at St. Stanislaus College in Tellabeg, Ireland. He is author of the recently published *Christ Unconquered,* a long epic poem on the passion and death of Christ (1935).

LONGFELLOW, HENRY WADSWORTH (1807–1882), was born in Portland, Maine, and educated at Bowdoin College and abroad, in France, Spain, Italy and Germany. In 1836 he accepted the professorship of modern languages and belles-lettres at Harvard, a chair he held for nearly eighteen years. His first book of original verse was *Voices of the Night* (1839), followed by *Ballads* (1841), *Poems on Slavery* (1842), *The Belfry of Bruges and Other Poems* (1846), *Evangeline* (1847), *Kavanagh,* a prose tale (1849), *The Song of Hiawatha* (1855), and *The Courtship of Miles Standish* (1858). Among his numerous other writings is *Christus, A Mystery* (made up of three parts already published, namely, *The Divine Tragedy, The Golden Legend* and *New England Tragedies,* as parts I, II and III respectively) published in 1872. The most fruitful part of his life was spent at Cambridge where he died March 24, 1882. *Michael Angelo* was published posthumously in 1883, and in 1884 a bust of the poet was unveiled in Westminster Abbey, the first American to be so honored.

LUKE, SAINT, THE EVANGELIST, companion of St. Paul, is mentioned in *Col.* 4:14 as "the beloved physician." He is reputedly a native of Antioch; his style proves him to have been a Greek. As a proselyte he acquired much knowledge of the Jewish peoples and customs, and also of the Aramaic tongue. His medical training was probably received at Tarsus, where he may have met St. Paul. He traveled a great deal and his writings evince a knowledge of the Mediterranean which would lead one to conclude that he may have been a doctor on board ship. *The Acts* reveal him first at Troas on his way to Europe with St. Paul, thence to Philippi, at the conversion of Lydia and at the arrest of Paul and Silas. At Philippi he evidently carried on the work after Paul's departure. Tradition records that he was unmarried and that he died a martyr's death in Boetia at the age of 74. The fact of his actual martyrdom is uncertain. He is one of the most extensive writers of the New Testament, and, with the exception of St. Paul in his *Hebrews,* surpasses the other Scriptural authors in literary excellence.

LYDGATE, JOHN (c.1370–c.1451), born probably at the Suffolk village of which he bears the name, became a Benedictine monk of Bury, St. Edmund's in his early boyhood. He was educated at both Oxford and Cambridge, and was ordained to the priesthood in 1397. He wrote much verse and enjoyed the patronage of Duke Humphrey of Gloucester. Much of his poetry is still in manuscript. His chief poems are: *The Troy Book* (written between 1412 and 1420 and first printed in 1513), *The Story of Thebes* (written c. 1420 and first printed c. 1500), *The Fall of Princes* (written between 1430 and 1438), some 36,000 lines in rime-royal, founded on Boccaccio's *De Casibus Virorum Illustrium,* *The Pilgrimage of Man,* a very prolix *Pilgrim's Progress* translated from Guillaume de Deguileville. A minor poem, "London Lickpenny" (edited for the Percy Society by Halliwell), gives an enlightening description of contemporary manners in London and Westminster.

LYNCH, JOHN W. (1904–   ), was born in Oswego, N. Y. (January 25); he attended Niagara University, Seminary of Our Lady (1925) and was ordained to the priesthood on May 25, 1929. He has been curate of St. Matthew's Church, East Syracuse (1929–32), St. Patrick's Church, Binghamton (1932–41), St. John the Baptist Church, Syracuse (1941). He is a contributing editor of *The Syracuse Catholic Sun,* and author of *A Woman Wrapped in Silence* (1941), a long lyric poem on the life of Our Lady.

MACGILLIVRAY, ARTHUR, S.J. (1912–   ), was born in Boston, Mass., and entered the Society of Jesus in 1932; he taught poetry and

415

English literature at Holy Cross College, Worcester, Mass., and was ordained to the priesthood in 1944. He has contributed prose and poetry to various periodicals. His volume of poetry, *Sufficient Wisdom* (1943) portrays "sensitiveness to beauty of thing and word." A. M. Sullivan has called him a poet who has "distinguished himself by his original statement and lyric discipline." At the present time he is pursuing studies at the University of Minnesota; he has recently prepared for publication an anthology of poems centered about the Spiritual Exercises of St. Ignatius, called *Poems for Retreat*.

McNABB, VINCENT, O.P. (1868–1943), was born at Portaferry on Strangford Lough, County Down, Ireland, the tenth of eleven children, and the seventh son. His father was a sea captain and much of the boy's childhood was spent at Belfast and Newcastle-on-Tyne. In 1855 he entered the Dominican novitiate at Woodchester, and was ordained to the priesthood in 1891. After taking the degree of Doctor of Theology at Louvain, he returned to Woodchester to teach philosophy. In 1897 he was appointed professor of dogmatic theology at Hawkesyard. From 1900 to 1906 he acted as Prior of Woodchester, at St. Dominic's, London; and later served as Prior at Holy Cross, Leicester. He made a preaching tour of the United States in 1913. His death occurred at St. Dominic's. His books include: *Some Mysteries of Jesus Christ* (1914), *Mary of Nazareth* (1939), *Eleven, Thank God* (1940) and *Old Principles and the New Order* (1942). His exquisite translation of *The Akathistos Hymn* from the Greek liturgy is included in this anthology.

MADELEVA, SISTER M., C.S.C., Mary Evaline Wolff (1887–), was born in Cumberland, Wis., and educated at St. Mary's College, Notre Dame, Ind., the University of Notre Dame and the University of California. She has taught and held executive positions in a number of the educational institutions of her Order, including St. Mary-of-the-Wasatch College, Salt Lake City, Utah, and St. Mary's College, Holy Cross, Ind., where she is now president. One of the foremost poets of our day, her volumes of poetry include: *Knights Errant* (1923), *Penelope* (1927), *A Question of Lovers* (1935), *Ballad of the Happy Christmas Wind* (1936), *Gates* (1938), *Four Girls* (1941) and *Selected Poems* (1939). She has also written a book of essays, *Chaucer's Nuns and Other Essays* (1925), and a scholarly treatise, *The Pearl—A Study in*

Spiritual Dryness (1925). A member of the Gallery of Living Catholic Authors and a charter member of the Catholic Poetry Society of America, she is now president of the latter organization.

MAGNIFICAT, THE, is the title given to the Latin text and vernacular translation of the Canticle or Song of Mary. It is the opening word of the Vulgate text (*Luke* 1:46–55). In ancient antiphonaries it was called "Evangelium Mariae" (the Gospel of Mary) and, because it appears in the Gospel, is called with the Canticles of Zachary and of Simeon, an evangelical canticle. Its thought content is similar to the Canticle of Anna (*Kings,* 2:1–10) and to various psalms. Its few lines compass the economy of God with His chosen people, pointing to the fulfillment of the ancient prophecy and prophesying anew. This first song of the New Testament was uttered (or not improbably chanted or sung) by the Blessed Virgin when she visited her cousin Elizabeth under the circumstances narrated by St. Luke in the first chapter of his Gospel. The second half of verse 48, "all generations shall call me blessed," proclaims a prophecy which has been fulfilled, and which adds to the overwhelming reasons for rejecting Elizabethan authorship of the canticle. The "Magnificat" is included in Vespers of the Divine Office. When sung in one of the eight modes of plain song, it is preceded and followed by an antiphon. Even in the Office of the Dead it is given an *initium* or intonation at every verse. Innumerable musical, as distinct from plain chant, settings have been given it. Its incomparable beauty has challenged the gift of almost every great composer. Settings by Palestrina, Orlando di Lasso and César Franck are extant. The Anglican service possesses 1,000 settings from which to choose.

MARIS STELLA, SISTER, S.S.J., Alice Gustava Smith (1899–   ), was born in Iowa (December 21). She was educated in public schools, Derham Hall, St. Paul, and the College of St. Catherine. In 1920 she was received into the novitiate of the Sisters of St. Joseph. She received her B.A. degree from the College of St. Catherine, 1924; B.A., Oxford University, 1929; M.A., Oxford, 1933. She is at present head of the Department of English at St. Catherine's College, St. Paul, Minn. Her poems have appeared in *The Commonweal, America, Poetry, The Sign, Spirit* and other publications, as well as in a number of anthologies. Twelve of her poems are included in *The Golden Book of Catholic Poetry,* selected

417

by Alfred Noyes (1946). Her one published book of poems is *Here Only a Dove* (1939); another volume is in preparation.

MARY CATHERINE, SISTER, O.S.U., Helen Margaret Vukmanic (1919–), the fourth of eight children, was born in Pittsburgh, Pa. (April 16). After completing studies at Schenley High School in 1935, she entered the Order of Ursuline nuns in Pittsburgh. In 1942 she received her B.A. degree from the College of St. Elizabeth. Graduate studies have kept her occupied at Duquesne University, Mount Mercy in Pittsburgh and Marquette University, Milwaukee. Since 1942 she has been teaching at the Ursuline Academy in Pittsburgh. Her poems have appeared in *Spirit, Ave Maria, Magnificat* and other periodicals.

MARY, THE VIRGIN MOTHER OF GOD, was born in the city of Nazareth, according to tradition, in the same house wherein the Word was made Flesh. The date of her birth is unknown. Nor have the year and day of the Annunciation been determined, though March 25 has been set as the feast depending upon the later feast of Christmas. The events in which she figures in the Gospel according to St. Luke were undoubtedly narrated by her to him. After Christ began His public life, she drops into obscurity, appearing in the Gospel narrative only at the Wedding of Cana, at the time when Jesus declined to cease his discourse to go to her on the outskirts of the crowd on the way to Calvary, and at the Crucifixion. Reliable tradition makes her the center of the post-pentecostal life of the early Church. The place of her death is uncertain. Baronius and Nirschl place it at 48 A.D. She was taken up into heaven bodily, the mystery of which is celebrated in the Church as The Assumption (August 15), though it is not yet formally defined as an article of faith. Mary, of all the children of Adam, was accorded the extraordinary privilege of being preserved from original sin, a mystery defined by the Church (Pope Pius IX, *Ineffabilis Deus,* 1854) as her Immaculate Conception. Her chief prerogative is her Divine Motherhood which survived the doctrine of Nestorianism and is the source of all her other prerogatives; by it she becomes the center of the hierarchy of rational creatures and an intermediary between God and the universe. Her titles Lady and Queen rest on her daughterhood of the First Person of the Blessed Trinity. She enjoys perpetual virginity, which means that she remained an inviolate virgin before, during and after the birth of her Divine Son. She is entitled to hyperdulia, that is, a worship which while essentially below that due to God, exceeds the ordinary dulia given the saints in precisely the same measure in which she outranks the angels and saints. Her name is genuinely Hebraic, and was first borne in the Old Testament by the sister of Moses. The Aramaic etymon is Lady. The Hebraic roots offer a variety of meanings: light-bearer, the refractory or stubborn one, myrrh, the strong, the tall, the bitter sea, or drop of the sea, and the sorrowful one. *Genesis* (3:15) prophesies her as the woman who was to be the enemy of the serpent and crush his head at least through her offspring; and *Isaias* (7:1–7) predicts her untarnished virginity in the conception of Emmanuel. Types and figures of her abound in Scripture and tradition. The second antiphon for Lauds on the Feast of the Circumcision likens her to Gideon's fleece, wet with dew amid dry ground, and the third antiphon sees in her the bush that was on fire and not burnt (*Exodus,* 3:2) because of her inviolate virginity after the birth of the Messias. The fourth Canticle sings of her as a "garden enclosed," a "fountain sealed up." Sara, Debbora, Judith, Esther and particularly Eve as the mother of all the living (*Gen.,* 3:20) prefigure her. Queen of Poets and Laureate of the Word are appropriate titles for the author of the most sublime poem in any language, The "Magnificat," which is her own song to God.

MAURA, SISTER, S.C., Mary Power (1881–   ), was born in Canada, daughter of Lawrence Geoffrey Power, sometime Speaker of the Canadian Senate. At her baptism her mother consecrated her to the Mother of God, and she wore blue and white until she changed it for the black and white of a Sister of Charity (Halifax Branch of Maryland community). She received her M.A. at Dalhousie; her Ph.D. at Notre Dame. She taught on the Notre Dame Summer School faculty from 1921 to 1925, and has been professor of English at Mount St. Vincent College, Halifax, N.S., since 1925. In addition to fugitive pieces not listed here, Sister Maura has written *The Angelus,* a prayer-play; *Chimes of the Immaculate,* a Litany of Our Lady; *Immaculata Revelata,* a liturgic play, published in the *Religious Journal of Instruction; A May Masque;* and *The Rosary in Terza Rima.*

MAURA, SISTER MARY, S.S.N.D., Catherine Mary Eichner (1916–   ), was born in Brooklyn, N. Y. (May 5). She received her education at the College of Notre Dame of Maryland in Baltimore, received an M.A. degree from the Catholic University of America, and is now doing graduate work at Johns Hopkins University and teaching in the department of English at the College of Notre Dame of Maryland. Her poems are seen frequently in current religious and secular journals. Her first volume of poems, *Initiate the Heart,* was published in 1946.

MAUROPUS, JOHN (d. 1060), came from Euchaita, a city of Hellesponte. He was surnamed Mauropus ("Blackfoot"). Living in the time of the Emperor Constantine X, he was made Archbishop of Euchiata. The *Carmina Joannis Euchaitensis* (published by Matthew Bust, Eton, 1610), is a volume of poems written on occasions of church festivals and commemorative of incidents in the lives of Christ and the saints. An *Officium,* or ritual service, composed by him and containing three canons or hymns is given by Nicolaus Rayaeus in his dissertation, *De Acolouthia Officii Canonici* (prefixed to the *Acta Sanctorum,* June, vol. 2). A number of his sermons and letters are also extant.

MENAEA, is the name of twelve books, one for each month, which contain the offices for immovable feasts in the Byzantine rite: feasts of Our Lord, the Blessed Virgin and the saints. They therefore correspond to the *Proprium Sanctorum* of the *Roman Breviary.* Used only in the Divine Office, the Menaea do not influence the liturgy. As the Byzantine year begins with September, that month forms the first of the Menaea, the year continuing to August. Translations, with additional offices for special feasts, are used in churches where Greek is not the liturgical language. The latest Greek editions were published at Venice in 1873 (Orthodox), and at Rome in 1888 (Uniate). Of obscure origin and gradual accumulation, a great part of the Menaea are attributed to Romanos, chief hymn-writer of the Byzantine church in the fifth century. The *Synaxarion,* evidently composed first, and containing short biographies of the saints and the histories of the feasts, are ascribed to Symeon Metaphrastes.

MENTH, ROBERT, C.SS.R. (1919–   .), was born at Whitestone, Long Island, N. Y. (April 21), and educated at St. Luke's Grammar School, Whitestone, St. Mary's College, North East, Pa., and Mt. St. Alphonsus, Esopus, N. Y. He made his profession as a Redemptorist on August 2, 1940, and was ordained to the priesthood on June 17, 1945. His poems have appeared in *Spirit.*

MERCIER, LOUIS (1870–   ), was born at Coutouvre near Roanne in the department of the Loire, France, and attended the seminary of St. Jodard, and later followed courses of the Faculté Catholique de Lyon. After three years military service in Tunis he returned to France in 1897, and settled in Roanne. At the outbreak of war in 1914 he again joined the service. He wrote both prose and poetry. His books of poetry include *L'Enchanté* (1897), *Voix de la Terre et du Temps* (1903), *Lazare le Ressuscité* (1910), *Les Pierres Sacrées Suivis des Poèmes de la Tranchée* (1922), *Les Cinq Mystères Joyeux* (1914) and *Virginis Corona* (1929). Louis Mercier is a religious poet who is sensitively aware of the Divine reference in the beauties of external nature. His verse is marked by the use of traditional symbols and a deep simplicity and integrity. His Marian poems are of a high order.

MERTON, THOMAS (1915–   ), was born in southern France, but has lived in Bermuda, Paris, England, the West Indies and the United States. He was educated in the French Lycée, an English public school, Cambridge University and Columbia University in America. After some graduate work at the latter he went to teach at St. Bonaventure College and Seminary. He is now a Trappist monk at Our Lady of Gethsemani, Kentucky. The modern poet, Robert Lowell, has called him the "most consequential Catholic poet to write in English since the death of Francis Thompson." To which F.X. Connolly writing in *Spirit* adds: "Supposing 'most consequential' to mean important, I feel the judgment is too cautious. Besides being important, Merton's poetry is importunate. An intrinsically valuable contribution to the body of creative literature, it demands the response of our admiration, our homage and our gratitude." Merton breaks sharply with traditional pattern and writes in modern rhythm and idiom. His poems have appeared in *View, The New Yorker,* and *Spirit.* His first volume of poems, *Thirty Poems,* was published in 1945, a second, *A Man in the Divided Sea* (1946).

MEYNELL, ALICE (1847–1922), was born Alice Thompson, in London. As a child she traveled with her family on the continent, mostly in Italy. When she was twenty she entered the Catholic Church. In 1875 she published her first book of poems, *Preludes,* and her talent was immediately recognized. In 1877 she married Wilfrid Meynell, the editor of her book of poems. For eighteen years she assisted her husband in his editorial work, besides writing essays and poetry. It was her sex alone that prevented her from becoming Poet Laureate in 1895 and again in 1914. As her life was long, reaching from the time of Newman to that of Chesterton, the names of Eric Gill, Joyce Kilmer and Thomas Walsh are among the many who profited by her "literary salon" and her inspiration. Her singular gifts, both in prose and in poetry, may be seen in her essays: *The Rhythm of Life* (1893), *The Color of Life* (1896), *The Children* (1896), *The Spirit of Peace* (1898), *Ceres' Runaway* (1910), *The Second Person, Singular* (1921), *Poems* (1893), *Later Poems* (1901), *A Father of Women* (1918) and *Last Poems* (1923).

MEYNELL, WILFRID (1852–   ), was born and educated in York. In 1870 he entered the Catholic Church, and in 1907 married the gifted poet, Alice Thompson. He will always be remembered for his great gift to Catholic letters—the poet, Francis Thompson whom he lifted out of the London slums, befriended, and set well on the way to literary fame. He edited *The Pen, The Weekly Register* (begun in 1881 at the request of Cardinal Manning) and *Merry England*. Among his writings are: *John Henry Newman* (1890), *Verses and Reverses* (1913) and *Rhymes with Reasons* (1919).

MICHAEL MARIE, SISTER, I.W.B.S., Pauline Kaiser (1923–   ), was born in Sterling, Col. (August 28). She attended the parochial grade and high school in Sterling, and at the age of seventeen entered the Convent of the Incarnate Word and Blessed Sacrament, Corpus Christi, Texas. There she made her final profession August 6, 1945. She is at present teaching at Our Lady of Consolation School, Riviera, Texas. Her poems have been published in *The Catholic World, The Sign, The Magnificat* and *Spirit*.

MILTON, JOHN (1608–1674), was born in London, and educated at St. Paul's School and Christ's College, Cambridge. He intended to take orders in the Anglican Church, but in 1632, finding himself out of sympathy with the Anglican hierarchy, decided to devote himself to literature. He retired to his father's estate in Buckinghamshire where he wrote "L'Allegro," "Il Penseroso," "Comus" and "Lycidas." Upon the establishment of the Commonwealth in 1649, he was appointed Latin secretary of state, an office which he continued to hold until the abdication of Richard Cromwell in 1659, despite the fact that he had been stricken with blindness in 1652. *Paradise Lost* had been begun in 1640 amid the bitter issue in Parliament between religious and civil liberty, whereupon he set it aside to write *Areopagitica* (1644), his plea for a free press. The former was not completed until 1665, published in 1667 in ten books and enlarged to twelve in 1674. *Paradise Regained* and *Samson Agonistes* appeared in 1671. His graceful *Hymn on the Nativity* (1629) is one of his best loved poems. His last years were clouded with difficulties with his daughters. He died quietly on November 8, 1674, and was buried in St. Giles's, Cripplegate.

MORTON, DAVID (1886–   ), was born in Kentucky (February 21), and educated at Vanderbilt University. For some years he did newspaper work, then taught English in Louisville, Ky., Morristown, N. J., and Amherst, Mass. He is the author of a dozen books of verse, the latest of which is entitled *Poems 1920–1945*.

MOSES (13th–14th centuries B.C.) was a Hebrew liberator, leader, lawgiver, prophet and historian. Rabbinical literature is filled with references to his colorful career. Of Levitic extraction, born when kingly decree militated against the life of every male Israelite, he became the hero of one of the Old Testament's most fascinating stories. After forty years of shepherd life, he heard the voice of God from the bush which burned and was not consumed, and listened to Him, Yahweh, "memorial to all generations." After the last plague had softened Pharaoh, together with 600,000 men, besides women and children, he made the long journey through the desert and over the Red Sea. On Mount Sinai he received from God the Ten Commandments. Before his death he uttered the three memorable discourses of *Deuteronomy*, and from Mount Nebo looked for a last time upon the Promised Land. Moses died at the age of 120 years. In later ages many of the learned found it difficult to admit that the person and personality of Christ eclipsed him, so unique and admired was he by all peoples.

MUSSER, BENJAMIN FRANCIS (1889–   ), was born in Lancaster, Pa., (February 3) of a family in which three generations of Episcopalians, seven of American Quakers and Mennonites, five of English, Welsh and German Protestants can be traced. He was educated at Yeates School, Episcopal Academy, Pa., Nashotah Seminary, Wis., and St. Joseph's College, New York. He became a Catholic in April of 1908, and in 1940 received the unusual honor of being made an affiliate of the First Order (Franciscans) by proclamation from Rome (only one other American layman has been so privileged, Paul Martin-Dillon). An Academy member of the Catholic Poetry Society of America, he also holds membership in the Poetry Society of America, Poetry Society of England (vice-president since 1937), and the Empire Poetry League. His published works include some forty-three volumes—

poetry, essays, history, biography, philology, devotional and mystical studies, liturgical treatises and Franciscalia. *Chiaroscuro* (1923), *Selected Poems* (1930), *Bucolics and Caviar* (1930), *Chaplet of Sanctuaries* (1934), *House of Bread* (1935), *Canticles for St. Francis* (1936), *and Bird Below the Waves* (1938) are among those best known.

NERSES IV (1098–1173), was born at Hromcla, Cilicia, and educated by his grand uncle, Patriarch Gregory Vkaiaser, and later by a doctor of theology, one Stephen Manuk. He is regarded as the greatest of Armenian writers, and is often called Klaientsi from the place of his birth, and Schnorkhali ("the Gracious"), from the elegance of his writings. He attended the Latin Council of Antioch in 1141, and in 1166 was elected patriarch. He labored to heal the breach between the Armenian and Greek Churches. Among his verses, the "Jesu Orti" is outstanding. His prose includes: *Prayers for Every Hour of the Day* (Venice, 1882); a Synodal Letter; and five letters to M. Comnenus (Venice, 1883). In his first letter to Comnenus is found his defense of the primacy of Peter.

NORTON, M.D. HERTER (Mrs. W.W. Norton), is connected with the publishing house of that name in New York, and her interest in Rilke is one of long standing. She has translated and published Rilke's *Letters to a Young Poet, The Tale of the Love and Death of Cornet Christopher Rilke, Stories of God, Sonnets to Orpheus and Letters of Rainer Maria Rilke* (1892–1910). A volume of the later letters of Rilke is now in preparation. Mrs. Norton has also published *String Quartet Playing* (Carl Fischer, 1925) and, in collaboration with Roy Harris, an edition of Bach's *Art of the Fugue for String Quartet* and a translation of Paul Bekker's *Story of Music.*

O'CONNOR, PATRICK (1899–   ), was born in Clontarf, Dublin, Ireland, (March 17). He was educated at Belvedere and University Colleges, Dublin, receiving his B. A. degree in 1919, his M. A. in 1922. On June 1, 1921, he entered the Society of St. Columban for Foreign Missions and was ordained at Dalgan Park, June 10, 1923. Since 1923 he has been editor of *The Far East*, at St. Columbans, Neb. He is the author of a book of poems, *Songs of Youth,* published in 1928; and is a frequent contributor to magazines.

O'DONNELL, CHARLES L., C.S.C. (1884–1934), was born in Greenfield, Ind., and received his educational training at Notre Dame Uni-

versity and the Catholic University of America. He received holy
orders in the Congregation of the Holy Cross, in 1910. From
1922 to 1926 he served as Provincial of his order, then president
of Notre Dame University until his death. A charter member of
the Catholic Poetry Society of America, and its first president, he
is considered one of America's outstanding priest-poets. His
works are: *A Rime of the Rood and Other Poems* (1928) and
Cloister and Other Poems (1922).

O'RIORDAN, CONAL (N. O'CONNELL) (1874–   ), was born in Dublin,
educated at Conglowes, and until 1920 wrote under the pen-
name of F. Norreys Connell. After a brief theatrical career he
became director of the Abbey Theatre. His works are: *In the
Green Park* (1894), *The House of the Strange Woman* (1895),
The Fool and His Heart (1896), *The Nigger Knights* (1900), *In
London* (1922) and *Rowena* (1925).

OX-BONE MADONNA, a poem by James J. Galvin, C.SS.R., and John
Duffy, C.SS.R., had its first impetus in a brief news item which carried the picture of a small madonna carved by a Polish soldier in
a Russian concentration camp, from a bone plucked out of the
soup. *Spirit,* in which the poem was first printed, placed the following footnote beneath it: "Beginning a poem with a news item,
one of the two poets above ran into difficulties after he had composed his first two lines, and took these to a confrère for advice.
The latter in the discussions that followed, gave certain suggestions, in turn 'took fire' and, using the basic idea of the whole
as well as the two lines, wrote a version of his own . . . an interesting insight into one aspect of poetic creation."

PARKER, DOROTHY ROTHSCHILD (1893–   ), was born in West End,
N. J., of a Jewish father and Scotch mother. She received her education at Miss Dana's School, Morristown, N. J., and Blessed
Sacrament Convent, New York. She worked for *Vogue* (1916–
17), married Edwin Pond Parker in 1917 and was dramatic critic
for *Vanity Fair* (1917–20). She perfected a light, humorous, cyni-
cal verse. In 1927 *Enough Rope* was published and she became a
member of the editorial staff of the *New Yorker,* as a book re-
viewer. *Sunset Gun* appeared in 1928; and in 1931, *Death and
Taxes.* She is also known as a prose writer and has published
Laments for the Living (1930), thirteen short stories and
sketches.

PATMORE, COVENTRY (1823–1896), was born at Woodford, Essex,
England, of a literary family. He was engaged as an assistant in

the printed book department of the British Museum. In 1864 he became a Roman Catholic. A friend of Tennyson, Ruskin and Thompson, he was also on intimate terms with the Pre-Raphael-ite coterie, to whose publication, *The Germ,* he contributed. Be-tween 1854 and 1862 he issued the four poems which constitute *The Angel in the House,* a long work designed to be an apotheosis of married love; in the words of Ruskin, it was "one of the most blessedly popular poems" in the language. In 1877 he published *The Unknown Eros,* odes on the sublime closeness of God to the human soul, and in 1878, *Amelia.* His collected works of poetry were published in 1886 with an appendix on English metrical law. *Principle in Art* (1889) and *Religio Poetae* (1893) contain articles contributed for the most part to the *St. James' Gazette. Rod, Root, and Flower* (1895) presents meditations on religious topics.

PÉGUY, CHARLES (1873–1914), was born at Orléans, France. When he was twelve he was sent to the Lycée at Orléans as a scholarship student, and in 1891, having passed his baccalaureate examinations, went to Paris that he might prepare for the École Normale. At this time he had lost all belief in the immortality of the soul. He entered the Lycée Lakanal at Sceaux, a suburb of Paris, but failed in the entrance examinations for the École Normale. Thereupon he decided to enlist in the army, a year before the required age. But in 1893, freed from military duties, he enrolled at the Lycée Sainte-Barbe, Paris, and the following year entered the École Normale Supérieure, a preparatory school for the training of university professors. In 1896 he left to marry, but in 1897 re-entered school and again failed in his final examinations. In 1901 he set up a publishing firm of his own and issued a fortnightly publication called *Les Cahiers de la Quinzaine,* in which he expressed his own views on the burning topics of the day. The years between 1892 and 1908 in the life of Péguy are shrouded in mystery. About 1892 he had declared himself an atheist, and in 1908, admitted to a friend that he had "found faith again," and was a Catholic. However, since he was not validly married in the eyes of the Church, it was impossible for him to receive the sacraments. It is said, however, that he did so a few weeks before his death. He was killed on the battlefield near Villeroy in the battle of the Marne. Foremost among his dramas is *Jeanne d'Arc* (1897), reminiscent of the medieval mystery plays. Among his best prose works are *Notre Patrie*

(1905), *Notre Jeunesse* (1910), *Victor Hugo* (1911) and *L'Argent* (1913). His *La Tapisserie de Sainte Geneviève et de Jeanne d'Arc* (1913) and *La Tapisserie de Notre Dame* (1913) are collections of poems written, one group to honor St. Genevieve, and one Our Lady.

PETRARCH, FRANCESCO (1304–1374), Italian poet and humanist, was born at Arezzo, Italy. Though his parents intended him for a legal career, he used every effort to free himself for an untrammeled pursuit of *belles lettres*. He had already received minor orders in 1323 at Avignon, when he met Laura (reputed by some critics to be legendary) who became the inspiration of his most famous work, the *Canzoniere*. The greater portion of his prose and verse was written in Latin: *Africa,* in hexameters, dealing with the Second Punic War; twelve eclogues, *Carmen Bucolicum;* the autobiographical *Epistolae Metricae;* the moral treatises, *De Contemptu Mundi, De Vita Solitaria, De Actu Religiorum, Psalmi Paenitentiales* and others. His fame, nevertheless, rests on his Italian verse, the *Canzoniere.*

PICKTHALL, MARJORIE LOWRY CHRISTIE (1883–1922), Canadian poet and novelist, was born in Oxford Road, Gunnersbury, Middlesex, England. In 1899 her family moved to Canada where she spent twenty-two of the thirty-eight years of her life. She contributed regularly to *The Atlantic Monthly, Century, Scribner's, McClure's* and *Harper's.* At her mother's death in 1910 she worked in the library of Victoria College, Toronto, and assisted in compiling the annual bibliography of Canadian poetry. She likewise edited a page in the *Canadian Courier.* In 1912 she went to England for her health, but in 1920 returned to Canada. The first edition of her book of poems, *Drift of Pinions* (1912), with its title taken from Francis Thompson, was sold out in ten days. Other volumes of her verse are: *Lamp of Poor Souls* (1916) and *The Wood Carver's Wife and Other Poems* (1922). Her fiction includes *Little Hearts* (1915), *The Bridge* (1920) and *Angel Shoes* (1923).

POE, EDGAR ALLAN (1809–1849), born in Boston, Mass., the son of actor parents, became an orphan in early childhood, and was brought up by John Allan, of Richmond. He was educated in Richmond, in England, and at the University of Virginia. At the latter place he ran into debt so heavily that Mr. Allan withdrew him from the institution, whereupon he enlisted in the United States Army. After two years' service he was given a cadetship at

West Point, but was dismissed a few months later. After 1831 he lived entirely by his writing. He served as editor of *The Southern Library Messenger*, 1835, and from then until 1845 was editor or associate editor of *The Gentleman's Magazine*, *Graham's Magazine* and *The Broadway Journal*, to which he contributed tales, poems and critical articles. His death, in Baltimore, occurred under mysterious circumstances. Important titles among his works are *Tamerlane and Other Poems* (1827), *Tales of the Grotesque and Arabesque* (1839), *The Raven and Other Poems* (1845). He is the first American poet to be received with enthusiasm by Europeans, who even today accord to him and to Whitman the distinction of being the greatest poetical geniuses who have come from the New World.

POWERS, JESSICA AGNES, Sister Miriam of the Holy Spirit, O.D.C. (1905–   ), born at Mauston, Wisconsin (February 7), was educated in the local school and St. Patrick's parochial school. Graduated from the Mauston High School in 1922, she attended Marquette University (1922–23), then went to New York where she acted as governess while writing poetry. She became a member of the Third Order of St. Francis in 1938, and was professed in 1939. In June of 1941 she entered the Order of Discalced Carmelites in Milwaukee, Wis., the first postulant to enter the newly founded Carmel of the Mother of God. In 1942 she received the brown habit and the name of Sister Miriam of the Holy Spirit, and in 1946 pronounced her final vows. A book of poetry, *The Lantern Burns*, published by the Monastine Press (1939), was widely acclaimed. A second volume of poems is in preparation.

PRAISE OF MARY (*Li Loenge Nostre Dame*), is taken from a thirteenth century manuscript preserved in the National Library of Paris. In 1840 the first five lines were used by P. Paris (*Mss. franc. III* 236), and later in the same year the first and last verses were published by F. Michel (*Chron. anglonorum* III, p. xxxv). There was no complete text of the poem published until that of Hugo Andresen (*Marienlob*) in 1891, annotated by its editor, and printed by Max Niemeyer. The scribe (or author) of the original manuscript, Perrot de Nerle, added to its text a rhyming analysis, as well as to the texts of the other pieces found in the same manuscript. The stanzas here translated by Father Henry Sorg retain their quaint medieval charm.

PROBYN, MAY, is an English poet and convert who wrote both fiction and poetry. After years of illness in London she retired to a Dominican community where she ceased her literary activity. There is present in her verse an unusual spiritual quality. *Poems* was published in 1881, and *A Ballad of the Road* in 1883. She is represented in Joyce Kilmer's *Dreams and Images* (1926) and Theodore Maynard's *Book of Modern Catholic Verse* (1926).

PRUDENTIUS, AURELIUS CLEMENS (348–413), born in the Terraconensis, in Spain, probably of Christian parents, was the greatest religious poet of the fourth and fifth centuries. He was first a lawyer, then served on two occasions as provincial governor and was finally summoned to Rome by the emperor. His works are lyrical, didactic and polemical. Among his lyrical works are two collections, the *Peristephanon* and the *Cathemerinon,* the latter a collection of twelve hymns varying in length from eighty to two hundred and twenty lines, written in a swinging rhythm admirably suited to their motif. Not meant for actual singing in the churches, these poems represent the most substantial addition made to Latin lyrical poetry since Horace. Their theology is that of the Nicene Creed. His most personal work is the *Contra Symmachum,* in which he shows how Christians reconciled their patriotism with their faith.

PSALMS, THE BOOK OF, known also as The Psalter is a collection of one hundred and fifty poems, divided into five books, and, according to the opinion of the Biblical Commission, written chiefly by David. In the Hebrew Bible the *Book of Psalms* is entitled "Praises," appropriately significant, since the psalms were used in the service of the temple—a service chiefly of praise. In the Septuagint manuscripts the book is called "Psalms." The word *psalm,* which in classical Greek meant the twang of a stringed instrument, is the translation of a Hebrew term occurring in the titles of fifty-seven psalms, signifying a poem of measured form. They are, therefore, poems of praise composed to be sung to the accompaniment of stringed instruments. *The Psalter* is considered the greatest hymn-book in the world. A manual of sacred songs primarily intended for use in the liturgy of the second temple, it has also become the hymnal of the Catholic Church. In the *Roman Breviary* the Divine Office is so arranged that the hundred and fifty psalms contained in the *Psalter* are usually recited within each week. In themes, the psalms run the entire gamut of religious feeling, "soaring to the topmost heights of Divine contemplation and sinking to the lowest depths of the human heart." The Hebrew poets have produced what Theodore Watts-Dunton styles the "Great Lyric," an outpouring of the soul from man to God. John Cowper Powys has proclaimed these lyrics "the most pathetic and poignant, as well as the most noble and dignified of all poetic literature."

PULCI, LUIGI (1432–1484), of Florentine birth, was an Italian poet, a member of a noted family which gave many literary artists to the world. He wrote the chivalrous romantic poem, "Morgante," which immortalized the peripatetic adventures of Roland, and was the first serious attempt at an artistic treatment of the Carlovingian epic matter imported from France. His lesser compositions are much inferior to this one work upon which his fame rests.

RAY, LOUISE CRENSHAW (1890–   ), was born in Greenville, Ala. (May 17), where she was educated and has spent most of her time. She is married to Benjamin F. Ray and has two daughters, Anne and Mary. Many awards have been given her for her splendid achievement in poetry. Her first poems appeared in *America,* later in the *North American Review, Forum, Century, Argosy, Spirit* and others. She is an Episcopalian. A volume of poems, *Color of Steel* was published in 1932.

REESE, LIZETTE WOODWORTH (1856–1935), was born in Waverly, Md., of a German mother and a father of Welsh ancestry. She taught school for forty-five years. Early in 1899 she wrote her famous sonnet, "Tears," which Robert Bridges printed in *Scribner's* magazine. She was a close friend of Louise Imogen Guiney. The literary arbiters of the day received her well. Her principal works are: *A Branch of May* (1887), *A Handful of Lavender* (1891), *A Quiet Road* (1896), *A Wayside Lute* (1909), *Spicewood* (1920), *Wild Cherry* (1923), *Little Henrietta* (1927) and *A Victorian Village* (1929).

REGINA COELI, THE, "Queen of Heaven," is an antiphon for Eastertide addressed to the Blessed Virgin. Its recitation is prescribed in the *Roman Breviary* from Compline of Holy Saturday until None of the Saturday after Pentecost, inclusively. Of unknown authorship, the antiphon has been traced back to the twelfth century. It was in use by the Franciscans in the first half of the following century. Together with other Marian antiphons it was incorporated in the Minorite-Roman Curia Office, which, through the activity of the Franciscans was widely popularized, and, by order of Nicholas III (1277–1280), replaced all the older Office books in the churches of Rome. The antiphon forms a syntonic strophe, depending on the accent of the word and not the quantity of the syllable. In it the *Alleluia* serves as a refrain.

REPPLIER, AGNES (1858–   ), was born in Philadelphia, Pa., and educated at the Sacred Heart Convent in Torresdale. She has been called America's most distinguished essayist, and holds the degree of Litt. D., from the Universities of Pennsylvania, Yale, Columbia, and Princeton, and the Laetare Medal (1911). Among her best known works are: *Books and Men* (1888), *Points of View* (1891), *Varia* (1897), *Points of Friction* (1920), *In Pursuit of Laughter* (1936) and *Eight Decades* (1937). Two biographies, *Père Marquette* (1929) and *Mère Marie of the Ursulines* (1931) have been immensely popular, the latter having been selected by the leading non-Catholic Book Club.

RILKE, RAINER MARIA (1875–1926), Austrian poet, was born in Prague, and educated at a military and business academy in Moravia, and the Universities of Prague and Munich. After much travel through Italy, Germany, Russia, France and the Mediterranean region, he settled in Italy where he wrote his *Life of the Virgin Mary* and the first two of the *Duiniso Elegies*. The former was inspired by two pictures—an Annunciation to Shepherds and a scene on the Flight into Egypt—in an old sketchbook given him by Heinrich Vogeler in 1900. Fascinated, he jotted down several lines of verse in his diary the next day. A plan to write a *Marienleben,* to be illustrated by Vogeler, never materialized. However, in 1912, Rilke wrote the cycle of poems on the Virgin Mary which was published in 1913. Rilke remarked of it: "It is a little book that was presented to me, quite above and beyond myself, by a peaceful generous spirit, and I shall always get on well with it, just as I did when I was writing it." The book contains thirteen pieces, the last poem being included in this anthology. The last seven years of Rilke's life were spent in solitude at the Tour de Muzot in Valois, Switzerland, where he completed his fifty-five *Sonnets to Orpheus*. W. H. Auden has said of him that he is "probably read and more highly esteemed by English and Americans than by Germans, just as Byron and Poe had greater influence upon their German and French contemporaries than upon their compatriots." His published works include: *Life of the Virgin Mary* (1921). *Later Poems* (1938), *Duiniso Elegies* (1939), *Fifty Selected Poems*

(1940), *Poems from the Book of Howe* (1941), *Sonnets to Orpheus* (1942). *Translations from the Poetry of Rainer Maria Rilke* was published in 1938 by Herter Norton.

ROSELIEP, RAYMOND F. (1917–   ), poet and critic, was born in Farley, Iowa (August 11). He studied at Loras Academy and Loras College, Dubuque, Iowa, and the Catholic University of America, Washington, D. C., where he took his seminary course and pursued graduate studies for an M. A. in English literature. He was ordained to the priesthood in Dubuque on June 12, 1943. From 1943 to 1945 he was assistant pastor at Gilbertville, Iowa; and in the June of 1945 he was appointed managing editor of *The Witness* (Dubuque archdiocesan organ), chaplain of St. Anthony Home, and area chaplain for the Northeastern Iowa section of Boy Scouts. In 1946 he was assigned to Loras College as instructor in Religion and English. His work has appeared in *America, The Catholic World, The Sign, Spirit, The Ave Maria* and *The Tidings*. A member of the Catholic Poetry Society of America, he is also well known as a literary critic. At present he is preparing for publication a collection of his poems —a *sacerdotalia*—centering on the sublime subject of the priesthood. Some have hailed him as this country's second great priest-poet—a worthy successor of Father Tabb.

ROSSETTI, CHRISTINA GEORGINA (1830–1894), the younger daughter of Gabriel Rossetti and the sister of Dante Gabriel Rossetti, was born in London. She contributed to *The Germ* under the pen name Ellen Alleyne. Cast in a decidedly spiritual and oftentimes melancholy mold, her poems are marked by a high degree of technical perfection; her short and intense lyrics, like "Uphill" and her sonnet "Remember," show the poet at her best. Her chief works are: *Goblin Market and Other Poems* (1862), *The Prince's Progress* (1866), *Sing-Song* (1872), *A Pageant and Other Poems* (1881), *Time Flies, A Reading Diary* (1883), and *New Poems* (1896) published after her death.

ROSSETTI, DANTE GABRIEL (1828–1882), was born in London, and educated at King's College, London, but soon turned to art for which he had great talent. Before he was nineteen he had composed two of his best-known poems—both published a few years later (1850) in *The Germ*—"The Blessed Damozel" and "My Sister's Sleep." As a founder of the pre-Raphaelite Brotherhood—though in many respects he stands outside it—he was closely as-

sociated with Holman Hunt, Millais and other young artists of
the day. In 1860 he married Eleanor Siddal, who died two years
later. His *Early Italian Poets* came out in 1861. *Poems by D. G.
Rossetti* (1870) contained the poems which in manuscript he had
placed in his wife's casket and which had now been taken from
her grave. *Ballads and Sonnets* appeared in 1881. Rossetti also
translated from the Italian, French and German writers, particularly from Villon. Many of his poems were composed as
commentaries on his own pictures. Walter Pater, in his essay on
Rossetti's poetry, calls attention to the seriousness of thought
underlying even his most fantastic poems, and illustrates this
quality by reference to "The Burden of Nineveh," a poem also
praised by Ruskin and Swinburne.

SAINT VIRGINIA, SISTER MARY, B.V.M., Virginia Berry (1907–   ),
was born in North McGregor, Iowa (December 5) and educated
at St. Mary's Academy, Prairie du Chien, Wis., and Fordham
University, New York. She entered the novitiate of the Sisters of
Charity of the Blessed Virgin Mary in 1932, and made her final
profession in 1940. Her poems have appeared in *America, The
Catholic World, The Commonweal, The Sewanee Review, The
Literary Digest, Poetry, The Sign, Spirit, The Tidings* and other
periodicals, and in the following anthologies: *Drink from the
Rock, Prose and Poetry of America, The Golden Book of Catholic Poetry* and *The Anthology of Magazine Verse for 1940–
1941.*

SALVE REGINA, "Hail, Queen," are the opening words of the most
celebrated of the four antiphons of the *Roman Breviary,* and is
sung from the first Vespers of Trinity Sunday until None of the
Saturday before Advent. Though the Bernardian legend still
clings to it, it is now generally ascribed to Hermann Contractus.
It was first sung processionally at Cluny in 1135.

SANNAZARIUS, ACTIUS SINCERUS (1458–1530), also known as Jacopo
Sannazaro, was an Italian and Latin poet, a satellite of Potanus
who gave him the title of Sincerus. Exiled by Louis XII of
France, recalled by Frederico, he lived and worked at Tours for
the remainder of his life. In his youth he produced *Arcadia,* part
verse, part prose, in which he described the pastoral life of the
ancients. Outstanding among his famous Latin works is the
De Partu Virginis, a poem in three cantos, which cost him
twenty years of labor and which, despite many digressions and
lavish allegorical personifications, won him the name of the

Christian Virgil. Hailed by Leo X when still unknown, the poem was dedicated to Clement VII who was enthusiastic in its praise.

SARGENT, DANIEL (1890–   ), was born in Boston, Mass., the son of Unitarian parents, and was educated at Groton School and at Harvard. His first intention was to study law but he changed his plan in favor of literature. While abroad he watched Germany mobilize and then returned to teach comparative literature at Harvard. A volume of lyrics, *Our Gleaming Days,* was published in 1915. He then went to France where he met Psichari and Péguy. At the close of the war he entered the Catholic Church, receiving baptism from the Rev. Martin J. Scott, S.J. He returned to Harvard to teach, and subsequently married Louise Collidge of Boston. In 1936 he was elected president of the American Catholic Historical Association, and in 1942 became a member of the Advisory Board of the Catholic Book Club. His books of poetry include: *Our Gleaming Days* (1915), *The Door* (1922), *The Road to Welles Perennes* (1925), *My Account of the Flood* (1929), *The Song of the Three Children* (1930) and *God's Ambuscade* (1935). His prose works are: *Thomas More* (1934), *Four Independents* (1935), *Catherine Tekakwitha* (1936), *Our Land and Our Lady* (1939), *Christopher Columbus* (1941) and *All the Day Long* (1941).

SAVONAROLA, FRA GIROLAMO (1452–1498), was born at Ferrara, Italy, and in 1474 entered the Dominican order at Bologna, making his first appearance as a preacher at Florence, in 1482. He became prior of the convent of San Marco, and from the pulpits of San Marco and the Duomo, he preached to crowds of avid listeners against the pagan-lived humanists in high places, pouring out upon them the vials of his just scorn. He urged the need of reform. Though a man of intense austerity, moral purity and holy motives, he became over-zealous and found himself involved in the party strife of Florence. When Charles VIII of France marched into Florence he hailed Savonarola as a new Cyrus, God's instrument for the punishment of the evil city. After the Medici had sought safety in flight, he set up a dictatorship, making Florence a democratic republic. The upper classes turned against him, as did the Medici, who plotted his downfall. They poisoned the mind of Alexander VI against him, and the Pope at once forbade him to preach to the people. When he ignored the mandate, he was excommunicated, but publicly claimed that the ban was null and void, a fact he promised to

434

prove by an ordeal of fire. When the prophecy did not take effect the people turned against him. An attack was made on San Marco, and he, with two other Dominicans, was tortured, hanged and burnt. Savonarola cannot be claimed as a precursor of the Reformation, for, though he refused to obey the Holy Father, yet he never preached or wrote a word contrary to the Catholic Faith. In his chief work, *Il Trionfo della Croce* ("The Triumph of the Cross") he states: "Whoever swerves from the unity of the Roman Church undoubtedly enters upon the path of error and turns his back upon Christ."

SCHAUMANN, RUTH (1899–   ), was born in Hamburg, Germany (August 24), daughter of a German cavalry officer whose ancestors had formerly been in service with the English Hanoverians. At the age of three she lost her hearing. As a young girl she studied art under Joseph Wackerle. Though her parents were strict Protestants she joined the Catholic Church when she was about twenty, and a short time later married Frederick Fuchs, an editor. She is an artist in wood, metals and etching, as well as a gifted poet. In 1932 she won the Munich Poetry Prize. Among her writings are prose legends, lyrical drama, and poetry, all distinguished by a deep note of mysticism and a charming simplicity. *Das Passional, Der Rebenhag,* and *Der Knospengrund* are her best known volumes of poetry. Her *Songs of Love and Marriage* and a *Lyric Sequence for Children,* illustrated by herself, are also distinguished literature. She is the mother of three children. Recently one of them, detained in a prisoner of war camp in Russia, was released through the kind services of a Russian doctor. When the young soldier was asked whether he knew Ruth Schaumann, since he was from Munich, and replied that he was her son, the doctor, an admirer of his mother's poetry, at once made efforts that he be sent home.

SCOTT, SIR WALTER (1771–1832), was born in Edinburgh, Scotland, and educated at the Edinburgh High School and University. Much of his childhood was passed in the country at Sandy-Knowe, where he assimilated the romantic backgrounds of Smailholm Castle and the songs and stories of the Border feuds. In 1792 he was admitted as a member of the faculty of advocates at Edinburgh, and in 1799 he married Charlotte Carpenter, daughter of a French refugee. His first literary works were translations from the German. In 1802–04 appeared his *Minstrelsy of the Scottish Border,* in 1805 *The Lay of the Last Minstrel,* followed by his many verse romances. It is said that Byron's rivalry caused him to seek a new form for his writing, and he opportunely chose prose fiction, to which he devoted his gift until his death. Among his Waverly novels *Ivanhoe* (1819), *Kenilworth* (1821), *Quentin Durward* (1823) and *The Talisman* (1825) are perhaps best known. He was made a baronet in 1820. The failure of the publishing house of Constable with which he was involved, cast him down and, refusing to take shelter behind the Bankruptcy Act, he endeavored to make good his losses by his pen. He succeeded, but his health broke. A journey to Italy was of little help and he returned home to die (September 21, 1832). His writings in verse include: *The Lay of the Last Minstrel* (1805), *Marmion* (1808), *The Lady of the Lake* (1810), *Rokeby* (1813), *The Lord of the Isles* (1815), *The Bride of Triermain* (1815), *Harold the Dauntless* (1816).

SEDULIUS, CAELIUS (5th century), was born probably at Rome. He became a convert to Christianity late in life but seems to have remained a layman. Best known of the poets of the early Church, he became the model for all Latin poets of the Middle Ages. The purpose of his writing was to reveal the superiority of the Christian story to pagan mythology. His principal work is his *Carmen Paschale,* in five books, of which forty-one different editions are extant. The poem, written in two thousand lines of hexameter, combines rhyme and alliteration to set forth its brief, dramatic episodes. The best known lines of Sedulius are the seven verses of the *Carmen Paschale,* addressed to the Virgin Mother of God, beginning, "Salve sancta parens, enixa puerpera regem," which were usually written in red characters in the manuscripts of the Middle Ages. The verses have been introduced into the liturgy.

SHELLEY, PERCY BYSSHE (1792–1822), was born at Field Place, near Horsham, Sussex, and was educated at Eton, where he rebelled against the flogging system, and at Oxford, from which he was expelled for having, jointly with Thomas Jefferson Hogg, a radical and atheistic thinker, written a pamphlet on *The Necessity of Atheism.* He then went to London and began the study of medicine. In 1811 he married Harriet Westbrook, a schoolfriend who shared his humanitarian dreams, and whom he wished to rescue from what he considered parental tyranny. When he proved unfaithful, Harriet took her life, whereupon he married Mary, the daughter of William Godwin. In 1818 he left England for Italy, where he spent the remainder of his brief life. He was drowned July 8, 1822, when his boat capsized in the Bay of Spezia. Shelley left writings both in prose and in verse. Among the latter are: *Queen Mab* (1813), *Alastor, and Other Poems* (1816), *The Revolt of Islam* (1818), *The Cenci* (1819), *Prometheus Unbound* (1820), *Epipsychidion* (1821) and *Adonais* (1821). His views on the poet and his mission he expressed in *A Defence of Poetry* (1821).

SKINNER, CORNELIA OTIS (1901–   ), was born in Chicago, Ill., the daughter of Otis Skinner, the actor. She received her education at Bryn Mawr College. One of our most distinguished and gifted artists of the stage, she is also known as a writer of both prose and poetry. Her books include: *Tiny Garments* (1932), *Excuse It, Please* (1936), *Dithers and Jitters* (1938), *Soap Behind the Ears* (1941), and *Our Hearts Were Young and Gay* (1942) with Emily Kimbrough.

SOLOMON was the second son of David, upon whom David conferred the throne when he was but eighteen years old. His reign of forty years was marked by internal and international peace. Under him was erected the magnificent temple at Jerusalem. According to the Hebrew historian, Solomon was unsurpassed for wisdom and knowledge. It is related that when Jehovah appeared to him at Gibeon in a dream, bidding him ask for anything he wished, the young king asked for wisdom, that he might rightly judge those committed to him. His request was granted, and to it were added riches, honor and length of days. Philosopher and poet, he spoke over three thousand proverbs, sang more than a thousand songs. *Ecclesiastes, Wisdom, The Canticle of Canticles* and some of the *Psalms* are attributed to him.

SORG, HENRY, S.D.S. (1899–   ), was born in the diocese of Rottenburg, Germany (August 13). He made his studies abroad, was ordained to the priesthood in the Society of the Divine Savior, December 31, 1923, at Passau, and was destined for the Chinese missions. But shortly before his departure, a serious throat disorder manifested itself, which prevented his going, and a confrère of his, Fr. Coleman, went in his stead, to be martyred a few years later by the Communists. In 1924 Fr. Sorg began his teaching career in Lochau, Germany; in 1926 he was transferred to America to the seminary staff at St. Nazianz, and three years later was appointed dean of studies. Pursuing graduate study at the Catholic University of America, he received his doctorate in philosophy and was offered a chair as instructor in the department of German literature. He declined the honor, and was appointed Superior and Rector of the newly opened Jordan Seminary at Menominee, Mich. He taught German literature and linguistics at the Catholic University summer school in Dubuque, Iowa, in 1942, and in 1943 was transferred to the Salvatorian Seminary at St. Nazianz, Wis., as director of studies, which position he still holds. He has published a critical study, *Rosegger's Religion*, 1938.

SOUTHWELL, BLESSED ROBERT, S.J. (1561–1595), was born at Horsham St. Faith's, Norfolk, of an old Catholic family, and was educated at Douai, Paris and Rome. In 1578 he entered the Jesuits, and in 1584 was ordained to the priesthood. He became Prefect of Studies in the English College at Rome, but in 1586, together with Father Henry Garnett, he went back to England, and shortly thereafter became domestic chaplain to the Countess of Arundel. For six years he ministered to the persecuted English Catholics, during which time he published not a little prose through his private press. But on June 20, 1592, while present as a guest of the Bellamys at Uxendon Hall near Harrow, he was betrayed into the hands of Topcliffe. He was tortured some fourteen times, later removed to Westminster Gatehouse, thence to the Tower, and the horrible dungeon in Newgate. He was condemned under the statute of high treason, despite his magnificent defense of his innocence, and sent to Tyburn for execution, February 23, 1595. He was beatified by the Church on December 15, 1929. Southwell's writings profoundly influenced the next generation. His chief works are: *Mary Magdalen's Tears* (1591), *St. Peter's Complaint* (1595), *Maeoniae* (1595). His poetical works were edited by W. B. Turnbull in 1856.

STODDARD, CHARLES WARREN (1843–1909), a native of Rochester, N. Y., was educated there and at the University of California. He made several trips to the South Seas and visited Father Damien at Molokai. For five years he was a European correspondent for the *San Francisco Chronicle*. He entered the Catholic Church in 1867. In 1885 and at subsequent periods until his retirement in Monterey, he was professor of English Literature at Notre Dame and at the Catholic University of America. Among his writings are: *South Sea Idylls* (1873), *Father Damien* (1901), *Exits and Entrances* (1903), *For the Pleasure of His Company*, an autobiographical novel (1903),

In the Footprints of the Padres (1912) and *Poems,* collected by Ina Coolbrith and edited by Thomas Walsh (1917).

STRASBURG, GOTTFRIED VON (13th–14th centuries), is one of the greatest of the Medieval High German epic poets. His *Tristan und Isolde,* written about 1210, is one of the most finished products of Middle High German literature. It is characterized by a courtly, polished style. He has likewise written a long poem on the Virgin Mary.

SULLIVAN, RICHARD WEBB (1917–   ), was born at Orange, N. J. (August 22). He has lived for the most part in Caribou, Maine, where he attended Caribou High School, Phillips Academy at Andover, and Harvard College. He works in the advertising field in New York City, and at present is likewise engaged in writing a novel. From 1940 to 1945 he served as an officer in the Merchant Marine and in the Navy. His poems have appeared in numerous periodicals, including *America, The Commonweal* and *Spirit.*

TABB, JOHN BANNISTER (1845–1909), born at Mattoax, Va., of an aristocratic Scotch-English family, is probably, next to Sidney Lanier, the best poet which the *post bellum* Southland produced. He had joined the Confederate forces shortly after the outbreak of hostilities and because of weak eyesight rather than his extreme youth did not become a fighter on the land, but served as the captain's clerk on the blockade-running ship, the *Robert E. Lee,* until its capture in 1864. Befriended by Sidney Lanier in the Union prison at Point Lookout, after his release he secured a position as instructor in St. Paul's Protestant-Episcopal School in Baltimore, and, five years later entered the Episcopal seminary at Alexandria, Va. Influenced by the Oxford Movement and the Newmanites, he became a Roman Catholic in 1872, and began studies for the priesthood at St. Charles College, Ellicott City, Md., where he was ordained in 1884. From that date until his death he remained at St. Charles College, teaching literature and a great array of grammar to seminarians. He acquired the reputation for being a wit and an epigrammatist, and began to write poetry. During the last two years of his life he was completely blind. The Rev. John J. Jepson, S.S., who knew him, and has made an intent study of his works, has called him "a reflective poet," who expresses a relationship that is not always obvious. "He sends us to think it over to see that the impression is true which something has made on his mind. He conveys a poetic aspect of things and does it in language that thrills and delights.

His predilection was not for the grand and the welling and the prolonged; it was for the quick, incisive thought melodiously expressed." His poem "To a Songster" is the philosophy of his own muse. Both his earlier published and his unpublished verse has been assembled by Francis A. Litz under the title, *The Poetry of Father Tabb* (1928). A volume of his prose writings, edited by Dr. Litz is to appear soon.

TATE, NAHUM (1652–1715), was born in Dublin and educated at Trinity College. He succeeded Shadwell as poet laureate in 1690, and died in the precincts of the Mint at Southwark, London, then a sanctuary for debtors. His name survives through the metrical version of the Psalms which he executed in conjunction with Nicholas Brady.

THÉRÈSE, SISTER M. SOR., D.S., Florence Mae Lentfoehr (1902–   ), was born in Oconto Falls, Wis., and educated at the Wisconsin and St. Joseph Conservatories of Music and Marquette University, Milwaukee, Wis. A member of the Gallery of Living Catholic Authors and a charter member of the Catholic Poetry Society of America, she is author of *Now There is Beauty* (1940) and *Give Joan a Sword* (1944).

THOMPSON, FRANCIS (1859–1907), was born at Preston, England, of parents who were both converts from Anglicanism. Shortly after his birth the family moved to a suburb of Manchester. In 1870 he was sent to Ushaw College where he remained for seven years, but with no aptitude for his studies toward the priesthood, a vocation which his parents had hoped he might follow. To their disappointment he returned to Manchester, and stolidly accepting his father's decision that he become a doctor, young Francis entered Owens College, Manchester. But neither did this appeal, and, after six years at Owens, he failed in his final examinations. His mother having died, his father put him to work with a manufacturer of surgical instruments, but after two weeks of work Francis fled to London, a copy of Blake's *Poems* and the plays of Aeschylus in his pocket. There, reduced to utter poverty, he sold matches and called cabs for a humble pittance. He was rescued from the London gutters by Wilfrid Meynell, to whose journal, *Merry England,* he had sent his poem "The Passion of Mary," and his essay, "Paganism New and Old." Mr. Meynell entered him as a border at the Premonstratensian Monastery, Storrington, Sussex, and after a period of convalescence from the effects of opium, Thompson began writing some of his best poetry. Alice Meynell, wife of Wilfrid, became his patron and muse, and to her he addressed the poems of *Love in Dian's Lap*. Between 1889 and 1896 he published *Poems, Sister-Songs* and *New Poems*. He likewise wrote magnificent prose, his *Essay on Shelley* is his best known work in this field, though his lesser known *Life of St. Ignatius* is of equal merit. He is perhaps best known for his "Hound of Heaven," an ode in which with poignancy and high lyricism he tells of the unending pursuit of the soul by God. A three-volume edition of his *Works* appeared in New York in 1913; *Poems of Francis Thompson*, a critical edition, was edited by Terence L. Connolly, S.J., in 1932, and the Newman Book Shop of Westminster, Maryland, is preparing a definitive edition of his works.

TOBIN, JAMES EDWARD (1905–   ), was born at Fall River, Mass. (January 17). He received his B.A. degree from Boston College in 1925, his M.A. from Fordham University in 1928 and his Doctorate in 1933. He was a member of the staff of the Associated Press, Boston and Baltimore, 1925–27; a member of the English department of Fordham in 1927; head of the department in the Graduate School, 1936; professor in 1942. He is the author of *Art in Boston College* (1924), *Contrast and Comparison* (1931), *Eighteenth Century English Literature* (1932), *To an Unknown Country* (1942), *Ardent Marigolds* (1933) and *An Approach to Study* (1937). *Thought, Comparative Literature* and *News-Letter* have benefited from his services as a staff member. He is a member of the Bibliographical Society of America, Medieval Academy, the Modern Humanities Research Association, Modern Language Association, National Council of Teachers of English and the Catholic Poetry Society of America.

TOWNSEND, ANSELM, O.P. (1901–   ), whose birthplace is Manchester, England, became a convert to Catholicism in 1924 while an Anglican seminarian. He studied at Providence College, at Dominican Houses in Illinois and Washington, D.C., and at the Catholic University of America. Having joined the Dominican Order in 1924, he was ordained to the priesthood in 1931. He is the general editor of *Dominican Library of Spiritual Works*. His translations include the following: *Dominican Spirituality* (1935), *Papers by French and Belgian Dominicans, Gifts of the Holy Ghost in the Dominican Saints* by A. Gardeil and *Hymn to the Blessed Virgin* by Geoffrey Chaucer.

UNKNOWN ALEXANDRIAN JEW, AN, is the author of *The Book of Wisdom*.

VAUGHAN, HENRY (1622–1695), known as the Silurist, was born at Newton, Brecknockshire, Wales, a twin brother of the famous alchemist, Thomas Vaughan. He received his M.D. degree at Oxford, and in 1646 published at London his first volume, entitled *Poems, With the Tenth Satyre of Juvenal Englished*. His *Silex Scintillans* ("Sparks from the Flintstone"), appeared in 1650 and *The Mount of Olives* a book of prose devotions, in 1652.

VERSTEGAN, RICHARD (ROWLANDS) (1548–1636), was born in London, of the Dutch Rowlands, and educated at Oxford, but because of his religion was forced to leave the University without a degree. His earliest known work was *The Post for Divers Partes of the World* (1576), a translation from the German with a dedication to Sir Thomas Gresham. He was in Paris in 1580. He married, and resumed his ancestral name. At his home in Antwerp, Verstegan, with the aid of his wife, accommodated English exiles, and put at their service a private printing-press. There he died, beloved by all who knew him. His closest friends had been such men, among Protestants, as Ortelius and Bochins, Sir Thomas Gresham and Sir Robert Cotton, the indexes of whose manuscript collections in the British Museum name Verstegan more than once. He was likewise a friend and correspondent of Fr. Robert Persons, S.J. Among his writings are: *The Cruelties of Contemporary Heretics,* written between 1583 and 1588, the first published English catechisms and prayerbooks, and the *Odes in Imitation of the Penitential Psalms* (1605). One of the poems in the latter is "Our Lady's Lullaby," the first four stanzas of which had appeared anonymously in Martin Peerson's *Private Musicke,* 1620. The eighth stanza is an early echo of Marlowe's pastoral lyric, first published incompletely and anonymously in *The Passionate Pilgrim* in 1599, and then completely as Marlowe's, in *England's Helicon* in 1600.

VINCENTE, GIL (1470–c.1540), was a Portuguese poet and dramatist, who abandoned law for literature, and wrote in Spanish as well as Portuguese. Many of his dramas celebrated religious festivals as held at that time, and are especially valuable for the songs with which they are interspersed. He is sometimes known as the father of Portuguese drama.

VILLON, FRANÇOIS (1431–1485), was born in Paris and educated there.

His life was disorderly in the extreme, and thrice he was under arrest for grave violations of the law. In 1457, as one of a group of burglars who broke into the Collège de Navarre, he was caught, tried, and with five others sentenced to be hanged, but the sentence was commuted to banishment. In 1461 he returned to France and passed the summer in the prison of Meung-sur-Loire but was released by Louis XI. After this he seems to have disappeared. Villon is considered the first and one of the greatest of the French lyric poets of the modern school. His chief writings are: *Le Petit Testament* (1456), *Le Grand Testament* (1461), and numerous shorter pieces, mostly ballades and rondeaux.

VIRGIL (Publius Vergilius Maro) (70–19 B.C.), celebrated Latin poet, was born near Mantua in Cisalpine Gaul, and was educated at Cremona, Mediolanum, Neapolis and Rome. He became one of the endowed court-poets who gathered around Maecenas. In 37 B.C. he published his *Eclogues,* ten pastorals modeled on Theocritus; at his villa in Naples he wrote the *Georgics,* which appeared in 30 B.C. The remaining eleven years of his life he spent on the composition of his *Aeneid,* the first printed edition of which appeared in Rome in 1469. In 1930 the Bimillennial Anniversary of his birth was observed with pilgrimages to his birthplace and to his tomb at Posillipo.

VOGELWEIDE, WALTHER VON DER (c.1160–1230), was a German medieval poet, born probably in the Tyrol. From 1180 to 1198 he was held in high favor at the court of Vienna, at that of the dukes of Austria, and later at Mainz and Magdeburg. In the poetical contest of the Wartburg in 1204 he eclipsed all his rivals. There are a number of editions of his works, notably those by Lachmann (1827), Wackernagel and Rieger (1862), Pfeiffer (1864), Wilmanns (1883), and Paul (1882); and translations by Simrock, Weiske, Schröter, Wenzel, and others. This great meistersinger is buried in the transept of Würzburg Minster. It is said that he left a legacy in his testament for the birds to be fed over his grave. In 1831, Heinrich Heine called him "the greatest German lyricist."

WALPOLE, BLESSED HENRY, S.J. (1558–1595), of the Norfolk Walpoles of Houghton, was educated at the Norwich Grammar School and at Peterhouse, Cambridge, which he left without a degree. In 1581 he was present at the execution of Bl. Edmund Campion at Tyburn, and it is said that Campion's blood was spattered upon his garments, which impressed him deeply. In

1582 he went to the English College at Rheims, thence to Rome where, in 1584 he joined the Society of Jesus. Ordained in 1588, he first served as military chaplain to "The English Regiment" in Flanders, then went to Spain (1592) where he assisted Fr. Persons in founding seminaries for the English mission. On his return the following year he carried with him a diploma from Philip II for the foundation of the College of St. Omers. In December 1593 he, his brother, and another companion landed secretly in England at Bridlington. They were at once arrested and imprisoned in York castle. After an examination by Topcliffe they were transferred to the Tower where, after four months solitary confinement, the examination of Henry Walpole was continued, interspersed with tortures. Only fragmentary details of the trial remain, but he was accused of abjuring the realm without a license, being ordained overseas, and entering England as a priest, and sentenced to death along with Fr. Alexander Rawlins. The time that remained before his execution, Walpole spent in prayer, and in the writing of verses, though his mutilated hands could scarcely hold a pen. He was executed at the Knavesmire outside Micklegate Bar on April 17. He was beatified by the Church in 1929. "The Song of Mary the Mother of Christ," with its ninety-five stanzas and intermittent refrain, is considered Walpole's because of its striking likeness to the opening stanzas of his first elegy on Campion.

WALSH, THOMAS (1875–1928), who also wrote under the names of Roderick Gill and Garrett Strange, was born in Brooklyn, N. Y., and received his education at Georgetown and Columbia Universities. A famous Hispanist, and pioneer in the Celtic Revival in America, he holds honorary degrees from Notre Dame and Marquette Universities. His publications include: *Prison Ships and Other Poems* (1909), *Pilgrim Kings* (1915), *Don Folquet and Other Poems* (1919), and the *Hispanic Anthology* (1920). He is especially known for his editing of the *Catholic Anthology*, which with added poems came out in a new edition (ed. by Geo. N. Shuster) in 1939. His *Selected Poems* with memoir by John Bunker and appreciations by Michael Williams and Edward Keyes, was published in 1930.

WEDDĀSÊ MĀRYĀM, is an excerpt from the complete translation of the famous Weddāsê Māryām manuscript. "The Book of the Praise of Mary," which consists of prayers which were daily recited to the Virgin in Ethiopian churches on the thirty-two days of festival celebrated in her honor. (The manuscript in the possession of the late Lady Meux was translated by Sir E. A. Wallis Budge, Litt.D., of the Department of Egyptian and Assyrian Antiquities in the British Museum, together with the Ethiopian manuscript of the legends of the Lady and her Mother Hanna). The date, assigned to the hymn of lyric praise of Mary, is set between the Councils of Ephesus, 431, and Chalcedon, 451. (From a note in *Carmina Mariana,* Shipley.)

WILDE, OSCAR (1856–1900), was born in Dublin, and studied at Trinity College, Dublin, and Magdalen College, Oxford, where he established a reputation for the founding of the Art-for-Art's-sake aesthetic cult. In London he lost his faith, was convicted of immorality and imprisoned. Later he fled to France, and before his death was reconciled to the Church. He published his first volume of *Poems* in 1881, followed by several works of fiction, including *The Picture of Dorian Gray* (1891). Of his scintillating comedies, the best known is *Lady Windermere's Fan,* produced in 1892. His play, *Salome,* written in French, was released in 1894. But the most literary of his works are perhaps "The Ballad of Reading Gaol" (1898) and "De Profundis" (published 1905), written after his sentence of imprisonment. Jacques Maritain says of his death: "In Paris, the priest arrived in time to save his soul, too late to save his art. Art is confined in the terrestrial duration; for it no mercy *in extremis.*"

WILKINSON, MARGUERITE (1883–1928), whose birthplace was Halifax, N.S., received her education in the United States where she came as a child: in Evanston High School, Evanston, Ill., the Misses Ely's School, New York, and Northwestern University. Her interest in writing began at the latter place. In 1902 she married James G. Wilkinson of New Rochelle, N. Y. A poet, lecturer and recognized critic of poetry, she wrote for the *New York Times Book Review.* Although an expert swimmer she tragically drowned off Coney Island. Her books are: *In Vivid Gardens* (1911), *By a Western Wayside* (1912), *The Passing of Mars* (1915), *Golden Songs of the Golden State* (1917), *New Voices* (1919) and *Citadels* (1926).

WILLIAMS, MOTHER MARGARET, R.S.C.J. (1902–   ), was born at Manchester Green, Conn. (July 2), and received her education at Manhattanville College of the Sacred Heart and at Oxford University, where she received her Master of Arts degree in 1939. She was professed in the Congregation of the Religious of the

Sacred Heart, February 9, 1933, in Rome, Italy. She is professor of English at Manhattanville College, New York. A distinguished English scholar, she has published *Word Hoard* (1940), passages from Old English literature from the 6th to the 11th centuries, a study which William Lyon Phelps has called "one of the most important works in the field of English scholarship"; and *Second Sowing* (1942), the life of Mary Aloysia Hardey.

WISDOM, THE BOOK OF, is one of the deutero-canonical writings of the Old Testament, placed in the Vulgate between the *Canticle of Canticles* and *Ecclesiasticus*. In the earliest records it is ascribed to Solomon, the Syriac reading, "The Book of the Great Wisdom of Solomon" and the Latin, "Sapientia Solomonis." In non-Catholic versions, the ordinary heading is "The Wisdom of Solomon," in contradistinction to *Ecclesiasticus,* which is usually entitled "The Wisdom of Jesus, the Son of Sirach." The book is in two sections, the first part dealing with wisdom from a speculative point of view, the second part from that of history. Though both the unity and integrity of the book are certain, its authorship is undetermined; the fact that it was composed in Greek seems to rule out its Solomonic authorship, though it may have been based on certain of Solomon's writings since lost. The monotheism permeating the work, the political allusions and local coloring of details, point to Alexandria as the place of its composition and it has been ascribed to an unknown Jew of that city. Its date falls either at the time of King Ptolemy IV, Philopator (221–204 B.C.), or Ptolemy VII, Physician (145–117 B.C.).

WORDSWORTH, WILLIAM (1770–1850), was born at Cockermouth, Cumberland, England, the son of a lawyer of that place. He was educated at Hawkshead Grammar School and at Cambridge. In 1790 he made a walking tour through France and Switzerland, and in November 1791 returned there to study, spending nearly a year at Orléans and Blois. An ardent supporter of the Revolution, only the interference of his friends deterred him from joining the Girondins and perhaps sharing their fate. Returning to England he published *An English Walk* (1793) and *Descriptive Sketches* (1793). He went to live at Alfoxden in Somerset, where he formed a close friendship with Coleridge, and with him published *Lyrical Ballads* (1798). After a winter in Germany he settled in the Lake district, first at Grasmere, then at Allan Bank, and finally at Rydal Mount. In 1802 he married Mary Hutchinson. For many years he wrote and published poetry and his public, at first indifferent, even contemptuous, began to look with favor on his writings. The Universities of Durham and Oxford honored him with degrees, and in 1843 he was named Poet Laureate. He died March 23, 1850. Among his many works are: *Lyrical Ballads* (with Coleridge, in 1798), *The Excursion* (1814), *Poems,* first collected editions (1807 and 1815), *Ecclesiastical Sonnets* (1822), and *The Prelude* (1850). He also published a number of volumes of prose.

ZEREA JACOB (15th century), was a Christian emperor of Abyssinia. He is known to have sent a delegation to the Council of Florence.

EDITOR'S NOTE: References to Mary as "goddess," "ador'd," "divine nature," and "priestly virgin," are not theologically accurate, but are, of course, to be understood as poetic epithets. Despite her divine motherhood Mary remained a mere creature, to whom veneration but not divine honors are due.

INDEX OF TITLES

449

INDEX OF POETS,
CONTEMPORARY TRANSLATORS,
AND LITURGICAL AND SPECIAL POEMS

457